Routledge Revision: Quest

# Company Law
## 2011–2012

## Routledge Q&A series

Each Routledge Q&A contains approximately 50 questions on topics commonly found on exam papers, with answer plans and comprehensive suggested answers. Each book also offers valuable advice as to how to approach and tackle exam questions and how to focus your revision effectively. New **Aim Higher** and **Common Pitfalls** boxes will also help you to identify how to go that little bit further in order to get the very best marks and highlight areas of confusion. And now there are further opportunities to hone and perfect your exam technique online.

New editions publishing in 2011:

| | |
|---|---|
| Civil Liberties & Human Rights | Equity & Trusts |
| Commercial Law | European Union Law |
| Company Law | Evidence |
| Constitutional & Administrative Law | Family Law |
| Contract Law | Jurisprudence |
| Criminal Law | Land Law |
| Employment Law | Medical Law |
| English Legal System | Torts |

For a full listing, visit http://www.routledge.com/textbooks/revision

Routledge Revision: Questions & Answers

# Company Law

## 2011–2012

**Michael Ottley**

*Senior Lecturer in Law, University of Greenwich*

Routledge
Taylor & Francis Group

LONDON AND NEW YORK

Seventh edition published 2011
by Routledge
2 Park Square, Milton Park, Abingdon, Oxon, OX14 4RN

Simultaneously published in the USA and Canada
by Routledge
270 Madison Avenue, New York, NY 10016

*Routledge is an imprint of the Taylor & Francis Group, an informa business*

© 2011 Routledge

Previous editions published by Cavendish Publishing Limited
First edition          1993
Second edition         1996
Third Edition          2001
Fourth Edition         2003

Previous editions published by Routledge-Cavendish
Fifth Edition          2007
Sixth edition          2009

Typeset in TheSans by RefineCatch Limited, Bungay, Suffolk
Printed and bound in Great Britain by TJ International Ltd, Padstow, Cornwall

*British Library Cataloguing in Publication Data*
A catalogue record for this book is available from the British Library

*Library of Congress Cataloging-in-Publication Data*
Ottley, Michael.
   Company law/Michael Ottley. — 7th ed.
     p. cm. — (Routledge questions & answers series)
   Rev. ed. of: Company law, 2009–2010/Michael Ottley. 6th ed. 2009.
   Includes bibliographical references and index.
   ISBN 978–0–415–59908–5 (pbk. : alk. paper) — ISBN 978–0–203–82952–3 (ebk)
1. Corporation law—Great Britain—Examinations, questions, etc. I. Ottley, Michael. Company law, 2009–2010. II. Title.
KD2079.6.O88 2011
346.41'066076—dc22                                            2010037442


ISBN 13: 978–0–415–59908–5 (pbk)
ISBN 13: 978–0–203–82952–3 (ebk)

# Contents

# Table of Cases

# Table of Legislation

## STATUTES

## STATUTORY INSTRUMENTS

# Guide to the Companion Website

http://www.routledge.com/textbooks/revision

Visit the Routledge Q&A website to discover even more study tips and advice on getting those top marks.

On the Routledge revision website you'll find the following resources designed to enhance your revision on all areas of undergraduate law.

## The Good, The Fair, & The Ugly

Good essays are the gateway to top marks. New to this edition, this interactive tutorial provides sample essays together with voice-over commentary and tips for successful exam essays, written by our Q&A authors themselves.

## Multiple Choice Questions

Knowledge is the foundation of every good essay. Focusing on key examination themes, these MCQs have been written to test your knowledge and understanding of each subject in the book.

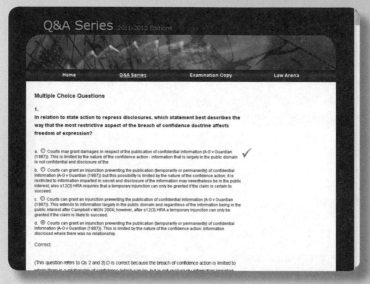

## Bonus Q&As

Having studied our exam advice, put your revision into practice and test your essay writing skills with our additional online questions and answers.

### Don't forget to check out even more revision guides and exam tools from Routledge!

## Lawcards

*Lawcards* are your complete, pocket-sized guides to key examinable areas of undergraduate law.

## Routledge Student Statutes

Comprehensive selections; clear, easy-to-use layout; alphabetical, chronological, and thematic indexes; and a competitive price make *Routledge Student Statutes* the statute book of choice for the serious law student.

# Introduction

Company law is less open to judicious question spotting than many others. If you are preparing for examinations, at least if you are sensible, you will ensure that you have an overview of the whole subject, even if you choose to concentrate revision in a limited number of areas. With this combined overview and specialised knowledge, you will be able to answer a question which is principally on topic X while pointing out that you realise that minor points Y and Z also arise – even if there is little that you can say on those points. An overview of company law also enables you to tackle general questions which cut across a major part of the syllabus, for example, questions on disclosure or the distinctions between public and private (particularly 'quasi-partnership') companies. When selecting specific areas for detailed revision, it is obviously sound practice to ensure that, where topics are linked, you study both; there is little point in knowing all about the rules relating to the duties of directors without being equally at home with the procedures for the enforcement of those duties.

Since no two syllabuses are identical and individual lecturers will have laid stress on particular topics, which they will have approached in differing ways, there can be no definitive list of typical examination questions. However, in this seventh edition, I have tried to produce questions which would be at home on an examination paper of any university or equivalent body and, I hope, the Legal Practice Course. The **Companies Act (CA) 2006** is fully in force, as of October 2009. However, some of the questions may demand a consideration of the proposals for reform of company law prior to the passing of the **CA 2006**. To this extent, reference to the work of the Law Commissions and the Company Law Review Steering Group may need to be made.

The answers featured in this book are not meant to be model answers that could be used to write a piece of coursework, rather, they are the type of answer which a good student could hope to achieve in the course of a written examination. Answers are around 1,800 words, which you should be able to write in about 40–45 minutes if you are well prepared. If you find that you cannot write this quickly, try to speed up, perhaps by using recognised abbreviations of standard terms, e.g. 'CA' for the Companies Act and 'IA' for the Insolvency Act. In suggesting answers to questions, I have assumed that a student is permitted to take statutes into his/her examination. Consequently, I have not cited anything other than section numbers as authority for propositions unless the wording of a statute is of particular significance. If you do not have access to the legislation, you can legitimately expect to receive some credit for remembering the content of relevant sections. I have also endeavoured to provide some useful 'tips' for a number of the questions in this book. These are designed to enable you to gain extra marks for your answers, either by following the suggestions given or by avoiding some common pitfalls.

All references to the model articles (2008) are to the **Companies (Model Articles) Regulations 2008**, which contain separate articles for private companies limited by shares (**Sched 1**), private companie limited by guarantee (**Sched 2**) and public companies (**Sched 3**). Any references to Table A are to Table A of the Companies (Tables A–F) Regulations 1985 (as amended), unless otherwise stated (for example, Table A of the First Schedule to the **Companies Act, 1948**). Table A has been superseded by the model articles of the Companies (Model Articles) Regulations 2008, as provided for by **s 20 CA 2006**. However, it should be noted that many existing companies may continue to have articles based on Table A.

Some areas in company law tend to be examined only by essays, while others tend to be assessed through the use of problems. The questions chosen in this book reflect this approach, although you should not assume that a particular topic cannot be assessed by either form of question.

Finally, to assist you further, do note the following suggestions that should help to improve your examination technique:

1   When tackling a problem question, do not repeat all the facts of the question at the beginning of your answer. This wastes valuable time, which is better spent on analysing the material facts in the light of the relevant law.
2   Avoid setting out large chunks of statutory material. When making reference to such material, try condensing the provision(s) using your own words.
3   Avoid using an impersonal style for both problem and essay type questions. Although sometimes it might be acceptable to use the word 'I' for an essay answer, this cannot said to be the case for a problem answer, where phrases such as 'it is submitted that' or 'it is arguable that' should be used.
4   In answers to essay-based and problem-based questions, make sure that you answer the actual question set. Simply setting out the relevant law, even if accurate and extensive, is unlikely to impress the examiner until you have

applied that law to the facts of the problem or related it to the question posed. An answer, therefore, should be balanced as between a statement of the law and application of the law.

My thanks go to Jennifer James who authored the first, second and fourth editions of this book.

*Michael Ottley*
*October 2010*

# Formation of Companies and Consequences of Incorporation

## INTRODUCTION

Questions are rarely set solely upon the rules relating to the formation of companies. However, in tackling questions on the consequences of incorporation, some appreciation of the rules of formation (and the different types of company) is appropriate. Factors which might influence the decision to incorporate, the effects of incorporation and 'lifting the veil' are common areas for questions. Questions involving 'lifting the veil' generally require some form of critical analysis rather than a mere recitation of decisions. Another, broader type of question regularly encountered involves advice about incorporation and running of companies and possible types of investment in a company either in general or for specified persons (e.g. a brilliant, but non-business minded, inventor). Material relating to formation should also be incorporated in questions relating to the different legal regime applicable to public and private (particularly quasi-partnership) companies and general questions about disclosure.

The law relating to promoters and pre-incorporation contracts can be regarded as part of the formation of a company. Questions on promoters may be linked with the liability of directors and a question could combine a pre-incorporation contract with a post-incorporation contract. However, the increasing use of 'off-the-shelf' companies for small private companies renders promoters and pre-incorporation contracts of diminishing importance. Some courses may require students to be familiar with methods of raising capital – such material is likely to form a small part of a problem or be examined by means of a simple essay which merely demands a competent recitation of facts; but, obviously, every question setter has their own hobbyhorse(s).

## Checklist ✔

Students should be familiar with:

- how a company can be formed and the different types of company;
- advantages and disadvantages of incorporation;

- effects of incorporation;
- circumstances in which the separate legal personality of a company can be disregarded, both at common law and by statute (particularly fraudulent and wrongful trading);
- promoters, particularly their duties and rights;
- liability for pre-incorporation contracts.

Students should be aware that related issues which could be linked to questions based on this area include:

- the distribution of power within a company;
- enforcement of the articles of association;
- liability and/or protection of directors/investors, including disqualification of directors;
- restructuring of share capital.

# QUESTION 1

Do the advantages of incorporation compensate for the bureaucracy involved in running a company?

## Answer Plan

A question such as this – a variant on the very well-worked theme of the advantages and disadvantages of incorporation – can only be tackled by someone who knows the material. It is very difficult to score high marks on such a question, since there is little scope for anything but a neat summary of the advantages of incorporation and a further summary of the bureaucratic requirements alluded to – a rare question where a list might be beneficial.

# ANSWER

Incorporation of an existing or projected enterprise (not necessarily a business) can be achieved either by forming a company in compliance with the procedure laid down in the **Companies Act (CA) 2006** or by buying a pre-existing company 'off-the-shelf' (the latter procedure accounts for about 60% of 'formations'). In either case, to incorporate a company, **s 9 CA 2006** requires the delivery, to the Registrar of Companies, of a memorandum of association (**s 8 CA 2006**), an application for registration (**ss 9–12 CA 2006**) and a statement of compliance (s 13 CA 2006). Articles of association are also required to be registered, by virtue of s 18 CA 2006. The content of the articles, which are the company's internal rules, are determined by the founders of the company. If articles are not registered or the articles that are registered do not exclude or modify the 'default' articles of the **Companies (Model Articles) Regulations 2008** for different types of companies, the default articles will apply (s 20 CA 2006). Previously, the default articles were **Table A** of the **CA 1985** if the company was limited by shares. The advantage of purchasing an off-the-shelf company is that the company already exists and there is no delay between deciding to form a company and the company coming into existence through the registration process; there is merely a transfer of shareholding. This obviates the problem of pre-incorporation contracts and the possibility of having stationery printed bearing a name which, by the time the company is registered, has been taken by another company. However, an off-the-shelf company would not have been formed with the specific requirements of the promoters in mind and alterations of the articles might be required. For most people interested in forming (or buying) a company, the appropriate form of company will be a private company limited by shares (ss 3(1), 3(2) and 4(1) CA 2006).

The UK has traditionally had more companies than other European countries of comparable size (there are more than two million limited companies registered in Great Britain and more than 300,000 new companies are incorporated each year). What are the attractions of incorporation? The principal advantage of incorporation, from which a variety of benefits flow, is that a company is a distinct legal entity with rights and duties independent of those possessed by its shareholders, directors and employees. In consequence, for example, business conducted in the name of a registered company is separate from the personal affairs of the human beings who act for the company, and separate also from the affairs of any other business that those human beings may conduct on behalf of another registered company. Corporate personality was created by statute in the first half of the nineteenth century, but the full significance of this provision was not appreciated until the famous case of *Salomon v Salomon and Co* in 1897.

In *Salomon*, S converted his existing, successful business into a limited company, of which he was the managing director. S valued his business at £39,000 (an honest but optimistic valuation) and received from the company, in discharge of this sum, a cash amount, a debenture (which is an acknowledgement of a debt) and 20,001 £1 shares out of an issued share capital of £20,007. S's wife and five children each held one of the remaining issued shares (seven being the minimum number of shareholders at that date), probably as his nominee. The company went into insolvent liquidation within a year with no assets to pay off the unsecured creditors. The issue for the courts was whether S was liable for the company's unpaid debts. The House of Lords, reversing the Court of Appeal, held that the company had been properly formed and was a legal person in its own right, separate from S, notwithstanding his dominant position within the company. The company was not S's agent and, consequently, S's liability was to be determined solely by reference to the **CA 1862**. The Act required a shareholder to contribute to the debts of a company only where he held shares in respect of which the full nominal value had not been paid. S had paid for his shares in full by transferring the business to the company, so he had no liability to the creditors of the company. Thus, the *Salomon* case established that legal personality would be recognised even when one shareholder effectively controlled the company and had fixed the value of the assets used to pay for his shares.

The effects of separate legal personality are many and include the following:

❖ a company can sue and be sued in its own name;

❖ a company has perpetual succession. A company cannot die simply because all its shareholders are dead, although it can be wound up or struck off the register by the Registrar of Companies if it appears to be moribund. Because a company exists unless and until it is wound up or deregistered, property, once transferred to the company, remains the property of the company, to do with as it pleases;

❖ the shareholders, directors and employees are not liable for criminal or tortious acts committed by the company, although they may incur personal liability concurrent with that of the company. For example, a company might, through the combined acts or omissions of several employees, establish and operate an unsafe system of work which caused the death of an employee. The company would be liable but an individual director or employee would not be liable unless he was personally negligent or the company was acting as an agent or employee of that individual;

❖ the shareholders, directors and employees are not liable on (nor can they enforce) contracts entered into by the company. As with criminal and tortious liability, an individual may incur personal liability concurrent with that of the company if he also enters into the contract. Furthermore, where the company acts as the agent of an individual, the individual is liable under the normal rules of agency;

❖ a company may be formed with limited liability (**s 3(1) CA 2006**). Limited liability allows the members of a company to limit their responsibility for a company's debts. Liability may be limited to a predetermined sum, payable on winding up (a company limited by guarantee – **s 3(3) CA 2006**), or to the nominal value of the shares held, unless this sum has been paid by the current or a former shareholder (a company limited by shares – **s 3(2) CA 2006**). Since most shares are issued fully paid, shareholders have, effectively, no liability for the company's debts;

❖ where a company has transferable shares, ownership of the company can be split or transferred without affecting the company itself;

❖ formation of a company may bring financial benefits. For example, a company can raise money to create floating charges and, perhaps, to minimise the tax liability of the shareholders.

There are drawbacks to separate legal personality, in that the property of the company, not being that of the members, cannot be insured by a member and the company cannot claim on an insurance effected by a person on property which he then owned but subsequently transferred to the company (see *Macaura v Northern Assurance* (1925)). Moreover, the assets of the company are the property of the company and a shareholder, even a controlling shareholder, cannot simply help himself to the company's cash. In addition, there is a limited number of situations where Parliament or the courts have decreed that corporate personality should be ignored, for example, where the directors have engaged in fraudulent or wrongful trading, they can incur personal liability under **ss 213–214** of the **Insolvency Act (IA) 1986**. But what bureaucratic drawbacks are there to incorporation? In return for the advantages of incorporation, Parliament requires the observation of mandatory rules on the operation of a company. These rules are lengthy and complex and there can be no doubt that, in most companies, many administrative rules, for example on the conduct of meetings, are largely ignored. Perhaps in recognition of the widespread lack of use of some of the rules, the government has sought to reduce the administrative burden on companies, especially smaller companies, by the passing of the **CA 2006**. The **CA 2006** permits a private company, for instance, to dispense with the holding of annual general meetings and to pass written resolutions by a bare or three quarters majority.

Such reforms are small measures, and even with the passing of the **Companies Act 2006** on certain administrative aspects of the formation and running of companies, there is still an immense amount of law imposing obligations upon companies, shareholders and directors which would not apply to a sole trader or to an ordinary partnership. These obligations fall into four broad groups:

(a)  Much of company administration is subject to statute (**CA 2006**) and there are rules relating to directors and the company secretary (**ss 154–259** and **ss 270–280 CA 2006**, respectively, although a private company is no longer required to have a company secretary). The conduct of meetings of shareholders and directors is subject to statutory control (**ss 281–361 CA 2006**), although the impact of such rules is lessened by the passing of the **CA 2006** in respect of small companies, reflecting the informal way in which most private companies are run.

(b)  The power of the directors, who in smaller companies will almost certainly be majority shareholders, are limited, in that certain things cannot be done while others can be done only with the agreement of the shareholders. For example, certain transactions between a director and the company require approval of the members, such as loans to directors – and 'substantial property transactions'.

(c)   The ability of the directors or shareholders to do as they wish with the shares of the company is restricted, so that, for instance, a company cannot buy its own shares, although there are exceptions (ss 658–659 CA 2006).

(d)   The major statutory requirement which imposes a continuing burden relates to company accounts. The financial results of the company must be presented to the shareholders in a balance sheet and profit and loss account (s 396 CA 2006). The length and technicality of the accounting rules mean that company accounts must, in effect, be prepared by a qualified accountant and a company must have its accounts checked (audited) by a qualified accountant (s 475 CA 2006 – see s 485 CA 2006 (private companies) and s 489 CA 2006 (public companies)). All companies must send their accounts to the Registrar of Companies, where they are open to public inspection, although small and medium sized companies, as defined by the CA 2006, can elect to send an abridged version instead. The obligation of a company to produce audited accounts in compliance with the CA 2006 imposes an annual financial burden on a company, although 'small companies' (defined in s 477 CA 2006) are exempt (s 475 CA 2006) from the statutory audit unless members holding at least 10% by value of a class of shares require the company to obtain an audit (s 476 CA 2006).

However, despite these obligations, there can be little doubt that a number of business people think that the bureaucratic drawbacks are more than outweighed by the benefits of incorporation.

# QUESTION 2

In forming a company, its shareholders may seek to minimise the liability of the company and themselves to creditors. To what extent, if at all, do the courts endorse this practice?

## Answer Plan

This question requires:

❖   discussion of whether shareholders and companies can minimise their liability to creditors; and

❖   a discussion of the case law in this area.

# ANSWER

The fundamental attribute of corporate personality is that the company is a legal entity distinct from its members – a company is a legal person. Corporate personality was created by statute in the first half of the nineteenth century, but the full significance of this provision was not appreciated until the famous case of *Salomon v Salomon and Co* in 1897.

In *Salomon*, S converted his existing, successful business into a limited company of which he was the managing director. S valued his business at £39,000 (an honest but wholly inaccurate valuation) and received from the company in discharge of this sum, a cash amount, a debenture and 20,001 £1 shares out of an issued share capital of £20,007. S's wife and five children each held one of the remaining issued shares (seven being the minimum number of shareholders at that date), probably as his nominee. The company went into insolvent liquidation within a year, with no assets to pay off the unsecured creditors. The issue for the courts was whether S was liable for the company's unpaid debts. The House of Lords, reversing the Court of Appeal, held that the company had been properly formed and was a legal person in its own right notwithstanding the dominant position of S within the company. The company was not S's agent, and consequently, S's liability was to be determined solely by reference to the **Companies Act (CA) 1862**. S had paid for his shares in full (by transferring the business to the company) and so his liability to creditors was exhausted – the full nominal value had been paid. Prior to *Salomon*, it had been suggested that the owner-managed type of company could not be treated as a separate legal person from its owner(s), but *Salomon*'s case established that, in the absence of fraud, legal personality would be recognised even when one shareholder effectively controlled the company and had fixed the value of the assets used to pay for his shares of the private company.

While not mandatory, the majority of companies are formed with limited liability. This does not mean that the liability of the company is limited – it is liable for all its debts. However, if a company is insolvent it has no money to satisfy creditors, and the creditors will look elsewhere for satisfaction of their debts. If a company is formed as a limited company, it means that the shareholders (even controlling shareholders and others engaged in the management of the company) can restrict their liability for the debts of the company which the company cannot pay. Most companies are limited by shares so that a shareholder who owns shares is liable only to the extent that he or a previous owner of those shares has not paid the nominal value of those shares to the company. Since, in practice, most shares have a low nominal value (generally 10 pence or £1) and it is paid when the shares are first issued, the amount which a shareholder has to contribute on the insolvency of the company is nothing. Of course, if a company is required to have a large share capital, then the company will at least have received a large sum during its lifetime, which may mean that it has fewer unsatisfied debts. Unfortunately, company law does not require private companies to have more than one share, so a private company might have as little as 1p share capital. Even public companies are not required to have a large share capital (**s 763 CA 2006** provides that public companies must have a share capital of at least £50,000 or the 'prescribed euro equivalent', of which, under **s 586 CA 2006**, at least a quarter must be paid). In addition, the rules relating to the payment for shares (**s 582 CA 2006**) allow private companies to sell their shares for non-cash consideration, which may be (as in *Salomon*) worth less than the nominal value of the shares allotted, provided the consideration is not 'wholly illusory'. The rules are slightly stricter for public companies so that, for example, they must have non-cash consideration professionally valued (**ss 593–609 CA 2006**). If a company is in financial difficulty it may be able to restructure itself (with court approval), which has the effect of discarding debts; but could it move all its assets to a new subsidiary, in order to avoid any potential or actual liability. Certainly, Parliament has not prohibited companies from setting up subsidiaries (probably wholly owned) which undertake risky enterprises on behalf of the parent company. If the risky enterprise fails, the holding company is unaffected and can ignore any debts of the subsidiary, while if it succeeds, the profits can be transferred to the holding company. Thus, in *Adams v Cape Industries plc* (1990), a UK-based company was not liable to pay damages to employees employed by a subsidiary company operating in South Africa who had been negligently exposed to asbestos and were suffering from asbestosis. Indeed, it is sound business practice to ring-fence risk in this way. Parliament has determined that the benefits of encouraging entrepreneurial activity outweigh the disadvantages of permitting undercapitalised companies to operate.

Parliament has, however, in a very limited number of cases, restricted the effect of incorporation. There are a number of minor provisions in which this is the case. The most important provisions are those relating to fraudulent or wrongful trading and the special rules for groups of companies. For instance, **ss 213–215** of the **Insolvency Act (IA) 1986** impose liability for the debts of a company where a person has engaged in fraudulent or wrongful trading (wrongful trading is limited to directors).

The courts have also been willing to lift the veil of incorporation, where a company has been used to avoid the existing liability of an individual. Such cases may be called cases where the corporate form is 'a mere façade' or a 'sham' but the description changes with the years. For example, in *Jones v Lipman* (1962), the owner of land contracted to sell it to the claimant but then transferred the land to a company which he controlled. When the claimant sought completion of the sale, the vendor said that he could not complete because he no longer owned the property; the court allowed the claimant to bring a claim against the company which had been set up simply to avoid the vendor's existing legal obligation. Similarly, in *Gilford Motor Co Ltd v Horne* (1933) H had worked for the claimant company and was contractually bound not to compete with it after leaving the company. H's wife set up a company which competed with Gilford and this company employed H. Gilford successfully sought an injunction against H and the new company. In both of these cases the courts imposed liability on the companies and so can hardly be said to have ignored corporate personality. A more common situation is where a company's controlling shareholders remove corporate assets from the company, leaving the company unable to satisfy its debts – in such a case, should the shareholders be ordered to return the assets or be personally liable for the unsatisfied claims of creditors? The courts have continued to adhere to the decision in *Salomon* and have been reluctant to disregard corporate statutes and treat the shareholders as directly responsible for the debts of the company or require them to return assets.

Both *Adams v Cape Industries plc* (1990) (mentioned above) and *Yukong Line Ltd v Rendsburg Investment Corp (No 2)* (1998) are clear authority for the proposition that where a company and its shareholders arrange its affairs in order to avoid potential liability (that is, liability that could arise) and in so doing transfer assets out of the hands of the company, there can be no claim upon those assets and no liability imposed on the shareholders. This appears to be the case even where the liability is imminent and will arise. For example, in *Yukong*, the company had entered into a chartering agreement with R which it broke, leaving it liable to pay damages for breach of contract. On the day of breach and shortly thereafter, but before R had commenced proceedings against the company, its assets were transferred to another company. The court refused to allow R to claim that sum of money from the transferee or bring a claim against the director-shareholder who had authorised the transfer (he might have been liable to the company for breach of a fiduciary duty, as codified by the CA 2006 or he might have been liable under the IA 1986, but any such liability would not have directly applied to R's benefit). A similar approach can be seen in *Ord v Belhaven Pubs Ltd* (1998), in which the claimant, O, had entered into a 20-year lease of a public house owned by the defendant (B). O was now alleging breach of contract and misrepresentation on the part of B. B was part of a group of companies which owned hotels and public houses, and, subsequent to O's claim, the group was restructured and ownership of the property leased by O was transferred from B to another company in the group, leaving B with no assets to satisfy any judgment which O might obtain. O sought to extend his claim to B's parent company and the other company which had taken over B's activities and assets. The court rejected O's claim, finding that the restructuring was a genuine commercial decision and not one designed to defeat O's claim (even if its effect was to make any judgment against B valueless). In the absence of some impropriety, the court would not lift the veil and allow O to bring a claim against the shareholder which had removed the asset from B or the new owner of that asset. Both *Yukong* and *Ord* rejected the earlier case of *Creasey v Breachwood Motors Ltd* (1993), in which the director-shareholders transferred all the assets of the company to another company which they controlled in order to ensure that if the claimant's legal claim against the company succeeded, it would have no funds to meet the judgment. Perhaps it is possible to reconcile these cases by treating *Creasey* as a case where there was no legitimate commercial reason for the transfer of assets, unlike the situation in *Ord*. However, this explanation does not apply to *Yukong*, where the sole reason for the transfer seemed to be to ensure that the company would not have to meet R's legal claim if it was successful. Further judicial support can be found in *Trustor AB v Smallbone* (2001), where the court took the view that the veil of incorporation will not be lifted simply because 'justice' would suggest that it should be done (see also *Adams v Cape Industries plc* (1990)). If the courts are to lift the veil, whether to protect creditors or others, there must, in the absence of statutory grounds, be such impropriety in the use of the company to justify the court disregarding an action which is otherwise legally effective. For instance, in *Kensington International Ltd v Republic of Congo* (2005), the court held that it was appropriate to pierce the corporate veil where a series of transactions within a structure of companies lacked legal substance and which was designed with a view to defeating the claimant's claim against the entity responsible for setting up the transactions and the structure of companies. The court was prepared to hold that the claimant was entitled to recover from one of the defendant companies a debt which was originally owed by the Republic of Congo.

## Common Pitfalls

While questions such as this one are fairly common, they are not well answered by saying that there are a large number of cases in which the courts will lift the veil and then listing them. This question calls for effective deployment of the relevant cases and a critique of those cases. Make sure, therefore, that you tailor the 'exceptions' to the question set.

## Aim Higher

With a question like this, you could expand on the policy reasons underpinning corporate personality and limited liability. You could, if relevant, discuss the proposals for reform in this area; see, for instance, the recommendation of the Company Law Review Steering Group for an 'elective' regime to be adopted in connection with groups of companies.

# QUESTION 3

Laura, a talented designer, and her husband, Bernard, are running a small business engaged in the printing and selling of silk scarves and ties. They are seeking to expand the business and have persuaded Laura's parents to provide funds for expansion. Laura's parents do not wish to participate in the day to day running of the business, nor do they need an income from their investment, but they would like to be consulted on major matters of policy and to be able to recover their capital in the future. Laura and Bernard wish to retain control of the business but want to give Laura's brother, Mark, who works for them, greater involvement in the business. Laura and Bernard have decided to form a company in which they will own the majority of shares and be directors. They seek your advice about how to structure the company and to accommodate the wishes of Laura's parents, Mark and themselves.

## Answer Plan

This is a fairly typical question which might apply to many small family businesses. The answer should address the specific concerns of those involved, rather than be a general description of company formation.

# ANSWER

Laura (L) and Bernard (B) wish to incorporate their existing business. The appropriate form of company will be a private company limited by shares (ss 3(1) and 4(1) of the Companies Act (CA) 2006). L and B may choose to establish a new company. The company will require a memorandum of association (ss 7(1)(a) and 8 CA 2006) and articles of association (s 18 CA 2006), together with an application for registration (s 9 CA 2006), the documents required by s 9 CA 2006 (as set out, where appropriate, in ss 10–12 CA 2006) and a statement of compliance (s 12 CA 2006), before it can be registered by the Registrar of Companies. The content of the articles, which can be called the company's internal rules, can be fixed by the founders of the company, but, if none is registered, the appropriate form of the Companies (Model Articles) Regulations 2008 will apply by default (s 20 CA 2006). Alternatively, they may choose to buy a pre-existing company 'off-the-shelf'. Perhaps the most important things for L and B to grasp are that a company is a separate legal person and that, by establishing it, they can no longer treat the business as entirely their own affair.

Turning to the mechanics of formation, the memorandum must state the names of the subscribers to the memorandum, who agree to be members of the company and, in the case of a company having a share capital, to take at least one share each. The application for registration must state the proposed name of the company, whether liability of the members is to be limited and, if so, whether limited by shares or by guarantee, whether the company is to be a public or private company and whether the company's registered office is to be situated in England and Wales (or Wales), Scotland or Northern Ireland. In the case of a private company, unless exempted, the final word of the company's name must be 'Limited', which can be abbreviated to 'Ltd' (s 59 CA 2006). There are restrictions upon the names which can be used (ss 65–76 CA 2006). The principal restriction is that the company cannot have the same name as an existing company, and a name which has been registered may, within 12 months of registration, be directed to be changed by the Secretary of State if it is too similar to the name of an existing company or is misleading (see *Association of Certified Public Accountants v Secretary of State for Trade and Industry* (1997), where the court held that the name suggested company's members possessed a level of qualification which was not in fact required). Other names are banned if the name would be a criminal offence or be 'offensive'. Yet further names can be used only if the Secretary of State gives permission, for example, names suggesting a connection with Her Majesty's Government or a local authority. It is possible to change the name of the company at a later date, if need be. Further provisions dealing with names and the use of particular words, letters or symbols are contained in the CA 2006 and subsequent regulations. These strengthen the provisions relating to company and business names.

The CA 2006 does not require that a company must have an objects clause. However, objects can be retained by a company in its articles (s 31 CA 2006). L and B may wish to have objects in the company's articles, as L's parents might wish to restrict the company's business to the existing trade, rather than see their money being expended on new schemes; restrictions in the articles may provide some protection for their investment, if they became shareholders, in that they could seek to restrain activities not sanctioned by the articles (s 40(4) CA 2006). The effect, however, of s 40(4) CA 2006 is that a shareholder can only restrain contemplated acts, not those already legally binding on the company. Alternatively, it might be better for L's parents to have a contract with L and B which determines what the money can be used for. If L's parents do become shareholders and the directors (likely to be L and B) overstep the restrictions in the articles in their dealings on behalf of the company, the company could sue them for breach of directors' duty (e.g. s 171 CA 2006 – duty to act in accordance with the company's constitution), although an issue of who has the power to bring legal proceedings on the company's behalf would likely arise. The objects of the company can, in any case, be changed, as an example of the company's power to amend its articles (s 21 CA 2006).

Sections 9–10 CA 2006 require a statement of the amount of the company's share capital, how the share capital is divided up and the 'value' of each share. This value – the nominal value – is an arbitrary figure which does not necessarily bear any relation to the asset value of the company or its earning potential. The minimum nominal value of a share is one penny and a company, public or private, can be formed by a single member (s 7 CA 2006). Thus, the company could have two one penny shares and I could buy one and D the other. These two shares have to be paid for in cash. Two shares create a rather inflexible share structure and most private companies have a share capital of £100 or £1,000 divided into £1 or 10p shares. L and B could give M a stake in the business by allotting shares to him. If L and B wish to retain control of the company, they need to ensure that their shareholding is at least 50% plus one vote (sufficient to pass an ordinary resolution) or, preferably, 75% (sufficient to pass a special resolution), although M might not regard less than 25% as a very worthwhile shareholding in the company. L's parents could also be given shares in the company but, unless they had a majority, which would not suit L and B, they would have no effective control over their investment.

Assuming that L and B are the principal shareholders, they may choose to pay for the shares by transferring the business to the company or by agreeing to work for the company – this is perfectly acceptable (s 582 CA 2006). Assuming that the value of the business is to exceed the modest nominal value currently encountered, L and B may be owed money for the business by the company. This debt could be secured by a debenture, giving, in theory, L and B priority over other creditors on winding up. Indeed, by incorporating, L and B appear to have removed their personal assets from the perils of the company's insolvency. In practice, the benefits of limited liability do not exist for founders of small private companies – the banks which form the major creditor for most businesses require personal guarantees (often secured on homes) from directors, etc, before extending the company credit.

Turning to the articles of association, s 20 CA 2006 provides for model, default articles, which, for new companies, replace the former articles of Table A (Tables A–F Regulations 1985). Table A applied to public and private companies alike. Section 19 CA 2006, however, provides for different articles to be prescribed by regulations for different types of companies – see the Companies (Model Articles) Regulations 2008. As a private company formed under the CA 2006, the prescribed model articles for a private company, contained in Sched 1 to the regulations, will become the default articles for the company, although as with any articles, the articles are amendable by s 21 CA 2006. A common provision in a company's articles is one restricting the transferability of a company's shares – in this case, L and B will not want M or any other shareholder transferring shares to outsiders. Other articles may vary the rules on quorums at meetings and the maximum number of directors. It is in the articles that L and B might choose to insert a provision permitting L's parents to block changes of policy. This could be achieved in one of two ways. L's parents could be given weighted voting rights (approved by the House of Lords in *Bushell v Faith* (1970)) in respect of certain transactions. Such a clause could be protected against amendment, as an entrenched provision under s 22 CA 2006. Alternatively, L's parents could be given a right to veto in the articles, as another entrenched provision, which, by virtue of s 33 CA 2006, gives them a contractual right of veto if they are shareholders.

The difficulty with the latter approach is that the ability of shareholders to enforce the contract which is contained in the articles is uncertain. The traditional view is that a shareholder can enforce the articles only insofar as the relevant article creates a 'membership' right, that is, a right attaching to each and every share which relates to the holding of shares. This view derives from the first instance decision of Astbury J in *Hickman v Kent or Romney Marsh Sheepbreeders' Association* (1915) and would appear to preclude the enforcement of a right vested only in L's parents. However, powerful arguments have been raised against this interpretation of the s 33 contract. Lord Wedderburn in particular relies heavily upon the House of Lords' decision in *Quin and Axtens v Salmon* (1909), where a shareholder was held to be entitled to enforce an article which required his consent to the sale of company land, to advance the view that a shareholder has a personal right to require the company to act in accordance with its articles. Variations on Lord Wedderburn's argument would restrict the shareholder to having a right to ensure that the appropriate corporate body carries on the affairs of the company. The uncertainty surrounding the s 33 contract makes this route an uncertain one for L's parents. Either of these proposals would limit L and B's ability to run the company as they wished. A freestanding shareholder agreement would provide a contractual means of restraining L and B's actions even if it did not bind the company.

Since L and B are forming a private company, they should be informed of the provisions for written resolutions (s 288 CA 2006) allowing decisions to be made by written agreement without the need to call a meeting. These provisions have been enhanced by the CA 2006.

If L and B are to be the first directors of the company (only one is required for a private company – s 154 CA 2006), no further directors are required, although there is no reason why M could not be invited to be a director. The proceedings of the directors will be governed by the articles. All directors are subject to rules pertaining to directors' duties. These duties, which derive from equity and the common law, are found in the CA 2006 and the directors should be advised of the need to seek proper legal advice before entering into transactions.

The final question to be addressed is how to protect the financial stake being provided by L's parents. Ordinary shares in a private company are not readily marketable and offer no protection against insolvency; they are not an appropriate choice. Preference shares are subject to the same handicaps, although redeemable shares would guarantee a return of capital if the company was still a going concern. The best solution would appear to be a secured loan, preferably redeemable at a fixed date, in their favour. Obviously, the company must have an asset of sufficient value to stand as security for the loan and a specified asset subject to a fixed charge is more likely to guarantee repayment than a floating charge.

> ### Common Pitfalls
>
> Since the decision to incorporate has been taken, there is no need to consider the advantages and disadvantages of incorporation. This would simply be padding out your answer without sticking to the question.

# QUESTION 4

Archie, Brian and Colin, who are all self-employed plasterers, agree to combine their businesses and to operate as a company, Cornice Ltd. A document is prepared which states: 'It is hereby agreed that all expenses incurred by Colin in the formation of Cornice Ltd shall be repaid from company funds within 12 months of the date of incorporation of the company.' It is signed: 'For and on behalf Cornice Ltd, as agents only, Archie and Brian.'

Upon advice by an accountant, Colin duly formed Cornice Ltd and its shares were divided equally among the three participants, who all became directors. The articles of the company provide that: 'Any person who has incurred expenses in connection with the formation of the company shall be entitled to reimbursement of those expenses by the company.' It has also emerged that Archie made a profit from the incorporation, which he did not reveal to Colin. Colin protested about the failure to pay the accountant and Archie's undisclosed profit. At a meeting of the board of directors, Archie and Brian resolved not to reimburse Colin for his expenses and to take no action to recover the profit from Archie.

▶ Advise Colin and the accountant.

## Answer Plan

Three principal issues arise in this question:

    (a)   whether Colin can initiate proceedings to recover the profit made by Archie;

(b)   whether Colin has any claim for the expenses which he incurred in forming the company; and

(c)   whether the accountant has any claim for his services.

## ANSWER

The law is a little hazy as to who is a promoter, it is a question of fact in all cases; there is no doubt that Archie (A), Brian (B) and Colin (C) are the promoters of Cornice Ltd. They are the people who decided to form the company, who set it going and who organised the registration, all of which are factors in determining whether a person is a promoter (see *Emma Silver Mining Co v Lewis* (1879) and *Whaley Bridge Printing Co v Green* (1880)). In contrast, despite any help he may have provided, the accountant is not a promoter if he merely acted in a professional capacity (*Re Great Wheal Polgooth Co* (1883)).

A promoter owes certain obligations to the company which he is forming – essentially, a duty of good faith in all dealings with the incipient corporation. This is because promoters are in a position of total dominance over the company and there is much scope for them to profit from the promotion. The courts have had to determine whether a promoter cannot derive a profit from the promotion or whether to allow the retention of profit in certain cases. The courts have adopted the second view. In *Erlanger v New Sombrero Phosphate Co* (1878), the House of Lords held that a promoter could keep any profit he made out of the promotion, provided that full disclosure was made to an independent board of directors.

While still valid, this test is almost impossible to satisfy. Promoters of private companies, as in this case, are likely to become the first directors and have a continuing involvement with the company; there is no independent board. Consequently, the courts have treated disclosure to the members as full disclosure (*Salomon v Salomon* (1897)), provided that the initial members do not intend to bow out once disclosure has been achieved.

A has not made full disclosure of his profit to all shareholders and, even if this is an indirect profit, he has broken the duty which he owes to the company. In *Gluckstein v Barnes* (1900), the promoters sold property (Olympia) to a company they were promoting, which profit was duly disclosed. The promoters did not reveal that, prior to their acquisition of Olympia, they had acquired certain debts (for less than face value, since it was generally thought that they would never be paid) secured on the property. Prior to transferring the property to the company, they arranged for these debts to be paid and the profit they made when the debts were discharged was not disclosed. The promoters were required to repay this profit to the company.

While there may be no doubt that A has broken his duty to the company, can C do anything about it? The duty is owed to the company and the company appears to have resolved to do nothing about A's action. Since a company is an abstraction, a person acting on behalf of the company must initiate litigation. By virtue of the **Model Articles (2008)** this power is vested in the board, which, in this case, has decided not to sue. C, as a shareholder, cannot force the company to sue A, nor has he the power to sack the board; but he may be able to bring a derivative action against the wrongdoer(s) (**ss 260–264** of the **Companies Act (CA) 2006**). However, given the inauspicious start to the joint venture, he might be better advised to seek a just and equitable winding up under **s 122(1)(g)** of the **Insolvency Act 1986** or to bring an action for unfair prejudice under **s 994 CA 2006** on his own account and seek to be bought out of the company.

C's next cause for complaint is the failure to obtain reimbursement for the expenses which he incurred in the course of promotion. A promoter is not entitled to reimbursement from the company unless he can establish a valid contract to pay. Is there such a contract? The document signed by A and B purports to bind the company to reimburse C, but the case of *Kelner v Baxter* (1866) has long established that a company cannot be bound by a contract entered into prior to its incorporation – the company did not exist at the relevant time, so it cannot contract. In *Kelner*, the promoters ordered wines and spirits on behalf of a hotel company they were forming. The goods were not paid for by the company; nor could they be recovered, since they had been consumed. The company was not liable on the contract, although the promoters were. Nor can the articles be said to ratify the pre-incorporation contract: *Kelner v Baxter* also held that a principal which did not exist at the time that its agent purported to act on its behalf cannot ratify the acts of the 'agent'. If the company was to enter into a new contract with C post incorporation, he could sue on the new contract, but he would have to show that he had provided consideration which was not past.

C may seek to rely on the provision in the articles authorising the reimbursement of promotion expenses. This article plainly authorises the directors to pay these expenses if they choose, but it almost certainly does not entitle C to demand payment. **Section 33 CA 2006** provides that the articles of the company bind the company and its members. The wording of the section seems tolerably clear – the articles create a contract between the company and its members. Since a contract exists – even if a rather odd one, in that it can be altered by one party (**s 21 CA 2006**) – it would seem that C could sue on the articles and obtain his due. Unfortunately, the courts have interpreted the **s 33** contract restrictively. The traditional view is that a shareholder can enforce the articles only insofar as the relevant article creates a 'membership' right, that is, a right attaching to each and every share and which relates to the holding of shares. This view derives from the first instance decision of Astbury J in *Hickman v Kent or Romney Marsh Sheepbreeders' Association* (1915) and would appear to preclude the enforcement of a right which, while vested in all shareholders (and others), does not relate to the ownership of shares. What constitutes a membership right is far from clear, but it seems clear that a reimbursement of promotion expenses does not fall into this category (*Melhado v Porto Allegre Rly Co* (1874)). However, powerful arguments have been raised against Astbury J's interpretation of the s 33 contract. Lord Wedderburn in particular relies heavily upon the House of Lords' decision in *Quin and Axtens v Salmon* (1909), where a shareholder was held entitled to enforce an article which required his consent to the sale of company land, to advance the view that a shareholder has a personal right to require the company to act in accordance with its articles. Variations on Lord Wedderburn's argument would restrict the shareholder to having a right to ensure that the appropriate corporate body carries on the affairs of the company. The conventional view seems likely to be applied to a case such as this and C would not be reimbursed.

C would, however, be able to bring an action against A and B personally for the reimbursement of his expenses. **Section 51 CA 2006** provides that a contract 'which purports to be made by or on behalf of a company at a time when the company has not been formed has the effect . . . as one made with the person purporting to act for the company as agent for it, and he is personally liable on the contract accordingly'. The courts have interpreted this section purposively and there seems little doubt that A and B will be liable. *Phonogram Ltd v Lane* (1982) illustrates the operation of the section. In this case, L had entered into a contract with the claimant on behalf of a company he was forming to manage a rock group (Cheap, Mean and Nasty) and had received approximately £12,000 on behalf of the intended company to aid his endeavours. The company was never formed and, even though it was accepted that the money had not necessarily benefited L personally, he was liable to reimburse the claimant.

The final issue concerns the accountant who has not been paid. Obviously, the accountant must establish some legal right if he wishes to bring an action to recover the sum due. First, he could seek to sue the company on the pre-incorporation contract, but this will not succeed, because:

❖ it is not clear that he was contracting with the company rather than with C personally;
❖ even if he was contracting with the company, the company, as we have seen, is not liable on a pre-incorporation contract.

Second, he could sue the company for non-payment and, if the company fails to pay, he might be able to seek a winding up order, although it is unlikely that the sums would justify this. He could not sue the company on the provision in the articles which seems to authorise the payment of incorporation expenses, because he is not a shareholder and is not a party to the s 33 contract. Indeed, even if he was a shareholder, he would face the same difficulties as C in enforcing what appears to be a non-membership right.

# QUESTION 5

Rendell Ltd has a number of wholly owned subsidiaries, including Barbara Ltd and Vine Ltd. The directors of Rendell Ltd are also directors of these two subsidiaries.

Land belonging to Barbara Ltd is being compulsorily purchased by the government for a road widening scheme; the amount of compensation has not yet been agreed.

Vine Ltd, whose business is house building, has incurred huge losses as a result of a downturn in the economy. The creditors of Vine Ltd are pressing Rendell Ltd to pay its subsidiary's debts. Without further support from Rendell Ltd, Vine Ltd will go into insolvent liquidation.

▶ Advise Rendell Ltd.

## Answer Plan

Your answer needs to address two main issues affecting Rendell Ltd. These are:

❖ Can Rendell Ltd obtain the best possible compensation for the land acquisition;
❖ Can Rendell Ltd escape liability for the debts of Vine Ltd.

# ANSWER

Rendell (R) Ltd wishes to maximise the compensation payable in respect of the road widening scheme which affects Barbara (B) Ltd, and to minimise its losses in respect of its subsidiary, Vine (V) Ltd.

## (A)  B LTD

B Ltd is a wholly owned subsidiary of R Ltd but, as a registered company, it is a separate legal person from its shareholder. Traditionally, a shareholder has no legal interest in the property of the company. Thus, in *Macaura v Northern Assurance* (1925), a shareholder was unable to claim on a policy of insurance which he had effected on certain of the company's assets and which had been destroyed by fire; one cannot insure another's property and the assets belonged to another – the company. Thus, the amount payable for the road widening scheme would seem to be limited to an appropriate sum under the legislation necessary to compensate B Ltd for its loss. However, the forfeiture of the land may also have an adverse affect upon other companies within the R Ltd group, resulting in greater loss than that which is payable to B Ltd.

Can R Ltd claim that the veil of incorporation cloaking B Ltd can be torn aside, so that R Ltd and B Ltd are treated as one company for the purposes of compensation? There are some circumstances in which a court will ignore the separate legal personality of a company. This disregard of corporate legal status may be required by statute or, in exceptional cases, be decreed by the courts. One statutory situation is pertinent. The statutes which permit compensation for persons whose real property is subject to a compulsory purchase order allow a court to disregard the separate legal personality of individual companies within a group and consider the effect of the order on the business of the group as a whole. This happened, with facts very similar to those of this case, in *DHN Food Distributors v Tower Hamlets LBC* (1976), but it cannot be said that in all such cases compensation will be awarded on this basis. See, for instance, the decision of the House of Lords in *Woolfson v Strathclyde Regional Council* (1978) and the view of the Court of Appeal in *Adams v Cape Industries plc* (1990).

## (B) V LTD

The situation in respect of this subsidiary is more complex. Once again, the existence of the corporate veil shields the shareholder, R Ltd, from the attentions of the disgruntled creditors of V Ltd. The situation is similar to that in *Salomon v Salomon and Co* (1897), in which S, who had converted his existing, successful business into a limited company of which he was the managing director and principal shareholder, was found not to be liable for the company's unpaid debts. This strict adherence to the separation of company (V Ltd) and its shareholders (R Ltd) causes loss to creditors but, as yet, this position has not been ameliorated by the courts (see the somewhat caustic comment on this by Templeman LJ in *Re Southard and Co Ltd* (1979)). Hence, unless there is some reason to disregard the corporate personality of V Ltd, the creditors have no call upon R Ltd. Grounds for lifting the veil include where a company is being used to conceal some fraudulent purpose, as, for example, in *Jones v Lipman* (1962), where the defendant sought to evade a binding contract of sale between himself and the claimant by conveying the subject matter of the contract to a company he controlled – the corporate status of the transferee was disregarded by the court.

However, where the claimant's right of action is against a company in the first place, the veil cannot be lifted so as to enable the claimant to bring proceedings against a person who controlled the company but who is not otherwise liable to the claimant (*Yukong Line Ltd v Rendsburg Investment Corp (No 2)* (1997); *Ord v Belhaven Pubs Ltd* (1998)). There seems to be no evidence of fraud by the shareholder in V Ltd in this case.

An alternative approach might be to claim that the company had engaged in wrongful trading and should contribute to the assets of V Ltd. However, wrongful trading becomes relevant only if V Ltd goes into insolvent liquidation. If such liability arose (see below for a fuller discussion of this point), R Ltd might also be liable if it could be regarded as a shadow director, that is, a person in accordance with whose directions the directors of a company are accustomed to act (s 251 of the **Companies Act (CA) 2006**). It seems probable that R Ltd exercised this degree of control over at least some of the directors and the section might apply.

While the contracts bind V Ltd, they are not enforceable against R Ltd, since to attempt to do so would disregard V Ltd's legal personality. Liability may sometimes be imposed upon the directors in respect of corporate activities. A director can incur liability for the company's debts where he was knowingly a party to a company's fraudulent trading. Fraudulent trading occurs when a director allows his company to continue trading in the knowledge that it cannot pay its debts at present and that there is no reasonable prospect that it will be able to pay them. Since fraud must be proved beyond reasonable doubt, actions for fraudulent trading are rarely successful (s 213 of the **Insolvency Act (IA) 1986**). It does not seem very likely here. It is wrongful trading, as contained in **s 214 IA 1986**, which appears more likely to be the basis for the imposition of personal liability upon the directors of V Ltd and R Ltd, if R Ltd is a shadow director. However, wrongful trading is applicable only where a company has gone into insolvent liquidation, which is not the case here. It might be worth R Ltd propping up V Ltd to avoid insolvency and the possible imposition of personal liability, which would mean that the creditors of V Ltd would be paid. The sums must be done carefully to see which is most beneficial. Where, in the course of the winding up of a company, it appears that a director is guilty of 'wrongful trading', the courts, on the application of the liquidator, may declare him liable to make a contribution to the company's assets of such an amount as it thinks proper.

The power to make a declaration under **s 214(1) IA 1986** applies in relation to a director if:

❖ the company has gone into insolvent liquidation;
❖ at some time before the winding up of the company, that person knew, or ought to have concluded, that there was no reasonable prospect of the company avoiding insolvent liquidation; and
❖ he was a director at that time.

However, the court must not make a declaration if, after the person concerned first knew or ought to have concluded that there was no reasonable prospect of the company avoiding insolvent liquidation, he took every step to minimise the potential loss to the company's creditors that he ought to have taken. Section 214(4) IA 1986 provides that, for the above purposes, the facts which a person ought to have known, the conclusions he ought to reach and the steps which he ought to take, are those which would be known, reached or taken by a reasonably diligent person with the general knowledge, skill and experience that may reasonably be expected of a person carrying out the same functions as are carried out by that director (that is, the director who is potentially subject to an order). This somewhat obscure provision seems to mean that what a director should have known or done is to be judged by reference to a theoretical director who possesses those skills that may 'reasonably be expected' of a director, unless the director is better qualified than this theoretical director, when he is to be judged by reference to his own qualifications.

The question is whether the directors of V Ltd have exercised sufficient skill – certainly, the inactive directors might be at fault if some degree of activity or active supervision could be expected from them. In *Re Produce Marketing Consortium Ltd (No 2)* (1989), it was found that, once the directors should have concluded from the falling profitability and increasing debts of the company that liquidation was inevitable, and they had failed to take all steps to minimise loss, since the directors had not limited their dealings to running down the company's stocks (which action might have been justified as an attempt to minimise liability to creditors), they were required to contribute £75,000 to the assets of the company, this being the loss which could have been averted by speedy liquidation.

## Aim Higher ★

Try providing a greater discussion of some of the cases in this area, in particular, *Yukong Line Ltd v Rendsburg Investment Corp (No 2)* (1997), *Ord v Belhaven Pubs Ltd* (1998), *Woolfson v Strathclyde Regional Council* (1978) and *Adams v Cape Industries* (1990).

# QUESTION 6

In May 2002, the shares of Large plc, a quoted international company, stood at £3. That month, the company issued listing particulars, in which the directors announced that the company was seeking finance to embark on gold mining in Siberia. The listing particulars contained a report by Bering Associates, stating that the area over which Large had the mining concession was rich in easily mined gold and that enormous profits could be expected.

Midas read the listing particulars and subscribed for 5,000 £3 shares at a total cost of £15,000. On the last day of June, Midas sold half his shares at £3.80 each to Croesus, who had also read the company's listing particulars. In early July, it was announced that a further survey revealed that, while there was gold in the area, it was extremely difficult to mine, making the project barely profitable, and the price of Large plc's shares tumbled to £1.80.

▶ Advise Midas and Croesus as to any remedies which may be available to them.

## Answer Plan

An answer to this question should differentiate between Midas, who will seek a remedy from the company and/or the directors and/or Bering Associates, and Croesus, who might seek to pursue a claim against Midas. In respect of each complainant, the statutory remedies under the Financial Services and Markets Act (FSMA) 2000 and the common law remedies should be considered.

# ANSWER

## (A)  MIDAS (M)

### FSMA 2000

When a company applies for listing of its shares which are to be offered to the public before admission to the Stock Exchange, a prospectus must be issued (s 84 FSMA 2000). Where a company applies for listing of its shares in other circumstances, listing particulars or a prospectus is issued (s 79 FSMA 2000). Here, listing particulars have been issued.

The remedy most easily available to M is that provided by the FSMA 2000, which is based upon certain EU directives (although criticism could be made of the adequacy of the implementation, thus leaving open the question of whether an individual could rely on a directive in preference to the Act). The FSMA 2000 provides for both civil and criminal sanctions against those who fail to comply with its provisions, or who induce subscription by false representations or engage in other improper practices. The first issue is whether there has been a false representation.

Section 80(1) FSMA 2000 imposes a general duty of disclosure in respect of listing particulars (and prospectuses) and provides that the listing particulars must contain:

all such information as investors and their professional advisers would reasonably require, and reasonably expect to find there, for the purpose of making an informed assessment of (a) the assets and liabilities, financial position, profits and losses, and prospects of the issuer of the security.

Further guidance is given on the information which might reasonably be expected in s 80(4) FSMA 2000. Is the information given to M about the mining operation, etc, information falling within sub-s (1)? It would seem so.

The second issue is, who incurs liability in respect of this false statement? **Section 80 FSMA 2000** states that the information to be included in the particulars is such information as is mentioned in **s 80(1) FMSA 2000** 'which is within the knowledge of any person responsible for the listing particulars or which it would be reasonable for him to obtain by making enquiries'. Liability is imposed upon the person(s) responsible for the listing particulars by **s 90 FSMA 2000**, subject to certain defences contained in **Sched 10** (s **82 FSMA 2000**, which allows the non-disclosure of certain information, does not apply here).

The persons responsible are set out in the **Public Offer of Securities Regulations (POSR) 1995.** They are:

* the company (**reg 13(1)(a)**);
* the directors (**reg 13(1)(b)**);
* each and every person who accepts (and is stated as accepting) responsibility for all or part of the particulars (**reg 13(1)(c)**); and
* each other person who has authorised the contents of the particulars or any part of it (**reg 13(1)(d)**).

Subject to **Sched 10 FSMA 2000** or **reg 15 POSR 1995,** there is little doubt that Large plc and its directors incur liability. Bering Associates would also appear to incur liability, that is, for the parts of the particulars for which they were responsible, if they have accepted responsibility for or authorised the contents. However, Bering Associates will not be liable unless the misleading material included in the particulars appeared in substantially the form and context to which Bering had agreed. Are any of the parties, who would appear to be liable, exempt? The **FSMA 2000** and **POSR 1995** exempt any person 'if he satisfies the court that at the time when the particulars were submitted . . . he reasonably believed, having made such enquiries (if any) as were reasonable, that the statement was true and not misleading', provided that he continued in his belief until the time that the securities were acquired, or he continued in his belief until after dealings in the shares had begun and they were acquired after such a lapse of time that he ought reasonably to be excused. This can be called the 'reasonable belief exemption' and it might apply here to Large and its directors – it seems unlikely to apply to Bering Associates.

Of greater relevance for Large and its directors are **Sched 10, para 2 FMSA 2000** and **reg 15(2) POSR 1995**. This provision exempts from liability those who relied upon a statement made by an expert (in this case, Bering Associates), provided that they can establish that they had reasonable grounds to rely upon the expertise of the provider of the misleading information (and the expert had agreed to its inclusion) and they continued to believe that Bering Associates were experts until after the shares had been bought, or they continued in that belief until after dealings in the shares had begun and they were acquired after such a lapse of time that they ought reasonably to be excused. Note that the mere fact that Bering Associates gave misleading advice does not necessarily mean that they are not competent. Even experts make mistakes.

There are special rules where misleading information is corrected, but these do not apply in the case of M. It should be noted that the onus of exempting themselves from liability falls upon those responsible for the particulars.

The third issue is the nature of any liability incurred. **Section 90 FSMA 2000** provides that those responsible for misleading listing particulars are liable to pay compensation to M for the loss he has suffered; the measure of damages is thought to be that applicable in tort, that is, restoration to his original position. Originally, M had £15,000 and no shares; he now has 2,500, worth £1.80 each (£4,500) and has received (it is assumed) £3.80 for each share sold to Croesus (£9,500), so that he needs £1,000 to restore him to his original position (plus any incidental expenses). If a contractual measure of damages was applicable, greater damages could be recovered (on the loss of expectation basis). It should be noted that M will not be able to claim compensation if he knew that the relevant statement was untrue.

## OTHER SOURCES OF LIABILITY

M should have no need to look beyond the **FSMA 2000**, but other possible sources of compensation are the tort of deceit (where there is conduct akin to fraud) or negligent misstatement either in tort or by virtue of s 2(1) of the **Misrepresentation Act 1967** (the last of these would only be available against the company). M could not rescind the contract, it seems, because he has sold half the shares. The fact that he could not rescind would not debar M from monetary compensation (**s 655** of the **Companies Act 2006**, reversing *Houldsworth v City of Glasgow Bank* (1880)).

# (B)  CROESUS (C)

The position of C is not dissimilar to that of M, in that he, too, may have a remedy under the **FSMA 2000**. The right to sue those responsible for the misleading listing particulars is not restricted to those who purchased the shares from the company. Now, anyone who has acquired shares and who can show that he has suffered loss as a result of the misstatement has a *prima facie* case for compensation. C will have to prove that there is a causal connection between the misstatement and the loss. Factors which will tend to negate such a connection are purchase after the true facts became known, which does not apply here, or such a lapse of time that the particulars can no longer be said to have any influence on the market. The gap between the publication of the misstatement and the purchase in this case does not seem so long as to debar C from seeking compensation.

Do any of those liable to M have a defence in the case of C? The only possibility would seem to be that the company or directors could establish that C bought the shares before it was reasonably practicable for them to bring a correction or inform people of the incompetence of the expert. The common law remedies seem unlikely to apply in this case, except, perhaps, with regard to M.

Whatever the outcome of any claim under the FSMA 2000, C has the usual common law remedies against M. Thus, if he can show that M knew the truth when he sold the shares, he may have a remedy for misrepresentation, but only if he relied upon an untrue statement made by M. If M knew the truth but kept quiet and made no statements, there can be no liability on the part of M – he is obliged to refrain from lies but has no obligation to disabuse C, unless he is in a fiduciary relationship with him.

# The Company and Insiders

## 2

## INTRODUCTION

In this chapter, students are directed specifically to the internal relationships within a company. This involves the rights and duties of the members in their dealings with each other and with the company (see, also, below, Chapter 5). The articles of association are the primary source of the provisions determining these internal relationships. The status of the articles and their enforceability (which touches on the rule in *Foss v Harbottle* (1843)) is a standard area for questions, both problem and essay. Specific regard will also be paid to the appointment, payment and dismissal of officers of the company and the division of power between the shareholders and the directors. Such material can form the basis of single question or can be combined with aspects of directors' duties, variation of class rights and s 994 of the **Companies Act (CA) 2006** or the external relationships of the company. Students should have at least background knowledge of the types of resolution and the majorities required, and of the conduct of meetings and votes. Arguably, the duties of the directors could form part of this chapter, but it is such a large topic that they are dealt with separately (see below, Chapter 4). The employees of the company are also insiders, but company law syllabuses rarely address issues relating to employees, other than directors, to say they have no *locus standi* to enforce either the company's constitution or the duty owed by directors to have regard to the interests of employees when acting bona fide to promote the success of the company for the benefit of its members as a whole.

## Checklist ✔

Students must be familiar with the following areas:

- the nature of the articles and their legal effect;
- amendment of the articles by the company (the **CA 2006** substitutes the word 'amendment' for 'alteration' as formerly provided for by the **CA 1985**);
- the appointment, payment and dismissal of directors; and
- the division of power in a company.

Students should be aware that related issues which could be linked to questions based on this area include:

- variation of class rights, reduction of capital and **s 994 CA 2006**;
- directors' duties and their enforcement; and
- the ability of officers of a company to bind the company.

## QUESTION 7

To what extent, if at all, does **s 33** of the **Companies (CA) Act 2006** give a shareholder enforceable contractual rights against a company?

### Answer Plan

Outline the contents of the memorandum and articles. Assess the efficacy of the s 33 contract and the ability of the company to alter the contractual rights of a shareholder, and tie up the law by reference to the question.

## ANSWER

A company's constitution includes the articles and any resolutions and agreements affecting a company's constitution (**ss 17** and **29 CA 2006**). Although **s 17(3) CA 2006** provides that references to the articles shall include the memorandum, the memorandum is of historic value only – merely setting out the names of the subscribers who wish to form a company and who agree to be members of the company (**ss 7–8 CA 2006**). While all companies must have articles of association (**s 18 CA 2006**), a company limited by shares may use the statutory form of articles provided for by **s 20 CA 2006** (as prescribed for by regulations under **s 19 CA 2006** – 'different model articles . . . for different descriptions of companies' – see the **Companies (Model Articles) Regulations 2008**) and, unless and to the extent that articles to the contrary are registered, the relevant model articles will apply by default (**s 20 CA 2006**). The articles, broadly speaking, define the internal relationships within a company – the division of power and the allocation of risk. **Section 33 CA 2006** provides that the provisions of the company's constitution:

> Bind the company and its members to the same extent as if there were covenants on the part of the company and of each member to observe these provisions.

The wording of s 33 CA 2006 has been changed from its predecessor (s 14 CA 1985) to reflect the fact that the constitution is binding on the company and the members 'to the same extent'. This was not clear entirely from the wording of s 14 CA 1985, although s 14 CA 1985 was interpreted in this way (see *Wood v Odessa Waterworks* (1889)).

What does s 33 CA 2006 mean? The first instance decision of Astbury J in *Hickman v Kent or Romney Marsh Sheepbreeders' Association* (1915) established that the memorandum and articles constitute a contract between the company and the members. Consequently, in *Hickman*, a provision requiring a member to refer any dispute with the company to arbitration was held binding on the member. The contract is bilateral and binds both the company and the members; it is also binding between the members (*Rayfield v Hands* (1960)).

It is a contract with a number of unusual features. First, it is subject to the provisions of the CA 2006, which include s 21 CA 2006. Section 21 CA 2006 provides that a company may amend its articles by special resolution (the memorandum is no longer alterable under the CA 2006). Thus, one party to the contract (the company) can alter that contract contrary to the wishes of another contracting party – a shareholder – provided that an appropriate majority of shareholders agree. Are shareholders, in voting to amend the articles by special resolution, entitled to vote with regard only to their own interests? Certainly, there are *dicta* in the cases which suggest that, on a vote to change the articles, the shareholders must vote '*bona fide* for the benefit of the company' (*Allen v Gold Reefs of West Africa Ltd* (1900)), but this is probably overstating the position. It seems clear that, where the proposed change of articles is designed to appropriate the shares of the minority, the court will strike down the amendment unless it is objectively in the best interests of the company. In *Sidebottom v Kershaw Leese* (1920), the Court of Appeal upheld an amendment which permitted the company to require a shareholder who had an interest in a competing business (as S, who was a director of the company, did) to transfer his shares to nominees of the directors for a fair price. The court held that this was beneficial to the company, thus indicating that, had they not reached this view, the judges would have struck the amendment down. In *Dafen Tinplate v Llanelly Steel* (1920), however, an amendment allowing any shareholder to be required to sell his shares was rejected by the court as going beyond that which was necessary to benefit the company.

Despite the use of the word 'may' in s 9 CA 1985, the predecessor to s 21 CA 2006, it was well established that it was not possible for a company to abrogate its right to change its articles. However, although the same language is used in s 21 CA 2006, under s 22 CA 2006, it is possible for the articles to contain 'entrenched' provisions, allowing for amendment or repeal of specified articles on condition that more restrictive requirements have been met. Alternatively, it is acceptable for the articles to provide that on a vote to alter the articles the shares of a particular member shall carry extra votes (*Bushell v Faith* (1970)). A weighted voting clause of this type could ensure that certain articles are entrenched. While a weighted voting clause in the articles is capable of change by special resolution, it could itself be entrenched by providing for more restrictive conditions to be satisfied before being amended or repealed.

It is the second feature of the s 33 contract which is more controversial. The ability of a shareholder (or the company) to enforce the contract which is contained in the articles is uncertain. The traditional view is that a shareholder can enforce the articles only insofar as the relevant article creates a 'membership' right, that is, a right attaching to each and every share, which relates to the holding of shares. This view also derives from the decision of Astbury J in *Hickman v Kent or Romney Marsh Sheepbreeders' Association* (1915) and would appear to preclude the enforcement of a right which does not fall into this obscure category. There are two difficulties with this decision. First, the precise nature of a 'membership right' is indistinct. It would seem that a right vested in only some of the membership (*Eley v Positive Life Assurance Co* (1876), where articles providing that E was to be company solicitor for life did not give E any contractual right of employment) or a right conferred, potentially, on all shareholders but relating to a shareholder in a non-member capacity is not such a right. For example, where the articles permit the reimbursement of promotion expenses, a member who, while acting as a promoter of the company, incurred such expenses could not rely on the articles to establish a contractual right to reimbursement (*Melhado v Porto Allegre Rly Co* (1874)) and, in *Beattie v E and F Beattie Ltd* (1938), a provision requiring members to submit disputes to arbitration did not apply to a dispute between the company and a shareholder in respect of his directorship. However, membership rights (or individual rights) are contractual rights and any attempt to ignore such a right is a breach of contract subject to legal action by the shareholder; in other words, membership rights are an example of a situation where the rule in *Foss v Harbottle* (1843), which restricts the right of a member to sue the company, does not apply. Examples of membership rights are the right to receive dividends when duly declared and payable, the right to attend general meetings and the right to participate on winding up.

The second, and more fundamental, objection to Astbury J's view is that the section does not differentiate between membership and non-membership rights and powerful arguments have been raised against this interpretation of the s 33 contract. Lord Wedderburn in particular relies heavily upon the House of Lords' decision in *Quin and Axtens v Salmon* (1909), where a director-shareholder was held entitled to enforce an article which required his consent to the sale of company land, to advance the view that a shareholder has a personal right to require the company to act in accordance with its articles (subject to those matters of internal management, breach of which is ratifiable by ordinary resolution). Lord Wedderburn would even argue that a shareholder can enforce an article which benefits an outsider or himself in a non-membership capacity. If a court was prepared to disregard the conventional view on the s 33 contract and hold that all the articles constituted contractual rights (or that a member had a right to have the articles complied with), an outsider would still have to depend upon a member suing on his behalf. This would cause no difficulty where an injunction was sought, but, where a member sued for damages on behalf of a third party, the rules of privity would seem to provide that any damages payable would reflect the member's loss and not that of the third party.

Variations on Lord Wedderburn's argument would restrict the shareholder to having a right to ensure that the appropriate corporate body carries on the affairs of the company – on this analysis, S succeeded in the *Quin and Axtens* case because the general meeting purported to take a decision which could only be taken by the board.

Other unusual features of the s 33 contract are that the 'contract' does not provide each party with a list of contractual duties, it is potentially infinite and it is not subject to rescission for misrepresentation.

The precise scope of the s 33 contract is still far from clear; these difficulties may be explained by the fact that the wording of s 33 CA 2006 (and its predecessors) derives from provisions relating to unincorporated joint-stock companies which are legally an entirely different type of being. It is certainly possible to conclude that a combination of Astbury J's interpretation of s 33 and the court's application of s 21 CA 2006 significantly diminish the rights of an individual shareholder. However, it could be argued that, at least in larger companies, it is entirely appropriate that the minority tail should not wag the majority dog. This is particularly true when an individual shareholder may be able to rely on s 994 CA 2006 to ensure that he is bought out of a company with which he is at loggerheads.

## Aim Higher ★

Extra credit can be expected for further discussion of the views of the Company Law Review Steering Group and considering other ways in which the s 33 contract differs from 'normal' contracts.

# QUESTION 8

It is a basic principle of company law that all the corporators, acting together, can do anything which is *intra vires* the company (*Cane v Jones* (1980), per Michael Wheeler QC).

▶ Consider the efficacy of, and the problems caused by, 'shareholder agreements'.

## Answer Plan

This is a question concerning the control of companies by reference to non-statutory documents – shareholder agreements. It simply requires a relatively factual description of the nature and function of such agreements in the context of company control. Some discussion of why shareholder agreements are used is also appropriate.

# ANSWER

A company is an association of persons in pursuance of some common object, generally, but not necessarily, for profit. The **Companies Act (CA) 2006** provides that the constitution of a company is based on the articles and any resolutions or agreements affecting the constitution. Although **s 17(2) CA 2006** provides that references in the Act to a company's articles include references to a company's memorandum, in effect, the memorandum no longer forms part of the constitution of a company. As can be seen, there is considerable freedom in the drafting of the basic constitutional framework of a company. This freedom is reduced when it is sought to change the articles. After all, it is argued, a shareholder has acquired shares in a company on the basis that his rights and liabilities are as set out in the articles and, while he knows from the outset that these rights and liabilities may be changed if a majority of shareholders so wish, the courts should be empowered to intervene to restrain the wish of the majority in certain cases. Others argue that, where an appropriate majority has sanctioned a change in the articles, the courts should not intervene to restrain such changes, however detrimental to the wishes of a shareholder, because Parliament has decreed that the shareholders can amend their mutual rights and duties as they see fit.

There are some statutory restraints placed upon the powers of the majority to alter the constitution of the company and consequently to run the company as they wish. For example, **ss 630–635 CA 2006** (variation of class rights) provide examples of specific restrictions or procedures on amendment of the company's constitution. The requirement that changes generally require a special resolution (**s 21 CA 2006**

75% majority of the votes cast) to implement them restrains the freedom of shareholders to amend the rights and liabilities of other shareholders. There are also rare examples of the courts requiring shareholders to exercise their right to vote in a manner which takes into account interests other than their own. For example, the courts have determined that they can reject an amendment of the articles, which complies with all statutory requirements, if the amendment is not '*bona fide* for the benefit of the company' (*Allen v Gold Reefs of West Africa Ltd* (1900)), although this seems to operate only where an expropriation of shares is involved (*Dafen Tinplate v Llanelly Steel* (1920)).

Where it is all the shareholders who wish to vary their mutual rights and duties, can there be any objection to them doing so? Obviously, the shareholders may choose to amend their respective interests by revision of the articles but, as indicated above, this may attract judicial intervention – although this is hardly likely if all shareholders agree. However, it is not uncommon for shareholders to supplement, suspend or amend the articles with 'shareholder agreements'. The majority may also use shareholder agreements to, for example, provide a 'voting block' to retain control of the company or evade provisions in the articles designed to protect the minority. It is the shareholder agreement between all shareholders which the case of *Cane v Jones* (1980) addresses.

In *Cane v Jones*, two brothers, P and H, formed a company, of which they were the 'life directors'; they were the only directors. All the shares were owned by close family members or on trust for such members. The articles provided that the chairman of directors had a casting vote at directors' and general meetings of the company. In 1967, all of the then shareholders agreed that the chairman would not use his casting vote and that, where the director-brothers could not agree, an independent chairman (with a casting vote) would be appointed. The two sides of the family fell out and P's side claimed that P, as chairman, had a casting vote. H's daughter, the claimant, who was not a party to the 1967 agreement (although trustees acting for her were), sought to rely on that agreement and petitioned for a declaration that P's casting vote had been abrogated. Michael Wheeler QC determined that P's casting vote had disappeared and held that the 1967 agreement was, in essence, a general meeting, which was effective to override the articles. The judge seemed to say that, where all the shareholders agreed to amend the articles, this could take effect as an amendment of the articles, despite the failure to comply with **s 21 CA 2006**, because **s 21 CA 2006** was merely a way, but not the only way, of amending the articles.

Whether this case should really be seen as an amendment of the articles can be doubted – if it was an amendment, it would now be subject to the official notification procedure (**s 1079 CA 2006**) so that the 'amendment' would only operate internally and would not bind third parties. Further, if it was an amendment of the articles, new shareholders would also be bound. This case should be treated as a shareholder agreement rather than an amendment of articles. What, then, is a shareholder agreement, and can such agreements outflank the statutory requirements?

Shareholder agreements fall into two broad groups:

(a) agreements between all or some of the shareholders and the company; and
(b) agreements between all or some (a majority) of the shareholders which do not involve the company.

Shareholder agreements will generally constitute contracts, the consideration being the agreement of the other parties to be bound by the agreement. Such agreements may be positive, for example, providing a method for the resolution of disputes between member and member or member and company; or negative, for example, an agreement that the articles shall not apply or that non-compliance with the articles will not be actionable. In some cases, a shareholder agreement may be regarded as an informal equivalent to a resolution of the members in general meeting, if it is unanimous and in writing, and the articles may expressly recognise this practice and treat such agreements as equivalent to formal resolutions. Where there is unanimous agreement to a proposal, there can be little objection to treating the agreement as binding between those who have agreed and as equivalent to a 'statutory' resolution, although official notification (s 1079 CA 2006), when required, would be necessary to bind third parties. Is this also the case when the informal agreement conflicts with substantive statutory rules (as opposed to procedural rules) designed to protect members? This issue is unresolved. It could be argued that a shareholder agreement should not be treated as an informal resolution where company legislation provides a substantive rule to protect shareholders (even though they have all agreed). Many shareholder agreements cannot be treated as informal resolutions of the company, either because that was not the intention of the parties or, it seems, because the Acts may specify that the formal route is the *only* method of doing certain things. However, it should be noted that, in *Re Barry Artist* (1985), the court approved a reduction of capital to which all members had merely given informal approval, despite s 135 CA 1985, which provided that a company may 'by special resolution reduce its share capital'. Where a shareholder agreement constitutes an informal resolution, it may, it seems, bind subsequent transferees of shares (unlike a pure shareholder agreement), subject to the official notification rules.

An agreement between all shareholders (and perhaps the company), as predicated in the question, can be compared with the articles of a company. The agreement can be said to govern the internal workings of the company. However, unlike the articles, all aspects of such an agreement are, presumably, mutually enforceable, and not merely those which create membership rights (provided the agreement is a contract), and the agreement cannot be changed without the agreement of all the parties to it unless the agreement so provides. A further contrast with the articles is that the agreement creates personal rights which bind parties to the contract as such, rather than as shareholders. Consequently, successors in title can neither enforce nor be bound by a shareholder agreement. However, it seems that a shareholder agreement, even if entered into by all of the shareholders, cannot fetter the directorial discretion of a director-member (*Boulting v ACTAT* (1963)) or the ability of a company to change its articles (*Allen v Gold Reefs of West Africa Ltd* (1900)). In respect of an amendment of the articles, the courts have held in relation to **s 9 CA 1985**, the predecessor to **s 21 CA 2006**, which provides that 'a company may by special resolution amend its articles', that a company cannot be restrained from amending its articles by special resolution even if the resultant amendment causes a breach of contract which may result in damages being payable (*Southern Foundries v Shirlaw* (1940)). In connection with **s 21 CA 2006**, however, **s 22 CA 2006** provides that the articles can provide for entrenched provisions for which amendment or repeal require more restrictive conditions to be met.

The House of Lords considered the effect of shareholder agreements in *Russell v Northern Bank Developments Corp Ltd* (1992). In this case, the bank had lent money to two companies – TP Ltd, which had incurred large losses, and TB Ltd, which had proved extremely successful. As part of a restructuring agreement devised by the bank, it was decided that the shares controlling the two companies would be brought together in a new holding company, Tyrone, which would run both companies and would be able to set TP's losses against TB's profits, thereby reducing the tax liability of TB. Four executives, including the claimant, were transferred from TB to run Tyrone and each of them was allotted 20 shares in Tyrone. The remaining issued shares (120) of Tyrone were allotted to the bank. One of Tyrone's articles allowed the company to increase its share capital but a shareholder agreement entered into by the bank, Tyrone and the four executives provided, *inter alia*, that no further share capital would be created or issued without the written consent of all parties to the agreement. Subsequently, the company sought to increase its share capital and the claimant, R, sought an injunction to restrain it from so doing, on the grounds that this was a breach of the agreement.

Despite the agreement of all the shareholders, it was not argued that this was an informal amendment of the company's articles. The majority would not have accepted that this was an informal amendment (had it been argued), saying that such a finding would be inconsistent with the company being a party to the agreement. The respondent bank argued that since the relevant statute (equivalent to **s 121(2)(a) CA 1985**) permitted a company to increase its share capital, provided that its articles sanctioned such an increase, which Tyrone's articles did, a shareholder agreement which fettered the statutory power must be invalid. The House of Lords decided that the shareholder agreement was separate and distinct from the company's articles and was of a purely personal nature.

Consequently, there was no objection to the shareholders making such an agreement as this, although it could not bind the company, because that would fetter the company's statutory right to issue shares. While the court declared the power to issue shares to be an inalienable statutory power, the effect of upholding this agreement was to render the company incapable of issuing shares. This is the first case to treat the power to issue shares as inalienable, even if the finding was nullified by the upholding of the shareholder agreement. The court did not provide any guidance upon which statutory powers are to be treated as inalienable and not subject to amendment or deletion even by unanimous agreement of the shareholders.

*Russell* stressed the primacy of certain statutory rights but then allowed the parties freedom to negotiate between themselves as to how to run the company, and could be seen as representing a non-interventionist approach by the court, allowing those who risk their money to outflank the intention of Parliament. The case would appear to allow a majority to decide to stymie the statutory rights of a minority by informal agreement – perhaps a case for the use of s 994 CA 2006.

## NOTE

Section 135 CA 1985 (reduction of share capital) and s 121(2)(a) CA 1985 (increase of share capital) have been replaced, with modification, by ss 617(2)(b) and 617(2)(a) respectively. The procedure is dealt with by Part 17 of the CA 2006.

## QUESTION 9

Sober Ltd was incorporated by Arnold in 1996 with the stated object to import and sell non-alcoholic fruit drinks; he was the sole director of the company. Arnold held 90% of the issued shares and his wife, Helen, held 10%. The articles of the company named Helen as company secretary 'for life'. On Arnold's death, his shares were inherited equally by his three sons, who became the directors of the company.

The sons are proposing to amend the objects of the company to permit the importation and sale of alcoholic drinks. Helen objects strongly to this proposal. Her sons tell her that they propose to employ a different company secretary and to insert a provision in the company's articles allowing the directors to require any shareholder whose statements or conduct is, in their opinion, detrimental to the company's future prosperity to transfer his or her shares to the directors at a fair price.

▶ Advise Helen.

**Answer Plan**

The issues that arise in this question are:

* ❖ can Helen prevent the amendment of the objects of the company?;
* ❖ is Helen entitled to be company secretary for life?; and
* ❖ can Helen object to the article permitting compulsory acquisition of the shares?

# ANSWER

It is not uncommon for a new generation which takes over a family company to have very different ideas about how the company should be run. The law will not intervene to restrain the directors from pursuing a different policy or business, even where it is a new venture in which the company has no expertise. For example, in *Re A Company (No 002567 of 1982) (1983)*, a minority shareholder in a company which was engaged in advertising failed in his attempt to prevent the company from using some of its surplus funds in opening a wine bar. However, where the change of policy necessitates a change of the articles (including those things, such as an objects clause, that, by virtue of the **Companies Act (CA) 2006**, are no longer permitted to be part of the memorandum, for anything contained in the memorandum prior to the passing of the **CA 2006** must be contained in the articles), there are appropriate statutory procedures which must be complied with and dissident shareholders may have the right to make their objections known to the court and sometimes to have the change struck down. The courts, in considering applications by disgruntled shareholders, have to balance the right of the majority of members to run the company (or have the directors run it on their behalf) as they wish and the question of whether there is any necessity, especially where statute does not give a remedy, to protect the interests of individual shareholders, even if this stymies the majority.

The first thing that the company wishes to do is to amend its objects, permitting the company to trade in alcoholic as well as non-alcoholic beverages. The objects are the purposes which the company is empowered to pursue and are a statement to potential shareholders of the type of business in which their money will be expended. Whether contained in the articles of a new company or in the memorandum of an existing company, the objects of a company, if any, can only be contained in the articles of a company (**s 31 CA 2006**). However, the objects of a company, like any other provision of a company's articles, can be amended by virtue of **s 21 CA 2006**, provided that the change is effected by special resolution. Helen (H) cannot block a special resolution, but she could apply to the court on the ground that the amendment is not *bona fide* for the benefit of the company as a whole. This judicial gloss, that the alteration must be *bona fide*, etc, on the apparently unfettered right of the shareholders to amend the articles is a rare illustration of a fiduciary duty being imposed on shareholders; shareholders are normally entitled to vote without regard to any interest but their own (*Welton v Saffery* (1897)). This *dictum*, which appears to place some limit upon majority power, derives from *Allen v Gold Reefs of West Africa Ltd* (1900). However, it should be noted that in this case a claimants' challenge to an amendment of the articles, which gave the company a lien over fully paid up shares in respect of any debt owed by a shareholder to the company, was unsuccessful. The claimant was the executor of the only shareholder with fully paid up shares. While the Court of Appeal may have expounded this limitation on the power of the majority to change the rules of the company, the operation of the limitation has proved somewhat disappointing to minority shareholders.

Apart from any general consequential amendments to the articles, H is objecting to the particular change which permits the expropriation of shares of a member who expresses views, etc, held, by the board, to be detrimental to the company. These issues can be considered together. Does *Allen v Gold Reefs* assist H? It seems clear from later cases that, where the proposed change of articles is designed to appropriate the shares of the minority, the court will strike down the amendment unless it is objectively in the best interests of the company. In *Brown v British Abrasive Wheel* (1919), the company was in urgent need of capital which the majority of shareholders were willing to provide. However, 2% of shareholders were not willing and the majority were willing to proceed only if they could buy out the 2%. The articles were changed to permit the acquisition of the objecting shareholders but was successfully challenged by one of them. The judge held that this alteration was for the benefit of the majority rather than the company. Even if one agrees with the idea that an amendment must benefit the company, this seems a strange application of the principle – the stymied majority, presumably, did not provide the needed capital and the company went into liquidation. *Brown* was distinguished in *Sidebottom v Kershaw Leese* (1920), in which the Court of Appeal upheld an amendment which permitted the company to require a shareholder who had an interest in a competing business (as S, who was a director of the company, did) to transfer his shares to nominees of the directors for a fair price. The court held that this was objectively beneficial to the company. Finally, in *Dafen Tinplate v Llanelly Steel* (1920), an amendment allowing any shareholder to be required to sell his shares was rejected by the court as going beyond that which was necessary to benefit the company. Consequently, if H can convince the court that this amendment is not for the benefit of the company, she may succeed in having it struck down.

Whether there is a general requirement that shareholders vote on proposals to amend the articles in a manner which is objectively in the best interests of the company is less certain. In *Greenhalgh v Arderne Cinemas Ltd* (1950), the majority shareholders in the company passed a special resolution which in effect required any shareholder, so directed, to transfer his shares to a nominee of the majority shareholders at a fair price. G, who was the only shareholder likely to be affected by this scheme, objected and the Court of Appeal, while rejecting G's case, seemed to suggest that all shareholder resolutions were subject to the *bona fide*, etc, test. The test requires a voting shareholder to 'proceed on what, in his honest opinion, is for the benefit of the company as a whole'. The Master of the Rolls, Lord Evershed, sought to explain what 'the company as a whole' meant by reference to whether the proposal was in the interest of a hypothetical member of the company not directly concerned in the contentious proposal. Given the uncertainty surrounding the nature of this test, and the fact that G was unsuccessful in his action, it is difficult to find much support for a general objective duty cast upon shareholders to act *bona fide*, etc. However, limited support for such a duty can be found in two first instance decisions – *Re Holders Investment Trust* (1971) (majority to consider interests of minority in deciding whether to vary class rights) and *Clemens v Clemens Brothers Ltd* (1976) (majority not able to issue further shares to deprive minority of negative voting control).

It seems improbable that H will be able to challenge the 'consequential amendments', which, even if the benefit of the company test applies, appear to be in the best interests of the company both subjectively and objectively. The statutory remedy for disadvantaged shareholders, **s 994 CA 2006**, may provide a remedy for H, but the courts have set their face against using the section to provide a remedy for shareholders who object to the board's *bona fide* actions if they do not impinge upon the 'legitimate expectations' of the shareholder; see, for example, *Re A Company (No 002567 of 1982)* (1983), the wine bar case mentioned above, and *Re Saul Harrison and Sons plc* (1995). In the latter case, Hoffman LJ accepted, however, that there are cases where the . . . articles do not represent the understandings upon which the shareholders are associated and, in such cases, it may be unfair applying equitable considerations to a shareholder for those who control a company to exercise the powers set out in the . . . articles if to do so denies the legitimate expectations of the shareholder.

The final complaint put forward by H concerns her dismissal as company secretary. H will have considerable difficulty, as we have seen, in blocking an amendment of the articles to delete this provision; but she may have an action for damages if the amendment (or dismissal without the amendment) is a breach of contract. However, H may not have an enforceable contract – there is no difficulty if she has a service contract independent of the articles (which is improbable) but, if she wishes to rely on the articles as providing the contract, she faces two difficulties. First, a contract based on the articles changes if the articles are validly amended (*Read v Astoria Garage* (1952));

and, second, even if the articles are not amended, it is unlikely that they give H an enforceable contractual right. The traditional view (which derives from the decision of Astbury J in *Hickman v Kent or Romney Marsh Sheepbreeders' Association* (1915)) is that a shareholder can enforce the articles only insofar as the relevant article creates a 'membership' right, that is, a right attaching to each and every share which relates to the holding of shares. It would seem that a right vested in only some of the membership is not such a right. For example, in *Eley v Positive Life Assurance Co* (1876), where the articles provided that E was to be company solicitor for life, E was held to have no contractual right of employment as solicitor. There seems little comfort for H here.

**Aim Higher** ★

Discussing the application of **s 994** of the **Companies Act (CA) 2006** in relation to the expropriation of Helen's shares and the dissipation of the company's traditional business could be useful here, although only the expropriation of her shares would suggest a strong ground for a successful petition under **s 994 CA 2006**.

# QUESTION 10

Robin, Swan and Turkey incorporated their existing printing business as Birdsong Ltd. They each hold 17% of the share capital and are the directors of the company. Four employees of the company each hold 5% of the share capital and the remaining shares are unissued.

The articles of the company depart from the **Model Articles (2008)** in the following respects:

(a) Robin, Swan and Turkey are named as directors for life and may only be removed by special resolution.
(b) On a vote to remove a director, that director would be entitled to three votes per share.
(c) In the event of any additional shares being issued, such shares must be offered to existing shareholders in proportion to their then shareholding.

The directors have decided to restructure the business and many processes will, in future, require appreciably less staff than at present. The employees are opposed to the restructuring and consequent reduction in the workforce. The directors propose to allot the unissued shares at a high price, knowing that it is unlikely that the employees will have the funds to purchase them.

▶ Advise the employees.

# ANSWER

## (A) LOCUS STANDI

The employees are seeking advice about the restructuring of the company. The first issue to consider is whether they have any *forum* for objection or *locus* to object either as employees or as shareholders in the company. While the **Companies Act (CA) 2006** requires the directors to have regard to the interests of employees, as part of a 'general duty' to act *bona fide* in a way that would most likely promote the success of the company for the benefit of the members as a whole (**s 172 CA 2006**), employees do not have *locus* to object to decisions of the directors and shareholders. Obviously, the employees can make their feelings known, but they have no status in company law. The employees who are also shareholders are in a different position: they are members of the company and can attend company meetings and vote on resolutions. However, a restructuring of the business by the board does not require approval by the shareholders unless it necessitates a change in the articles for which a special resolution would be required (**s 21 CA 2006**). For example, if the restructuring needed a change in the objects of the company, as specified in the articles, a special resolution would be necessary. The employees have sufficient votes to block a special resolution (20 out of the 71 issued). If no shareholder approval is required, it is likely that the restructuring falls within the general power to manage the company vested in the board, in accordance with the **Model Articles (2008)** which, in this case, would be **Sched 1, art 3**.

Can the shareholder-employees require a meeting to be held to discuss their objections? **Section 303 CA 2006** permits members holding not less than 10% of the issued share capital to require the directors to call a general meeting. On receipt of such a requisition, the directors have 21 days to call a meeting to discuss those matters specified in the requisition. Thus, the shareholder-employees can obtain a meeting. Can they do anything more?

## (B) RESTRUCTURING

At the meeting, the shareholder-employees can raise their objections to the restructuring but cannot block it; nor have they the power to sack the board (a simple majority is required – s 168 CA 2006). They could argue that the proposals are unfairly prejudicial to them, but the courts have been reluctant to use s 994 CA 2006 where there is a dispute between shareholders as to the policies of the company with no allied impropriety. For example, in *Re Saul Harrison and Sons plc* (1995), a shareholder failed to prevent the directors of a company, who had substantial assets but a revenue deficit, from continuing to operate the company, rather than, as she wished, winding up the company and distributing its assets. The Court of Appeal held that unfairness for the purposes of s 994 CA 2006 was primarily governed by the constitution of the company and, if they had been complied with, the section was unlikely to be operative. Here, the majority of shareholders (the directors) approve the new policies, so the fact that it does not suit others is unlikely to give the disgruntled individuals a remedy. If, however, the directors are exercising their powers of management for an improper purpose, an action under s 994 CA 2006 might succeed.

## (C) ARTICLES OF ASSOCIATION

We must now turn to the provisions in the articles relating to the terms of employment of the directors; first, the weighted voting clause which effectively renders a director impregnable unless all other shareholders vote to dismiss him (he has 51 votes and the rest of the issued shares could muster 54) using s 168 CA 2006. Despite powerful objections, it is well established that a weighted voting clause of this type is valid (*Bushell v Faith* (1970)), at least in companies of this type which are small and private, as are entrenched provisions generally under s 22 CA 2006. Such a clause could be deleted using the procedure set out in s 21 CA 2006, which states that a company can change its articles by special resolution. However, this would require all the shareholders except a single director to vote in favour of the change, which may be difficult to achieve. The court is even less likely to upset the clause than in *Bushell*, since, even with the clause, s 168 CA 2006 is not nullified, as all the shareholders together could dismiss any one director. Nor will the fact that the directors' service contracts exceed two years (contrary to s 188 CA 2006) aid the shareholders. It may be that the contracts were approved in advance by the shareholders in general meeting – in which case they are unchallengeable. However, breach of s 188 CA 2006 does enable the company to terminate the contract by the giving of reasonable notice, but such notice is given by the company and it is the directors of the company who determine the company's decision to give notice.

# (D) ALLOTMENT

Finally, can the shareholder-employees block the proposed allotment of shares? Whether it is the board or the general meeting which has the power to allot shares, s 550 CA 2006 allows the directors to issue shares in a private company which has one class of shares, unless prohibited by the articles. In all other respects, directors' power to allot shares must come from the articles or by company resolution (s 551 CA 2006). The three directors between them can control the general meeting, and so they, as the general meeting or the board, have the power to allot these shares.

Section 561 CA 2006 requires shares to be offered to existing shareholders in the proportion of their current holding; this the directors seem willing to do, confident that the shareholders cannot take up the offer. Even if the pre-emption right was ignored, the allotment would be valid and the disadvantaged shareholders would be limited to an action for damages. An alternative course would be for the directors to offer the shares in return for non-cash consideration when the pre-emption right is inapplicable, or to act where the articles or a company resolution provide for the disapplication of the pre-emption right under s 569 CA 2006 (private company with only one class of shares). However, the ability of the directors to allot shares is subject to the requirement that the directors, as fiduciaries, exercise their power *bona fide* for the benefit of the company and for a proper purpose (s 171 CA 2006). The so called proper purpose test has been interpreted by the courts as giving judges the power to determine the purpose for which a power has been allocated to the directors by the shareholders and to strike down any attempt to use the relevant power for other purposes. Thus, in *Bamford v Bamford*, the Court of Appeal ruled that an attempt to block a takeover bid by allotting shares to associates was an improper use of directors' powers. In a case similar to this one, *Pennell v Venida* (1974), a rights issue which the directors knew could not be taken up by one impoverished shareholder was struck down as designed to emasculate the shareholder who objected to certain proposals by the board.

While, *prima facie*, these cases seem to stymie the directors, there is no doubt that an act which is for a collateral purpose can be ratified by the company in general meeting by ordinary resolution (s 239 CA 2006 – see *Bamford v Bamford* (1970); *Hogg v Cramphorn* (1967)), and the majority could achieve this. While ratification of the rights issue may be possible, it would seem to be an obvious case for an application under s 994 CA 2006. While a blatant attempt to emasculate one group of shareholders appears to be a clear case of unfair prejudice which would leave a court with an unfettered discretion to devise an appropriate remedy, it might be thought that the shareholders in this case were merely trying to impose their view of the company's future on the majority and, consequently, the s 994 application could fail. If an action were to succeed, the most likely remedy would be an order for the purchase, by the majority shareholders or the company, of the dissenting member's shares (s 996 CA 2006).

In conclusion, the position of the employees appears less than hopeful.

## Aim Higher ★

You could comment on the practical and financial difficulties associated with a company in general meeting using **s 168 CA 2006** as a means of removing a director.

# QUESTION 11

(a) 'Corporate power lies with the board of directors.' Comment on this proposition.

(b) The shares of Rail Nostalgia Ltd are owned equally by its five shareholders, A, B, C, D and E. A, B and C make up the board of the company. The company needed to purchase iron chairs and agreed to buy them from Alpha Bros, of which A is a partner. A disclosed to the board that he was a partner of Alpha Bros but did not reveal that he would receive a commission on the sale. On discovering the truth, D proposed to the board that the company should seek to rescind the purchase, but the board refuse to do so. At a subsequent general meeting, D and E vote to take legal action against A but the board have refused to act. What is the legal position?

## Answer Plan

Part (a) is essentially a description of the division of power within a company, with a concluding paragraph to be added as comment.

Part (b) involves a possible breach of director's duty by A and the power to sue.

# ANSWER

## (A) CORPORATE POWER

The shareholders are the owners of the shares of a company and can, generally, do what they wish with their property. They are free to run the company as they see fit (subject to the rules of company law), either in person or by appointing representatives to act on their behalf. In practice, the shareholders appoint such representatives – a board of directors. The directors of a company may be co-extensive with the shareholders (for example, in small family owned and run companies), be existing shareholders on appointment (majority or minority), acquire shares on appointment, or own no shares in the company. When the shareholders in general meeting and the board are not co-extensive, even if there is an overlap in membership, there is potential for conflict. The issue that then arises is who makes the decisions for the company. Early cases suggested that the power to run a company must be vested in its members – the shareholders – but the Court of Appeal in *Automatic Self-Cleansing Filter Syndicate Co Ltd v Cunninghame* (1906) made it clear that the division of power between the board and the shareholders in general meeting depended on the articles of the company. Where the articles had vested power in the board, it was the board, said the court, and the board alone which ran the company. This view was affirmed by later cases including the House of Lords' decision in *Quin and Axtens v Salmon* (1909), and it is now well settled that, where the articles give the power to manage to the board (for example, **Sched 1, art 3 or Sched 3, art 3** to the **Model Articles (2008)**), they have an exclusive power to do so, subject only to the provisions of company law and any restrictions upon their powers contained in the articles themselves. This does not mean that the board's authority is inalienable; a power given in the articles can be changed or deleted by amending the articles. However, amendment of the articles requires a special resolution (a three-quarters majority of those present and voting – s 21 **Companies Act (CA) 2006**), so that changing the articles is not easy; indeed, if the board members hold 25% or more of the votes, it is impossible without the agreement of the board.

Where the general meeting is unable to amend the articles, the drastic step of dismissing all or some of the directors and the substitution of more pliable office holders might be possible. **Section 168 CA 2006** provides that the general meeting can dismiss a director by ordinary resolution (that is, a simple majority of those present and voting). While easier to achieve than amendment of the articles, dismissal of the directors, even where possible, will leave any new directors with the same powers of management as those possessed by the former board. Moreover, directors of small companies can effectively nullify s 168 **CA 2006** by the use of a weighted voting clause, which gives their shares extra votes where there is a proposal to dismiss a director (*Bushell v Faith* (1970)). Such a clause could be deleted using the procedure set out in s 21 **CA 2006** but this requires a special resolution. Consequently, one can conclude that the board is not susceptible to the control of the general meeting *unless* the articles provide a method of control.

Since 1906, the majority of companies have adopted the equivalent provision of the **Model Articles (2008)** to determine the division of power between the general meeting and the board: the current provision is contained in **arts 3** and **4** of **Scheds 1** and **3** to the **Model Articles (2008)**. These provide that, subject to the articles and any special resolution of the members of the company, directing the directors on the taking, or refraining from taking, specified action, the business of the company shall be managed by the directors who may exercise all the powers of the company. Thus, it can be seen that the shareholders can give the directors instructions on how to manage – but only in compliance with any particular provision in the articles or by special resolution. Where directions are given, they cannot invalidate any prior act of the directors but can, presumably, instruct the directors not to implement that prior act if it is still executory. The wording of the articles seems also to allow the shareholders to instruct the directors to undertake a course of action which the board had resolved not to pursue. It might be thought peculiar that the board can be sacked by ordinary resolution but cannot be instructed other than by special resolution, particularly where the company is small or of the quasi-partnership type.

From the above discussion, it can be concluded that the board always runs the company, but, where the board cannot or will not exercise the power vested in it, the general meeting regains, at least temporarily, the power to run the company. For example, in *Barron v Potter* (1914), the two directors of the company were not on speaking terms and board meetings could not be held – the power to conduct the company's affairs vested in the shareholders until an effective board was in place. Note that the default powers of the general meeting operate only where the board is completely incapable of acting and not when a minority of directors use their powers to block a decision by the majority of the board (see, for example, *Breckland Group Holdings v London and Suffolk Properties* (1989)), for, in the latter case, the board is precluded from acting by the operation of the articles, not by an incapacity to act. Moreover, an individual shareholder can commence legal proceedings on behalf of the company even if that is not the wish of the board or the general meeting if he is able to bring a derivative claim in accordance with **ss 260–264 CA 2006**.

This is a situation where shareholders might be wise to agree to a shareholder agreement which could provide remedies against the other shareholders, even if it did not bind the company.

## (B)  RAIL NOSTALGIA LTD

Assuming Rail Nostalgia Ltd has articles in the form of the **Model Articles (2008)** the directors have the power to manage the company. The directors of the company, A, B and C, own 60% of the shares of the company and are, while united, immune from dismissal or the giving of directions as to how the company should be run. As directors, they owe statutory duties (**ss 171–177 CA 2006**) which are based on the case law derived duties of care and skill and fiduciary obligations. These duties are generally owed to the company and not to the shareholders (s 170(1) CA 2006 – *Percival v Wright* (1902); *Peskin v Anderson* (2001)). Here, D and E are seeking to initiate litigation against A, alleging that, in breach of his director's duty, he failed to make adequate disclosure of the circumstances surrounding the contract to buy iron chairs from A. Any attempt to sue a director raises two issues: first, who has the *locus* to sue; and, second, is there a breach of duty?

Since a breach of duty by a director is a wrong done to the company, the person who can sue the director is the company. The relevant body to determine whether to sue is the body with the power to run the company – in this case, the board, in accordance with **Sched 1, art 3** to the **Model Articles (2008)**. Consequently, it might be concluded that, since the board is not in favour of litigation, A is immune from suit. Certainly, D and E cannot instruct the board how to act (only 40% shareholding, whereas 75% is required to give directions), nor could they sack A, B and C. Where the company declines to sue, the rule in *Foss v Harbottle* (1843) generally precludes litigation by a minority shareholder. However, in order to vindicate the company's rights, a shareholder can bring a derivative claim on behalf of the company where a wrong committed by a director is caught by **s 260 CA 2006**. This provision replaces generally the common law exception to *Foss v Harbottle* (1843) of 'fraud on a minority'. However, an applicant bringing a derivative claim would need the permission of the court to continue with the claim (**ss 261** and **263 CA 2006**) (see *Iesini v Westrip Holdings Ltd* (2009); *Kiani v Cooper* (2010)) and the common law rules on authorisation (**s 180(4) CA 2006**) and ratification (**s 239(7) CA 2006**) are preserved. In *Daniels v Daniels* (1978), a shareholder was given *locus* to sue a director who had sold land to herself at an alleged undervalue. Templeman J ruled that a director who was negligent might not be the subject of a derivative action but that a director whose negligence resulted in a profit of £115,000 to herself could be so liable. Under **s 260 CA 2006** negligence is no longer a bar to bringing a derivative claim, but permission of the court to continue with the action is required (ss 261 and 263 CA 2006). In this case, the 'wrongdoers' control the company (by virtue of both the articles and their 60% shareholding). In *Smith v Croft (No 2)* (1988), Knox J held that, where an independent organ of the company rather than a wrongdoer was blocking litigation, the shareholder had no right to drag the company into litigation – the denial of proceedings was entirely proper. This does not seem to apply here and, presumably, a derivative action could be brought. What, then, is the 'wrong' committed by A and ignored by B and C?

A, as a director, is subject to a number of statutory duties, derived from equitable principles, to ensure that there is no conflict between his duty to the company and his own personal interest (**ss 175–177 CA 2006**). One area where the possibility of such conflict arises is when a director benefits either directly or indirectly from a contract made by the company of which he is a director. In *Aberdeen Rly Co v Blaikie Bros* (1854), the House of Lords ruled that a director cannot benefit from a contract entered into by the company, even if the contract is perfectly fair. This strict approach was extended to indirect contractual benefits, as in this case, by *Imperial Mercantile Credit Association v Coleman* (1873). However, directors are not trustees and they are not prohibited from benefiting from their directorship, provided that any benefit is revealed in advance to the shareholders or, where permitted, to some other relevant body. Where there is no disclosure, the transaction is voidable at the company's option (*Hely-Hutchinson v Brayhead* (1968)), a rule preserved by **s 178 CA 2006**. However, the transaction is not voidable where, in the case of **s 175 CA 2006** (duty to avoid conflicts of interest) the directors have authorised the transaction. Where a director has an interest in an existing transaction or arrangement (**s 182 CA 2006**), which has not otherwise been disclosed under **s 177 CA 2006** (duty to declare interest in a proposed transaction), failure to disclose that interest renders the director liable to a fine (**s 183 CA 2006**). In addition to a possible breach of **s 182 CA 2006**, the transaction might amount to a substantial property transaction, in which case A must comply with **s 190 CA 2006**, that is, the transaction must be approved by a resolution of the members of the company and failure to so do renders the contract voidable (**s 195 CA 2006**). This, however, seems unlikely.

In conclusion, it seems that D and E may have *locus standi* to sue in the company's name, but that, should they seek so to do, A, B and C will simply ratify the disputed transaction, making it difficult for litigation to proceed.

## Common Pitfalls

Two-part questions always call for effective time management. Here, the first part of the question demands an essay type answer, while the second part of the question involves problem solving. Some cross-referencing should ameliorate the time problem.

## Aim Higher ★

Ensure that you cover the issue of breach of duty in both parts of the question with reference to *locus standi*, as simply establishing breach of duty in your answer is insufficient if you fail to comment on the ability or inability of the general meeting to instruct the board to initiate litigation.

# QUESTION 12

Christie Ltd was incorporated in 2006. The articles of the company contain the following provisions:

1. As long as he remains a member, Marple shall be entitled to be a director of the company and to be the company secretary.
2. Marple shall be paid such remuneration as a director as the board shall determine and he shall be paid not less than £20,000 per annum as company secretary.

Marple holds 15% of the issued shares of the company, the remainder being held by his brothers, Battle and Poirot. The three brothers are the only directors of the company but Poirot takes no active part in management. Marple quarrels with Battle over the future of the company: Battle enters into an agreement with Poirot whereby, in consideration of a payment of £10,000, Poirot agrees to vote with Battle at all board and general meetings. After appropriate notice, a general meeting is held and **Art 1** is deleted by special resolution.

The remuneration of the directors has never been fixed; Marple received about £75,000 in total for the years 2006–2008 'for services rendered'. He received no money in 2009 for his services as a director of the company but has always been paid for his work as company secretary. The company is profitable but has never declared a dividend.

▶ Marple is worried about his position and seeks your advice. Advise him.

## Answer Plan

Marple has, presumably, a number of concerns. First, the deletion of the article by virtue of which he had a right to be a director and to be the company secretary. Second, has he any entitlement to be paid while he continues to act as director and/or company secretary, and has he any claim for the period prior to the amendment of the articles? Third, is the voting agreement between Battle and Poirot valid?

In addition to any specific remedy open to Marple, consideration should also be given to overall remedies, for example, use of **s 994** of the **Companies Act (CA) 2006** or, less likely, **s 122(1)(g)** of the **Insolvency Act (IA) 1986**.

# ANSWER

In advising Marple (M), consideration must be given to his specific concerns relating to the change of articles, but also to the possibility of a more general remedy being open to him.

## (A)  DELETION OF ART 1

Companies are able to amend their articles by special resolution (s 21 CA 2006). M lacked a sufficient shareholding to block the passing of a special resolution to amend the articles of the company, so the deletion of Art 1 appears unchallengeable. However, shareholders, in voting to amend the articles, may not have an unfettered right to cast their votes with regard only to their own interests. There are *dicta* in the cases which suggest that, on a vote to change the articles, the shareholders (Battle (B) and Poirot (P)) must vote '*bona fide* for the benefit of the company' (*Allen v Gold Reefs of West Africa Ltd* (1900)). Could this apply in this case, so that M could seek the reinstatement of Art 1? There are two objections to such a proposal. First, the scope of this *dictum* is uncertain, although it is clear that, where the proposed change of articles is designed to appropriate the shares of the minority, the court will strike down the amendment unless it is objectively in the best interests of the company. For example, in *Dafen Tinplate v Llanelly Steel* (1920), an amendment to the articles which allowed any shareholder to be required to sell his shares in the company was rejected by the court as going beyond that which was necessary to benefit the company. However, whether there is a *general* requirement that shareholders vote on proposals to alter the articles in a manner which is objectively in the best interests of the company is uncertain. In addition, B and P could argue that this proposal *is* in the best interests of the company.

A further argument of which M should be apprised is that the deletion of this article may not affect his rights, in that Art 1 gave him no rights. B and P could then argue that, since M was no worse off, there could be no objection to the deletion of Art 1. Certainly, despite Art 1, M could have been sacked by ordinary resolution (s 168 CA 2006). Where dismissal using the statutory format constitutes a breach of contract, the sacked director would be entitled to compensation. However, if Art 1 did not give M any enforceable contractual rights as a director, M would be no worse off if he was dismissed by ordinary resolution before or after the deletion of Art 1. M might try to argue that Art 1 created a contract between himself and the company, which entitled him to be both a director and company secretary, because s 33 CA 2006 provides that the articles constitute a contract between the shareholders and the company. However, the scope of the s 33 contract and the ability of M to enforce it in his capacity as director/secretary is likely to disappoint him. The traditional view is that a shareholder can enforce the articles by virtue of s 33 CA 2006 only insofar as the relevant article creates a 'membership' right, that is, a right attaching to each and every share and which relates to the holding of shares. This view derives from the decision of Astbury J in *Hickman v Kent or Romney Marsh Sheepbreeders' Association* (1915) and would appear to preclude the enforcement of a right which does not fall into this category. In this case, it is difficult to see that a right conferred on M to be a director or to be company secretary could be regarded as a membership right. For example, in *Eley v Positive Life Assurance Co* (1876), where the articles provided that E was to be company solicitor for life, E was held to have no contractual right of employment as solicitor and, in *Beattie v E and F Beattie Ltd* (1938), a provision requiring members to submit disputes to arbitration was held not to apply to a dispute between the company and a shareholder in respect of his directorship.

# (B) ENTITLEMENT TO BE PAID

While M continues to act as company secretary, he is entitled to be paid for this work. If he has a service contract, that will define his entitlement. If M had an express service contract in respect of his role as company secretary, the deletion of **Art 1** would have no effect on that contract and any attempt to dismiss him in breach of the independent contract would allow M to sue for damages. Any amendment of **Art 2** could not affect a separate service contract or any entitlement already earned (*Swabey v Port Darwin Gold Mining Co Ltd* (1889)). **Section 21 CA 2006** could be used by B and P to amend the articles (for example, to change the salary in **Art 2**), even if the amendment resulted in breach of M's service contract, although damages would then be payable (*Southern Foundries (1926) Ltd v Shirlaw* (1940)). If the terms of M's service contract are expressed to be as set out in the articles, any amendment of the articles would amend the service contract (*Read v Astoria Garage Ltd* (1952)). If he has a service contract whose terms on the relevant issue (in this case pay) are deficient or non-existent, the articles may be treated as implied terms of the contract and, as terms, the articles would be enforceable under the normal rules of contract. If this applied here, M could rely on **Art 2** to claim £20,000 a year. In such a case, it would seem that amendment of the articles does not change the service contract because the usual rule in contract is that contract terms cannot be changed without the agreement of all parties to the contract. If M has no separate contract but is relying upon **s 33 CA 2006** to provide a contractual right to remuneration, he will be disappointed – see *Eley v Positive Life Assurance Co* (above) – in that the **s 33** contract does not apply to rights which are not membership rights.

While M remains a director, has he any entitlement to be paid? If he has an express service contract, his rights are parallel to those outlined above in respect of his role as company secretary. If M has a service contract, the terms of which are expressly based on the articles (terms subject to change using **s 21 CA 2006**) or a service contract into which the articles are implied (terms subject to change only with M's consent), his entitlement to remuneration is determined by **Art 2**. In *Re New British Iron Co ex p Beckwith* (1898), the directors were held entitled to claim the sum specified in the articles as remuneration because the relevant article was 'embodied in and formed part of the contract between the company and the directors'. This case was approved, *obiter*, by the House of Lords in *Guinness plc v Saunders* (1990). If M does not have a service contract, he cannot rely on **s 33 CA 2006** to confer a contractual right based on **Art 2** (see the arguments above). However, even if M can claim that the article gives him a contractual right, his right is limited to that provided by the contract which, in this case, is what the board decide. Thus, if the board decide to pay M nothing, he will receive nothing. Further, the House of Lords in *Guinness v Saunders* (1990) held that, where a provision in the articles was the implied contract term as to pay, the contract term was the exclusive definition of a right to pay, even if, as in that case and here, it effectively deprived the director of any remuneration.

## (C)  THE VOTING AGREEMENT

M may challenge the validity of any decisions by B and P acting as directors or shareholders, in that B has bought P's votes and P has exercised no independent judgment in voting. It has been repeatedly laid down that votes are proprietary rights which the holder can do with as he wishes and there seems little doubt that, as a shareholder, P can bind himself to vote in a particular way (*Alexander Ward and Co Ltd v Samyang Navigation Co Ltd* (1975)). However, in a limited number of cases, the courts have held that this freedom to deal with one's assets (votes) as one sees fit must be restricted in the wider interests of company law. Nevertheless, the situations where a shareholder is subject to an inalienable duty are mainly concerned with expropriation of company property or the shares of other members and do not seem to apply here. It can be concluded that in respect of the decision to delete **Art 1**, P's decision to sell his shareholder votes to B is unchallengeable.

The situation is different when M seeks to challenge P's sale of his votes as a director. P as a director owes general, statutory duties to the company. One duty is to act in good faith in a way that is likely to promote the success of the company for the benefit of the members as a whole, which requires the director to be free to vote at board meetings as he wishes; the director must be 'left free to exercise his best judgment in the interests of the company' (*Boulting v ACTAT* (1963)). Presumably, an agreement to fetter one's directorial discretion is a breach of duty, allowing M, a minority shareholder, to bring a derivative claim, prima facie at least, under **s 260 CA 2006**. While the agreement between B and P could be challenged by M, it would appear to be binding as between B and P themselves (*Dawson International v Coats Paton plc* (1989)). Not all agreements by directors to fetter their discretion are improper. If the directors take a decision, *bona fide*, to act in a particular way in the future, such a decision may be perfectly proper (see, for example, *Fulham FC v Cabra Estates plc* (1994)).

## (D)  GENERAL REMEDIES

Given the uncertainty of the remedies which apply to the specific difficulties faced by M, it would be wise to advise him of the possibility of pursuing a general statutory remedy. The statutory remedies open to shareholders are to apply for a just and equitable winding up under **s 122(1)(g) IA 1986** or to seek a declaration of unfair prejudice under **s 994 CA 2006**. The just and equitable winding up route will be open to the court where the company is of the appropriate type – traditionally called a 'quasi-partnership' company – and it is plain that there is such a breakdown in the relationship of the corporators that the company cannot function as intended.

In *Ebrahimi v Westbourne Galleries Ltd* (1973), the House of Lords ordered the winding up of a small company where one of the founder members was, lawfully, excluded from management. As, in this case, the clear intention of the parties was that all would participate in running the company and all profits were paid as directors' fees and not as dividends, so that dismissal of one director from his post meant that the underlying assumptions upon which the company was founded were destroyed and winding up was necessary. Of course, winding up is a very drastic remedy and M might prefer to use **s 994 CA 2006**. In *Re Kenyon (Swansea) Ltd* (1987), the court held that an attempt to exclude from management a director who had the legitimate expectation that he would continue to be involved in management was unfair prejudice. However, the fact that M hoped his involvement in management would continue may not be sufficient to found a 'legitimate expectation'. In *O'Neill v Phillips* (1999), the House of Lords stressed that such expectations must be based on a contract independent of the constitution or where equitable considerations meant that such expectations should be honoured. If **s 994 CA 2006** applied, the court could award a remedy – possibly the exclusion of B from management or, more likely, an order for the company or the respondent shareholder(s) to buy M's share at a fair price (**s 996 CA 2006**).

# 3 The Company and Outsiders

## INTRODUCTION

A company, if it engages in any business at all, must necessarily have dealings with persons who are not members of the company and may have dealings with members in a non-member capacity (for example, many shareholders of Sainsbury Ltd buy their groceries from the company). It is the ability of the company to deal with outsiders and the legal implications of such dealing that this chapter addresses.

There are two main issues. First, what is the company entitled to do in its capacity as a company and, if there are restrictions on its power to operate, what is the effect of overstepping these constraints? Second, since a company exists only as a matter of law and must necessarily act through human agents, what is the position where the human agent engages in an activity on behalf of the company which the company was authorised to do but which the agent was not authorised to transact on the company's behalf?

In both of these areas, there has been a considerable amount of statutory tinkering with the common law rules. With respect to the first issue (the powers of the company), this has simplified the law, but, in the second (the ability of individuals to bind the company), the law remains something of a mess.

### Checklist ✔

Students should be familiar with:

- the rules relating to the determination of the powers of a company and the consequences of non-compliance with any limitations on these powers;
- the rules relating to the ability of representatives of the company (or those purporting to represent the company) to bind the company.

The latter issue overlaps with the provisions pertaining to the liability of a director for breach of duty.

# QUESTION 13

The Consultation Document from the Company Law Reform Steering Group (*Modern Company Law for a Competitive Economy: Company Formation and Capital Maintenance* (London: DT1, 1999)) posed the following question:

> Do you agree that a company should henceforth have unlimited capacity, regardless of anything in its constitution, including its objects, but a member should continue to be able to take proceedings to restrain the doing of an act contrary to the constitution?

▶ Discuss.

## Answer Plan

In answering this question, a student should consider:

- ❖ the history and purpose of a company's objects;
- ❖ the effect of unlimited capacity;
- ❖ the position of the shareholders;
- ❖ the changes introduced by the Companies Act 2006.

# ANSWER

Under the Companies Act (CA) 2006, every company must have a memorandum of association which must be submitted to the Registrar of Companies prior to registration, except that, unlike previous Companies Acts, the memorandum is of historic value only. The CA 1985 stated that a company's memorandum had to state the 'objects of the company' (s 2(1) CA 1985), a provision which had been present in company legislation since 1856. The legal effect of the objects clause was determined by the House of Lords in the famous case of *Ashbury Railway Carriage Co v Riche* (1875), in which R sued the company for money owing to him in respect of his supervision of a project entered into by the company to build a railway in Belgium. The company sought to deny liability for this debt by pointing out that the objects of the company were to build railway rolling stock and not railways, and asking the court to hold that the objects clause defined the contractual capacity of the company, thus denying the company the capacity to engage in contracts relating to building railways. The House of Lords accepted the company's argument and held that since the company did not in law have the ability to enter into a contract to build a railway, it could have no capacity to employ R to supervise such a project – it was beyond the powers of the company, that is, it was *ultra vires*. Consequently, R had no contract and no contractual right to be paid.

The rationale behind this decision was that shareholders and creditors must know what they were putting their money into. While this might be true of shareholders, although one might argue that they would have no objection to their money being used in non-authorised but profitable purposes, it is difficult to see how this rule protects creditors. One could say that creditors whose debts are incurred in the company pursuing authorised debts are protected by the inability of the company to waste its money on paying debts incurred on unauthorised business, but this is a somewhat remote benefit. Interestingly enough, the decision in *Ashbury* was no more popular with companies than it was with *Riche*, and means were soon adopted to try to evade the effect of the decision. This unpopularity stemmed from the fact that a company might expand into new areas without realising the need to amend its objects so that the company, or others who had financed the change of direction, would find that they had entered into a series of unenforceable transactions. The difficulties of the rule itself were compounded by the doctrine of constructive notice, which meant that the objects clause, once registered, was constructively (that is, in law) notified to everyone. Thus, a person who made transactions with a company could not claim not to know that a transaction was not within the company's objects since, in law, he knew the contents of the objects clause. The doctrine of constructive notice in relation to the objects clause was abolished by s 711A CA 1985, as introduced by the CA 1989, although the section was not implemented, but its absence did not appear to cause any appreciable difficulty for a third party due to general reform of the doctrine of *ultra vires* by the CA 1989.

Prior to reform, companies sought means to evade the effect of the rule. This self-help approach generally took the form of adopting extremely long objects clauses, embracing everything the founders of the company and their advisers could think of with a view to authorising every conceivable activity. The judicial attitude to such self-help was mixed. In *Cotman v Brougham* (1918), the House of Lords reluctantly accepted the validity of an objects clause authorising the company to do almost anything. However, in later cases such as *Re Introductions* (1970), the Court of Appeal held that a list of registered 'objects' could be divided by the courts into 'true' objects and mere powers. A mere power did not give the company an absolute right to do something; it only gave a right to do something provided it promoted a true object. The situation was a mess. The rule existed but companies sought to evade it – sometimes with success and sometimes without. Parliament sought to amend the effect of the *ultra vires* rule in a series of statutory reforms. Initially, a company remained authorised to engage in activities which were permitted by its registered objects, but a third party dealing with a company could, if certain conditions were satisfied, enforce an *ultra vires* contract.

Despite the recommendations of the Prentice Report, the CA 1985, as amended by the CA 1989, did not abolish *ultra vires* either wholly or in part; rather it mitigated and marginalised the rule. In addition to s 711A CA 1985, three sections were inserted into the 1985 Act by the CA 1989. First, s 3A CA 1985, which might ultimately have rendered the *ultra vires* rule obsolete for all but charitable companies. This section provided that a company could adopt as its object 'to carry on business as a general commercial company' and that, in such a case, the company, has as its object, 'to carry on any trade or business whatsoever'. This section, which overturned case law that had rejected similar objects clauses, was strangely worded but it clearly allowed a company to adopt a general object so that a company which had such an object could be authorised to do practically anything. This general objects clause could not be adopted by non-commercial companies, for example, charities. Section 3A CA 1985 allowed, therefore, trading companies to adopt an object which authorised the pursuance of any lawful activity, so rendering the *ultra vires* rule moribund. However, such companies did not substitute this general object for their lengthy objects clauses, they merely added it to the list. Secondly, s 4 CA 1985 allowed a company to change its objects, for example to that authorised in a s 3A clause, by special resolution. This simplified the previous scheme for the alteration of objects and was designed to encourage existing companies to move to the new all-purpose objects clause.

Thirdly, s 35 CA 1985 provided for the enforcement of *ultra vires* transactions if certain conditions were satisfied. Section 35(1) CA 1985 provided that: 'The validity of an act done by a company shall not be called into question on the ground of lack of capacity by reason of anything in the company's memorandum.' This section, if it stood alone, would have given companies legal capacity comparable to that enjoyed by natural legal persons of full age and understanding; unfortunately, it did not stand alone. While s 35(1) CA 1985 said that the validity of an act done by a company cannot be called into question on the grounds of lack of capacity by reason of anything in the memorandum, it was thought to extend to an action not mentioned by the memorandum, that is, an act not restricted by the objects clause but not authorised by it either. Further, it was assumed that the section also covered a decision not to act by the company despite the reference to an act done.

Turning to the restriction on the operation of s 35(1) CA 1985: s 35(2) CA 1985 allowed a member of a company to restrain the company from doing an act which, but for s 35(1) CA 1985, was beyond the company's capacity. This provision was designed to retain a member's ability to ensure that his investment is used in a manner authorised by the objects clause. However, s 35(2) CA 1985 was itself restricted, in that it only permitted a member to restrain the directors from a proposed action unconnected to any 'legal obligation' arising. Thus, a shareholder could stop a contract which it is proposed shall be entered into, but could not stop the carrying out of a contract which had been entered into.

Perhaps to reinforce the idea that a member should have some control over the use of his money, s 35(3) CA 1985 provided that the shareholders could by special resolution ratify a transaction which was beyond the capacity of the company but for s 35(1) CA 1985. This allowed shareholders to decide whether to authorise, albeit retrospectively, the company to spend their money on *ultra vires* activities. If the shareholders did not ratify a transaction entered into by the company, s 35(1) CA 1985 still protected the person dealing with the company. The failure of the directors to observe the objects clause amounted to a breach of directors' duty and ratification of their action did not absolve the directors from liability. However, the shareholders could absolve the directors from liability by special resolution.

The changes introduced by the CA 1989 reduced the effect of the objects clause in a way which self-help could never achieve, even though they did not apply to statutory companies and registered charitable companies.

In the light of the difficulties associated with Review *ultra vires* rule and the complexity of the statutory reforms, the Company Law Steering Group proposed that private companies should no longer have an objects clause and would have unlimited capacity. This is the case for limited liability partnerships, as provided for by the Limited Liability Partnerships Act 2000. This seems an entirely sensible suggestion. The *ultra vires* rule was designed to have an internal effect (to allow members to know where their money was going), but there is no need for this rule of internal management to have any effect on third parties who deal with the company. However, the Steering Group wished to retain the ability of shareholders to restrain the doing of an act contrary to the constitution of the company. The effect of the CA 2006 is that a company is no longer required to have an objects clause. However, the CA 2006, which retains s 35(1) CA 1985 in the form of s 39(1) CA 2006, does provide that a company can have objects, but such restrictions have to be contained in the articles (s 31 CA 2006). The CA 2006 also provides for a measure of shareholder protection, as directors are under a duty to observe the company's constitution (s 171 CA 2006). It seems entirely sensible that shareholders can restrain the actions of directors in appropriate cases, but this does raise the usual problem with directors' duties – who enforces them and how.

# QUESTION 14

The main business of Cambridge Ltd is the publication of academic books and journals, as provided for by the company's objects clause. Following a downturn in the economy, the company plans to diversify. Cambridge Ltd's board of directors resolve that the company should produce sporting goods. For this purpose, the directors enter into the following transactions on behalf of the company:

(a) A loan of £1m from Bank plc with security granted over the company's assets in favour of Bank plc.

(b) The purchase of plant and machinery from London Ltd in order to manufacture a range of sporting products. The directors of London Ltd are aware that Cambridge Ltd's constitution does not contain any reference to the purchase of plant and machinery.

On being made aware of shareholder disquiet as to their activities, advise the directors of Cambridge Ltd as to whether the contracts are valid and binding and the extent, if any, of their liability.

## Answer Plan

An answer requires an analysis of the principles dealing with the capacity of the company and the board of directors to enter into binding arrangements of the kind that have taken place. In particular, there is a need to consider the provisions of the Companies Act (CA) 2006, which amends further the law relating to the doctrine of *ultra vires*, a process which was undertaken by the Companies Acts of 1985 and 1989. There is also a need to consider the position of the company in respect of any breach of duty by the directors and forms of corporate action.

# ANSWER

The first issue to comment on, giving the passing of the CA 2006, is that a company is no longer required to have an objects clause. Any restrictions relating to its objects, although permitted, must be contained in the company's articles (s 31(1) CA 2006). This provision applies to both new and existing companies, so that, although Cambridge (C) Ltd's objects are in its memorandum, the effect of the CA 2006 is that the objects are treated as being contained in the company's articles and the company's articles will need to be amended accordingly (s 31(2) CA 2006).

Given the restrictions on the company's activities, the next issue to consider is whether the transactions between C Ltd and Bank (B) plc and between C Ltd and London (L) Ltd are valid and binding. There may be a concern that the transactions are *ultra vires*, i.e. beyond the powers of the company, and, therefore, void and unenforceable.

Section 39 CA 2006 provides that no act (which includes contractual arrangements) can be questioned on the ground of a lack of capacity in the company's constitution. Therefore, from an external perspective, the contracts between C Ltd and B plc and C Ltd and L Ltd are valid and enforceable. This is due to the effect of s 39 CA 2006 which abolishes the doctrine of *ultra vires* – i.e. there is no limitation on a company's capacity to enter into contracts.

Similarly, where an act of a company is within the company's powers but outside the powers of the directors, a third party dealing with the company can assume that there is no limitation on the powers of the directors or those authorised by the directors (s 40(1) CA 2006). It is a requirement of s 40 CA 2006 that the third party is acting in good faith. However, the section states that a third party is not bound to enquire as to any limitation on the directors' powers and neither is mere knowledge on the part of the third party that the directors have exceeded their powers sufficient to amount to a lack of good faith (s 40(2) CA 2006). To that extent, L Ltd's knowledge that C Ltd's directors have acted beyond their powers does not affect the application of s 40(1) CA 2006 in protecting the third party. Section 40(4) CA 2006 enables a shareholder to seek an injunction to prevent the company from acting beyond the powers of the directors. The chances of success in obtaining an injunction however are limited, as relief is subject to (a) any 'legal obligation' arising from the act of the company (s 40(4) CA 2006); (b) ratification of the act by the company (s 239 CA 2006); (c) whether the act *is* beyond the directors' powers; and (d) the fact that any injunctive relief is discretionary. The facts of the question suggest that the two contracts have been entered into, so subjecting the company to legal obligations. On that basis, it would be too late for a shareholder to restrain the company.

There have been two reported decisions on s 40 CA 2006, dealing with the meaning of 'person' within s 40 CA 2006 and the extent to which a third party is protected by the section – *Smith v Henniker-Major & Co* (2002) and *EIC Services Ltd v Phipps* (2004). In *Smith*, in a mistaken, but honest, breach of the articles, a director entered into a contract with the company at an inquorate meeting of the board of directors and he attempted to rely on s 40 CA 2006 to validate the transaction. The Court of Appeal held, by a majority, that although a requirement for a quorum of directors was a limitation on the powers of the board of directors and that s 40 CA 2006 was wide enough to include a director of the company, s 40 CA 2006 could not protect a director relying on his own mistake in order to validate something which had no validity under the company's constitution. In *EIC Services*, the Court of Appeal held that a shareholder of a company, as an 'insider', could not rely on s 40 CA 2006 in respect of an issue of shares that was beyond the powers of the directors of the company. The share issue was void and unenforceable.

Section 41 CA 2006 provides a different conclusion as to the issue of contractual validity, where a third party to a contract with a company is a director of the company or is connected to a director of the company. Although possible, it seems unlikely that B Ltd or L Ltd are connected to one or more of the directors of C Ltd. Under s 41 CA 2006, any transaction between the company and the director (or connected third party) is deemed voidable, at the instance of the company, where the transaction exceeds any limitation placed on the powers of the board of directors or is beyond the powers of the company. It will cease to be voidable, however, where the company affirms the transaction or some other limit to rescission operates (s 41(4) CA 2006). The section further provides that the third party or the directors of the company who authorised the transaction are liable to indemnify the company for any loss or damage resulting from the transaction and to account to the company for any gain made from the transaction (s 41(3) CA 2006).

Where transactions involving third parties are valid, action can be taken against the directors for breach of duty in failing to act in accordance with the company's constitution (s 171(a) CA 2006). By acting beyond the company's objects, have the directors breached this duty? Further, the directors are under a duty to act *bona fide* in a way that is most likely to promote the success of the company for the benefit of the members as a whole (s 172 CA 2006). The duties are owed to the company and not to any individual shareholder (s 170(1) CA 2006, see *Percival v Wright* (1902) and *Peskin v Anderson* (2001)). These statutory duties of a fiduciary nature require a director to exercise his powers in a way which has regard to the interests of the person to whom the duties are owed and not to abuse his position of trust and influence within the company.

Although the directors may normally have the power to sue, as part of a general power of management (art 3 of the Model Articles (2008)), where the directors are the wrongdoers, the shareholders can exercise a residual power to sue on behalf of the company. Section 260 CA 2006 also provides that a member can bring a derivative claim on behalf of the company against a director for breach of duty, but such a claim requires the shareholder to establish a *prima facie* case (s 261 CA 2006) and to obtain the permission of the court to continue with the claim (s 263 CA 2006). Section 260 CA 2006 provides that the shareholder must establish that the directors are in breach of duty and the company has a cause of action arising from such a breach. Assuming that the conduct of the directors amounted to a breach of duty, e.g. in accordance with s 171 CA 2006 or s 172 CA 2006, the shareholder must then establish a *prima facie* case under s 261 CA 2006. If the court is satisfied that there is a *prima facie* case, it has the power *inter alia* to give directions as to the evidence to be provided by the company and, on hearing the application, to give or refuse permission to continue the claim (s 261 CA 2006). Under s 263 CA 2006, the court must refuse to give permission where the court is satisfied that a person acting in accordance with s 172 CA 2006 (duty to promote the success of the company) would not seek to continue with the claim (*Iesini v Westrip Holdings Ltd* (2009)) or where the act has been authorised or ratified by the company (s 263(2) CA 2006). Where this is not the case, s 263 CA 2006 sets out factors the court can take into account in deciding whether to allow the claim to proceed. These include whether the shareholder is acting in good faith (*Kiani v Cooper* (2010)); the importance that a person acting in accordance with s 172 CA 2006 would attach to continuing the claim (*Franbar Holdings Ltd v Patel* (2008); *Kiani v Cooper* (2010)); how likely in the circumstances the act would be authorised or ratified by the company; whether the company has decided not to pursue the claim; whether the member could pursue an action in his own right; and the views of other members who have no personal interest (s 263(3)(4) CA 2006). The Secretary of State has the power to add to the circumstances in which permission is to be refused or given (s 263(5) CA 2006). Any decision by the company to ratify the conduct of the directors amounting to a breach of duty must be taken by the members, the votes of the directors as shareholders not counting (s 239 CA 2006), unless the consent is unanimous (s 239(6) CA 2006). The common law and equitable rules on acts which are incapable of ratification are preserved by s 239(7) CA 2006. For example, a derivative claim did not lie at common law where the shareholder participated in the fraud or had benefited from it (*Nurcombe v Nurcombe* (1985)), has sued for an ulterior motive (*Barrett v Duckett* (1995)) or has failed to establish that it is the wrongdoers who are blocking litigation by the company (*Smith v Croft (No 2)* (1988)).

It would appear therefore that a shareholder of C Ltd would be faced with a number of significant hurdles to overcome in order to succeed with a derivative claim under the CA 2006.

## Common Pitfalls

Avoid stating a lot of the past law on the doctrine of *ultra vires*. The abolition of the doctrine is significant, but there is no need to review all the past cases and rules in this area. Ensure you understand the difference between 'external' and 'internal' effect – i.e., keep the two aspects separate, even if the facts might relate to both.

## Aim Higher ★

Demonstrating a good understanding of the difference between 'external' and 'internal' aspects of corporate transactions is important. The former deals with the validity of company acts and contracts between the company and a third party, i.e. whether the company is 'externally' bound to a particular act or contract with an outsider or insider. The latter, however, deals with the liability of directors for exceeding their powers, which is a matter 'internally' between the company and its directors.

# QUESTION 15

Epsom Eels Ltd and Newbury Nosh Ltd are companies set up to provide catering services at racecourses. The following events have occurred:

(a) Alf, the company secretary of Epsom Eels, has been buying alcohol from Zak. Alf has charged the alcohol to the company but he has used it in another business with which he is connected. Zak has demanded payment from the company.

(b) Bryony, a shareholder in Newbury Nosh, has written derogatory comments about the board in the press. The other directors have suggested that it would be in the best interests of the company if either they or the company purchased Bryony's shares.

(c) Charlie, a shareholder in Epsom Eels, has discovered that the company entered into a transaction which was beyond the company's objects as set out in the company's articles. Charlie has insisted that the company withdraw from the transaction and wishes to initiate litigation against the directors for disregarding the constitution of the company.

▶ Advise Zak, Bryony and Charlie respectively.

## Answer Plan

This question addresses a number of issues conveniently set out in the three parts of the question:

(a) Is the company bound by this contract?

(b) Can the company or the directors insist on Bryony selling her shares to either the directors or the company?

(c) Can Charlie insist that the company withdraws from this transaction and can he obtain a remedy for a breach of duty by the directors?

# ANSWER

## (A) IS THE COMPANY BOUND BY THE ALCOHOL CONTRACT?

Zak, the supplier of alcohol, wants to be paid. He can claim against Epsom Eels (EE) Ltd if the company was authorised to purchase alcohol and the person who negotiated the contract was authorised to act on behalf of the company in a transaction of this type. There is little doubt that EE Ltd was authorised to enter into this contract given its line of business, but even if this was not the case, Zak could enforce the contract under **s 39 Companies Act (CA) 2006**. However, in order to enforce the contract, Zak must also establish that Alf had authority to enter into a contract for the supply of goods.

If Alf was given express authority to purchase alcohol, then EE Ltd must pay Zak even though Alf has converted the alcohol for his own use: EE Ltd could pursue a remedy against Alf if it chose to do so. If we assume that Alf does not have express authority, then Zak must show that he had usual or ostensible authority in order to make EE Ltd liable. Usual authority can be defined as the degree of authority which it would be normal for a person occupying a particular post or office to possess. Thus, Zak needs to establish what could be regarded as 'normal' transactions which a company secretary could undertake and see whether the purchase of goods is among them. In *Panorama Developments Ltd v Fidelis Furnishing Fabrics Ltd* (1971), the usual authority of a company secretary (the position held by Alf) was held to include the hiring of cars to transport visitors to the company's premises. Consequently, the company was liable for the car-hire charges even when the secretary had used the cars for his own purposes. In that case, the court considered that the company secretary has usual authority to run the administrative side of a company's affairs: this could involve purchasing office equipment, hiring staff and generally ensuring the smooth running of the support side of a business. Thus, Alf could be said to have usual authority to purchase goods, but probably not goods relevant to the commercial operations of EE Ltd. It seems likely that Alf did not have usual authority to enter into this transaction. Could Alf have ostensible authority? When those authorised to run a company (that is, those with actual authority) hold a person out as having authority to undertake particular tasks, then a third party who relies upon that representation is entitled to assume that the person held out has authority to act – the person held out has ostensible authority. In the important case of *Freeman and Lockyer v Buckhurst Park Properties Ltd* (1964), the Court of Appeal laid down four conditions for ostensible authority to operate:

❖ a holding out;
❖ by those with actual authority;
❖ on which the third party relied;
❖ with no restrictions on the authority of the person held out (or the ability to hold out) in the company's constitution (now subject to **s 40 CA 2006**).

We have no evidence to suggest any holding out in respect of this purchase by those with actual authority (the board), so it seems unlikely that Alf would have ostensible authority unless Zak could show that Alf had often purchased alcohol before and that EE Ltd had happily paid up in the past. There is no doubt that the board had the power to buy alcohol and it might be possible that the articles of EE Ltd authorised delegation of board powers to others. However, Zak cannot rely on this power of delegation to claim that he assumed that the board delegated power in this respect to Alf unless he could establish that he had read (rather than having constructive notice of) the articles (*British Thomson-Houston Co Ltd v Federated European Bank Ltd* (1932)). Even if Alf did have usual or ostensible authority, EE Ltd would not be bound if the transaction was so manifestly suspicious that Zak should have inquired as to the extent of Alf's authority (*Underwood Ltd v Bank of Liverpool* (1924), where a bank liable to reimburse a company when a director signed cheques drawn on the company's account into his own account). This purchase does not seem so suspicious as to require further inquiry. In conclusion, it seems unlikely that Zak can claim repayment from EE Ltd.

## (B) CAN BRYONY BE FORCED TO SELL HER SHARES?

It may be that the articles of the company provide that a shareholder can be required to sell his or her shares to the company (or the directors) in certain defined circumstances. If this is the case then **s 33 CA 2006**, which gives contractual effect to the articles, would allow the company to rely on that provision, although the court would not enforce the provision if it provided for acquisition without compensation, even if the conduct of the shareholder was detrimental to the company. However, directors who are not shareholders would not be able to enforce such a provision as individuals because they are not parties to that contract. Even if the directors were shareholders, the traditional view is that they could not enforce the articles other than in respect of provisions which related to their rights as shareholders. For example, in *Beattie v E and F Beattie Ltd* (1938), a provision requiring members to submit disputes to arbitration did not apply to a dispute between the company and a shareholder in respect of his directorship. Whether the **s 33** contract does extend to rights conferred other than in a capacity as a member remains controversial, but it seems unlikely that the directors acting for themselves could enforce such a provision in the articles.

If there is no power in the articles to require Bryony to sell her shares to the company, the company could seek to amend the articles (**s 21 CA 2006**) to insert such a provision. A change in the articles must, at least, be passed by special resolution. Even if Newbury Nosh (NN) Ltd succeeded in amending its articles, the courts have the power to strike down the amendment since shareholders, in voting to amend the articles, do not have an unfettered right to cast their votes with regard only to their own interests. There are *dicta* in the cases which suggest that on a vote to change the articles the shareholders must vote '*bona fide* for the benefit of the company' (*Allen v Gold Reefs of West Africa Ltd* (1900)). The scope of this *dictum* is uncertain, although it is clear that where the proposed change of articles is designed to appropriate the shares of a minority shareholder, the court will strike down the amendment unless it is in the best interests of the company. For example, in *Dafen Tinplate v Llanelly Steel* (1920), an amendment to the articles allowing any shareholder to be required to sell his shares in the company was rejected by the court as going beyond that which was necessary to benefit the company. A court might not overturn insertion in the articles of the right to require shareholders whose actions are detrimental to the company to sell their shares to the company at a fair price (for example, *Sidebottom v Kershaw, Leese and Co Ltd* (1920)). However, if the company has (or acquires) such a right, the court could still rule that making derogatory comments about the board is not sufficient to allow the company to exercise that right.

# (C) HAS CHARLIE ANY PROSPECTS OF SUCCESS IN HIS CLAIMS?

Under the **CA 2006**, a company is no longer required to have an objects clause. However, the Act does allow for a company to have objects but these must be contained in the articles (**s 31 CA 2006**). We are told that the transaction about which Charlie is complaining is beyond the objects of the company, so it is *ultra vires* and at common law unenforceable by or against EE Ltd. However, the common law has been amended by **s 39(1) CA 2006** which provides that: 'The validity of an act done by a company shall not be called into question on the ground of lack of capacity by reason of anything in the company's constitution.' Hence, it appears that the party with whom EE Ltd contracted can enforce the contract and that Charlie can do nothing to prevent it.

However, while Charlie may not prevent the contract from proceeding, he is entitled to complain that the actions of the directors in ignoring the objects clause are a breach of directors' duty (**s 171 CA 2006** – duty to act in accordance with the constitution). While the directors may be in breach of duty, Charlie has to establish that he is entitled to bring an action against them – he must show that he has *locus standi*. In *Foss v Harbottle* (1843), Wigram VC laid down the basic principle that a shareholder could not sue in respect of wrongs done to a company, since where a wrong has been done to the company, the proper claimant is the company. Hence, if disregard of the constitution of the company is a wrong done to the company, then Charlie has no right to sue on behalf of the company. However, there are exceptions, and the **CA 2006** sets out the means by which a shareholder can bring a derivative claim (previously available at common law) on the company's behalf for a wrong done to the company caused by breach of duty by a director (**s 260 CA 2006**). However, C would have to seek the permission of the court to continue with such a claim in accordance with **ss 261** and **263 CA 2006** and the difficulties such shareholders were faced with at common law are likely to be replicated in connection with proceedings brought under **Part 11 CA 2006**.

**Common Pitfalls**

This question comprises three scenarios, each involving issues of similar complexity, so make sure that your answer is appropriately balanced between the three parts.

**Aim Higher** ★

When discussing that part of the question dealing with agency, credit will be given for attempting to discuss the relevant cases in the light of the facts of the question. This can be equally said of the cases in connection with a derivative claim under **s 260 CA 2006** and its common law predecessor.

## QUESTION 16

The articles of Fish Ltd state that:

(a)  the board of directors may delegate all or any of its powers;
(b)  any transaction with a value of £40,000 or more must have the prior approval of the company in general meeting;
(c)  company cheques must be signed by two directors.

The board, recognising that the company is in need of new business, appoints Shark to the board, with particular responsibility for marketing, and instructs him to 'make things happen'. Without reference to the rest of the board, Shark immediately organises a 'sales conference' for potential clients at a luxury hotel in the Bahamas, at a total cost of £50,000. Shark pays a deposit of £5,000 to the hotel by means of a company cheque which he alone signs, having forged the signature of a second director, since he is keen to book the conference before the hotel implements a proposed price rise.

Shark has just reported his actions to the board. The board, horrified by the proposed expenditure, wishes to dismiss him from his post of Marketing Director and terminate his directorship, and intends to cancel the conference.

▶  Advise Shark and the luxury hotel.

## Answer Plan

Shark (S) and the luxury hotel have different concerns. S does not want to be dismissed from either his executive post or his office of director, or at least wants compensation for loss of office. The luxury hotel is concerned with the enforceability of the contract negotiated by S – issues of agency and effect of forgery arise. In the alternative situation, the hotel is looking at the enforceability of a contract negotiated by the board – the impact of the articles on enforceability and s 40 Companies Act (CA) 2006 are at issue.

# ANSWER

### S's DIRECTORSHIP

S should be advised that, in forging a signature on the cheque, he has committed a serious criminal act, for which he could be prosecuted. Even if prosecution, conviction and imprisonment ensued, this would not automatically terminate his non-executive directorship, although it might well terminate his executive directorship, since he would be unable to act as an effective marketing director from prison. Indeed, his conduct might be found to be evidence of fraud, which could lead to disqualification under the **Companies Directors Disqualification Act 1986**. Whether prosecution or imprisonment arises, S should be informed that he has broken the terms of his executive directorship by acting as he has and that it is likely to be a breach which entitles the company to terminate his contract of service. If this is so, there is no requirement to pay compensation, so that, even if there are more than four years of the service contract to run, there will be nothing, other than salary already earned, to pay S on termination of his executive role. The power to dismiss S from his executive post is vested in the company. As in most companies, this means that the power is vested in the board of directors (**art 3** of the **Model Articles (2008)**).

As to his non-executive role, this would continue unless and until terminated by the company. The articles of the company do not give the board power to dismiss a director (there is nothing in the **Model Articles (2008)** to this effect), so for the board to try to do so would be ineffective. However, there is no reason why the shareholders should not dismiss S by using **s 168 CA 2006**. **Section 168 CA 2006** allows the shareholders to dismiss a director by ordinary resolution, provided that appropriate notice of the meeting has been given and the director has had the chance to put his case to the shareholders and to speak at the meeting. The shareholders can use their powers under **s 168 CA 2006** even if a director has done nothing wrong and they just feel like a change – it is not a power which must be exercised for a proper purpose.

However, termination of office using **s 168 CA 2006** does not prevent the director from seeking compensation for loss of office (**s 168(5) CA 2006**).

### THE LUXURY HOTEL

Regardless of who negotiated the contract with the hotel, there is little doubt that Fish (F) Ltd had the contractual capacity to enter into such a contract, as a company is no longer required to have objects (**s 31 CA 2006**). Where, however, a company chooses to have objects, which by virtue of **s 31 CA 2006** must be contained in the articles, the contract would be valid and binding by virtue of **s 39 CA 2006**. However, simply because the company has the capacity to contract does not mean that the contract is binding on F Ltd. Since F Ltd is an artificial legal person, its decisions and actions have to be taken by natural persons acting on its behalf. These acts and decisions may fail to be taken by the board or the shareholders in general meeting or by agents or employees of the company. Whether a particular person (or persons) can bind the company to this contract is essentially a question of agency – the principal (F Ltd) is bound by acts entered into on its behalf by a person with actual, usual or ostensible authority so to do. In this company, it is the board of directors which has the power to make the decisions as to how the company is to operate (**art 3** of the **Model Articles (2008)**) subject to the need for approval from the general meeting for contracts valued over £40,000. Does this mean that S's agreement cannot bind the company?

## (A) CONTRACT NEGOTIATED BY S

The hotel wants the contract entered into by S, a single director, to be binding on F Ltd. In order to enforce the contract, the hotel must establish that S had authority to enter into this contract and bind F Ltd. Alternatively, F Ltd would be bound if it ratified an unauthorised act, but it seems obvious that the board has got cold feet about S's activities and has made it plain that it does not wish to ratify S's contract. Has S authority to bind the company?

Plainly, S has not got express authority to enter into this transaction unless the instruction to 'make things happen' confers express authority to do anything on S. Nor can the hotel rely on the articles to claim that S was impliedly authorised by the articles, in that the board could have delegated power to him, since the cases seem to accept such reasoning only where the third party has read the articles (*British Thomson-Houston Co Ltd v Federated European Bank Ltd* (1932)). This would raise difficulties for the hotel, since, if it had read them, it would know of the restriction on S's powers, although the hotel might be able to argue that it was entitled to assume that the general meeting had given permission in accordance with the principle enunciated in *Royal British Bank v Turquand* (1856). It is unlikely that the hotel has read F Ltd's articles.

More promising for the hotel is the possibility that S has usual authority to enter into this transaction. The extent of S's usual authority to enter into a transaction is determined by reference to the position which he holds, that is, he has the powers which the holder of such a post within a company would usually possess. For example, a company secretary has usual authority to run the administrative side of a company's affairs. This could involve purchasing office equipment, hiring staff and generally ensuring the smooth running of the support side of a business. In *Panorama Developments Ltd v Fidelis Furnishing Fabrics Ltd* (1971), the usual authority of a company secretary was held to include the hiring of cars to transport visitors to the company's premises, so that the company was liable for the car-hire charges even when the secretary had used the cars for his own purposes. The question for the hotel in this case is, what is the usual authority of a 'marketing director'?

S is a properly appointed director, so the problems of *de facto* appointments do not arise. There are no cases on the usual authority of a marketing director, so one can merely speculate on the scope of his usual authority. It can be assumed that S has authority for matters concerning marketing, but at some point the magnitude of the transaction might indicate that board approval is required – the sums involved in this case do not seem so large (but see the articles) that the hotel should instantly be suspicious; nor do there seem to be any suspicious circumstances which should have put it on its guard. If there are suspicious circumstances, the hotel will not be able to claim that it relied upon S's usual authority unless it 'made such inquiries as ought reasonably to be made' (*Underwood Ltd v Bank of Liverpool* (1924)).

Even if, *prima facie*, S has usual authority, the hotel has deemed notice of the limitation on the powers of individuals contained in the articles, because registration of the articles is constructive notice of their contents to the whole world. However, if the hotel can rely on s 40 CA 2006 (see below), the restriction on S's power contained in the articles does not bind it (s 40(2)(b) CA 2006). In addition to usual authority, an agent may have ostensible authority, whereby an agent of the company is held out by those with authority (for example, the board) as having wider powers than those normally possessed by an agent of that type (ostensible authority also has other meanings), but there seems to be no question of S possessing such authority. The scope of ostensible authority, if any, would also be curtailed by the articles unless the hotel could rely on s 40 CA 2006 to abrogate any restriction on S's authority.

The act of forgery committed by S should not destroy his usual authority, provided that he was simply carrying out an authorised task (conference organising) in an unauthorised way (*contra* the case of *Ruben v Great Fingall Consolidated* (1906)).

However, even if S is found to have authority to enter into the hotel contract, F Ltd is not criminally liable for the forgery committed by S.

Thus, the hotel could enforce the contract against F Ltd only if not bound by the restriction in the articles.

## (B) CONTRACT NEGOTIATED BY THE BOARD

There is no doubt that, if the board had decided to embark on organising a sales conference for less than £40,000, the company would have been bound. Even if such a decision had been a breach of directors' duty, for example if it had not been made *bona fide* (s 172 CA 2006) or for a proper purpose (s 171 CA 2006), that would not affect the validity of the transaction as far as the third party was concerned. However, in this case, the board has exceeded its powers by not referring the contract to the shareholders.

The hotel can rely on **s 40 CA 2006** if it wishes to enforce the conference contract despite the wishes of the shareholders. **Section 40(1) CA 2006** provides that, 'in favour of a person dealing with a company in good faith, the power of the board of directors to bind the company . . . shall be deemed to be free of any limitations under the company's constitution'. In interpreting this section, s 40(2) CA 2006 provides some guidance. A person 'deals with a company' if he is a party to a transaction or other act to which the company is a party – the hotel has no difficulty in satisfying this test. **Section 40(2) CA 2006** then provides that it is assumed that a person dealt in good faith unless the company proves the converse. Cases on earlier versions of s 40 CA 2006, which would probably remain applicable, ruled that good faith was a subjective test. Nourse J in *Barclays Bank Ltd v TOSG Trust Fund* (1984) stated that 'A person acts in good faith if he acts genuinely and honestly in the circumstances of the case'. There seems to be no evidence of any lack of good faith on the part of the hotel in this case and the hotel would appear to be protected by s 40 CA 2006. Moreover, s 40(2) CA 2006 provides that the hotel is not bound to enquire as to any limitation on the powers of the directors. Thus, the hotel can be advised that its contract with F Ltd is enforceable against the company.

## Aim Higher  ★

When discussing that part of the question dealing with agency, extra credit can be expected for discussing the relevant cases in the light of the facts of the question. Applying the law of agency is equally important to stating the law of agency.

# QUESTION 17

The objects of Mansfield Park Ltd, as contained in its articles, provide that Mansfield Park Ltd is to purchase a specific stately home, Mansfield Park, and convert it into luxury flats for rent, and that the company can also purchase and convert similar properties. The articles of the company are based on the **Model Articles (2008)** except that:

(a) the board of directors may delegate all or any of their powers or functions to any director or directors; and

(b) any contract to purchase land for the company's use must be approved by the company in general meeting.

At the outset, the company had three shareholders, Austen, Bingley and Collins, who each held 25% of the company's share capital. Austen and Darcy were appointed as directors; Darcy has always acted as managing director but has never been formally appointed to the position. Later, Elton was appointed to manage the flats at Mansfield Park. Recently, Elton ordered a car costing £25,000 in the company's name, to be used by him primarily for company business. Elton, in conjunction with Austen, has just negotiated the purchase, at a price of £500,000, of another property for conversion, Kellynch Hall, which Elton has just inherited.

Bingley and Collins do not wish the purchase of the car or Kellynch Hall to proceed and wish to dismiss Elton and restrict Austen to a non-executive role in the company.

▶ Advise Bingley and Collins.

## Answer Plan

The first issue is the ability of a manager to enter into a contract which can bind the company (the car) and whether he can be sacked. The second issue is whether Elton and Austen together bind the company to purchase Kellynch, and, if they can, does the fact that it belonged to Elton affect the validity of the contract?

# ANSWER

The power to run a company, which includes the right to sue errant directors, dismiss employees and seek to evade contracts, is determined by reference to the articles. This company has the **Model Articles, 2008**, so that it is the directors who decide whether to exercise legal rights on the company's behalf (**art 3**). The directors of this company are Austen (A) and Darcy (D). Bingley (B) and Collins (C) cannot instruct the directors as to how to run the company, because such instructions are operative only if given in the form of a special resolution (**art 4**), which they cannot muster (they hold 50% of the share capital, or 66% if only 75% is issued). However, B and C do have sufficient voting strength to obtain an ordinary resolution, which would enable them to dismiss A under **s 168** of the **Companies Act (CA) 2006**, which would terminate both the non-executive and executive roles. Should they do so, they may then seek to appoint new directors, run the company themselves (they would then be treated as the directors, even if not formally appointed – **s 251 CA 2006**) or reappoint A with limited powers.

While A remains in charge, the shareholders cannot engage in legal activity on behalf of the company, because the famous case of *Foss v Harbottle* (1843) provides that the power to act on behalf of the company lies with the company itself and, given the usual practice of adopting the **Model Articles (2008)**, the exercise of that power lies, in the main, with the directors. However, majority shareholders can exercise a residual power to sue where the wrong done to the company is committed by the whole board, or a shareholder can bring an action where *Foss v Harbottle* does not apply, an example of this being when the company has acted *ultra vires*. However, *ultra vires* is limited to cases where the company has exceeded its powers and is not in issue when the company itself is authorised but the particular human intermediary was not authorised to act.

The purchase of a car and the purchase of Kellynch clearly fall within the express or implied powers of the company, so that these contracts cannot be called *ultra vires*. Another exception to *Foss* arises when there is 'fraud on the minority', that is, where an unratifiable wrong has been done to the company and the wrongdoers control the company so that there is no effective champion of the company's rights. This was the common law position and the procedure in bringing such a claim is provided for by **s 260 CA 2006**. If the purchase of the car or Kellynch is such a wrong, then B and C have power to initiate litigation in the name of the company by means of a derivative action. This looks like being a remarkably long-winded way of outflanking A, whom they can sack, and it is difficult, although not impossible, to see why under **s 263 CA 2006** a court would allow B and C to act for the company while ignoring their alternative remedy. However, B and C might argue that it was more appropriate for them to sue rather than sack, if sacking A might jeopardise the existence of the company, in that A's dismissal could trigger a claim by him for just and equitable winding up. **Section 122(1)(g)** of the **Insolvency Act (IA) 1986** allows such an action if the company has the hallmarks of a 'quasi-partnership' company and the relationship of the parties has irretrievably broken down. This could well apply here.

If B and C dismiss A (or persuade him to fall in with their views), they may seek to evade the car and Kellynch contracts. Since there is no doubt that a company such as this has an implied power to purchase a motor car for a senior employee, even if he also uses it for non-company business, the company is bound by this contract unless it can establish that the person who negotiated the contract, E, had no power to bind the company to a contract of this type. Since Mansfield Park, as an incorporated company, is an artificial legal person, its decisions and actions have to be taken by natural persons acting on its behalf.

Whether E can bind a company is essentially a question of agency – the principal (the company) is bound by acts entered into on its behalf by a person with actual, usual or ostensible authority so to do. E does not appear to have actual authority to enter into this contract but he may have usual authority – that is, the authority that can be assumed to arise from the position he holds within the company. A senior manager must have some ability to bind his company but there is little case law on the usual authority of senior employees. It is a moot point whether a third party is entitled to allege that he was entitled to assume that E had the power to buy a car of relatively high value on behalf of the company.

Alternatively, E may have possessed ostensible authority. Ostensible authority allows a person to bind the company: those with actual authority, the board, have indicated to the world that E possesses such power, that is, they have given the impression that he has the relevant power and the car dealer has no reason to doubt the impression that the board has given him. The fact that the directors can delegate all or some of their powers does not mean that a third party is entitled to assume that a power has been delegated; there must be some indication by the board that E has the authority to bind Mansfield Park.

If E does not have usual or ostensible authority, it seems that the company is not bound by the car contract and it should be noted that **s 40 CA 2006** would not affect this. **Section 40 CA 2006** merely permits a restriction, which would limit an authority which would otherwise exist to be ignored; it does not confer authority where none existed previously.

E can be sacked by his employer, the company, provided that the decision to sack him is taken by the appropriate organ of the company – the board. The consequences of this will depend upon whether he was in breach of his contract of employment, which would allow dismissal without compensation, or whether there was no such breach, so that the company would have to compensate him on normal legal principles.

Finally, have B and C, either as the new board (or a new set of directors appointed by them) or as shareholders, any power to challenge the purchase of Kellynch? The question of authority again arises – can A (the sole legitimate director) and E (a manager) bind the company? Clearly, the company has the ability to undertake such a purchase, since the objects of Mansfield Park permit the purchase and conversion of other properties of a similar type to Mansfield Park itself. Kellynch would appear to be such a property. Whether B and C can prevent the contract of sale proceeding to completion without exposing the company to an action for breach of contract depends upon the authority possessed by the negotiators and the effect, if any, of the close relationship of the vendor with one of these negotiators. Plainly, neither A nor E, either together or singly, had actual authority to bind the company. While a manager must be regarded as having some usual authority by virtue of his position (see above), it cannot extend to a transaction of this magnitude (*Armagas Ltd v Mundogas SA* (1986)) so that the company is bound only if A has usual authority or A and/or E had ostensible authority.

Generally, the usual authority of a single director who is not a managing director is very limited, and in this case, D, however improperly, has been acting as managing director, so that A cannot be regarded as filling that post. Perhaps it could be argued that, since D is not a director (he has no shares), then A is the board, and that since the board could negotiate this contract, A could bind the company by virtue of being the only director; or that A, as the board, could hold himself out as able to bind the company. If A has no authority, he cannot bind the company; if he has authority, E may still appear to be defeated by art (b). Article (b) provides, in effect, that the purchase of land without the approval of the general meeting cannot bind the company. However, **s 40(1) CA 2006** provides that, 'in favour of a person dealing with a company in good faith, the power of the board of directors to bind the company . . . shall be deemed to be free of any limitations under the company's constitution'.

E, as vendor of Kellynch, falls within the section, especially since **s 40(2) CA 2006** provides that it is assumed that a person dealt in good faith unless the company proves the converse. Cases on earlier versions of **s 40 CA 2006**, which would probably remain applicable, ruled that good faith was a subjective test. Nourse J in *Barclays Bank Ltd v TOSG Trust Fund* (1984) stated that 'A person acts in good faith if he acts genuinely and honestly in the circumstances of the case'. Thus, the fact that the vendor is an employee of the company (even one who was involved in negotiations) does not mean that there is a lack of good faith on his part in this case and the vendor might well be protected by s 40 CA 2006. Neither s 190 CA 2006 nor s 195 CA 2006 apply to employees, so the transaction is not voidable on the basis of either of those sections. However, if E could be treated as a shadow director (s 251 CA 2006), although this appears unlikely, then s 190 CA 2006 (which applies to substantial property transactions) would apply and the sale would be voidable unless approved by the company in general meeting.

Entry into the land transaction is a breach of directors' duty on the part of A (and breach of his duty as employee on the part of E), but this simply gives the company a remedy against A and does not allow it to disregard the contract if it is rendered enforceable by s 40 CA 2006.

# Directors

# 4

## INTRODUCTION

There are few aspects of company law which do not, in some way, involve a discussion of the directors and their powers. Every company must have at least one director (two in the case of a public company) and they have a multifaceted role within a company. The directors may be employees, they have duties as directors and they generally act on behalf of the company in its dealings with the outside world (that is, they act as agents). This variety of functions means that any question can include an aspect relating to the directors. For example, a question on shares might raise issues of the power to allot (**s 549** of the **Companies Act (CA) 2006**), a question involving litigation might touch on the division of powers within a company, almost any transaction might be challengeable as an improper use of directorial power and, as discussed above in Chapter 3, the validity of a company's contract can turn on the authority of the director who purported to act on behalf of the company. In addition, questions might arise, although rarely as the only issue, on the validity of the appointment, the amount of remuneration or the legitimacy of a dismissal of a director.

The most likely area for questions solely on directors is that of the extent of their statutory duties. Prior to the passing of the CA 2006, these duties were based on case law, but it is expected that they will be interpreted and applied in the same way as the common law rules and equitable principles (**s 170(4) CA 2006**). Students must not become too narrow minded in addressing the issue of directors' duties. For example, a question may require consideration of a contract between a director and the company – obviously, the usual rules on disclosure, the nature of the disclosure and the effect of non-disclosure (including possible ratification) arise, but students must also consider the nature of the contract. Ask yourself whether the transaction is a substantial property transaction (**s 190 CA 2006**) or whether it involves a loan, etc (**ss 190–214 CA 2006**) or a service contract (**s 188 CA 2006**). Entry into a contract may also be attacked as an improper use of directors' power. Any question on directors' duties may raise the issue of *locus standi*; is the person seeking to sue the director authorised to do so? *Locus* involves the case of *Foss v Harbottle* (1843), its exceptions and the derivative claim procedure of **Part 11 CA 2006**, and it may be that a litigant denied *locus* on behalf of the company has an alternative remedy under **s 994 CA 2006** or **122(1)(g)** of the **Insolvency Act 1986**.

Linked to questions of directors' duties may be questions about the liability of third parties who have been involved in misappropriating corporate property. The ambit of constructive trusteeship in respect of third parties arises in such cases.

# QUESTION 18

The combination of *Percival v Wright* (1902) and *Foss v Harbottle* (1843) means that the directors' power of management contained in the **Model Articles (2008)**, as provided for by the **Companies Act (CA) 2006**. Effectively frees directors from any risk of litigation for breach of duty being brought by minority shareholders or creditors.

▶ Discuss.

## Answer Plan

First, discuss what the decisions and the statutory provisions provide, then turn to the effect of the law on potential actions by minority shareholders or creditors. Sum up by determining whether directors are right to feel fearless.

# ANSWER

Private companies are required to have at least one director, public companies must have at least two (**s 154** of the **Companies Act (CA) 2006**). When a company is registered, the shareholders of the company possess the authority to determine how the company will operate and be operated, and they are not required to bestow all or any of their powers on the board of directors. The shareholders generally give away their power to run the company in the articles (e.g. **art 3** of the **Model Articles (2008)**) but the degree of delegation is a matter for the shareholders to determine, either in the articles or subsequently. In practice, most companies adopt the model articles, which effectively gives the power to operate the company, which would otherwise be vested in the shareholders in general meeting, to the directors. Consequently, the shareholders (majority or minority) cannot complain if the directors exercise the powers which have been delegated to them unless the articles of the company, or other provision giving power to the directors, restrict the apparently unfettered use of such powers. The articles can, of course, be changed by special resolution (**s 21 CA 2006**) but this will not avail a minority shareholder (who will be unable to muster the requisite number of votes) or a creditor (who has no right to attend company meetings or vote off the officers of the company). Directors who upset their shareholders can be dismissed by ordinary resolution (**s 168 CA 2006**) but a minority shareholder may find even this lowered hurdle too high to scale. The general power of management provided by the **Model Articles (2008)**, does contain a provision permitting the shareholders to instruct the board how to act, provided that such directions are given by special resolution (**art 4**), but this is of little practical value to minority shareholders and of none at all to creditors. It can be concluded that, in most companies, the directors have a relatively unfettered right to run the company, although their right to do so is hedged by statutory obligations.

A minority shareholder or a creditor might seek to restrain the proposed acts of the board or sue in respect of past acts, alleging breach of a statutory duty. Potential litigants have two cases with which to contend: *Percival v Wright* (1902), which provides that the board, in exercising its powers (or duties), is generally responsible to the company and not to individual shareholders or creditors (or the employees); and *Foss v Harbottle* (1843), which held that a breach of duty owed to a company can be litigated only by the company. Since the power to litigate on behalf of the company will normally reside in the board (by virtue of **art 3** of the **Model Articles (2008)**, or its equivalent), the directors would appear to be able to determine whether to sue themselves in respect of wrongs which they have done to the company. While the board might be willing to sue a director (or former director) with whom the majority had fallen out, it is difficult to imagine a united board voluntarily agreeing to sue itself or one of its members. The issues which must be considered are whether *Percival v Wright* precludes a director from owing a duty to a shareholder or creditor and whether *Foss v Harbottle* is subject to exceptions.

In *Percival v Wright* (1902), the directors of a company were privy to confidential information which, once released, was likely to increase the value of the company's shares. P, a shareholder, offered to sell his shares to the directors, who accepted his offer. When the confidential information was released, P sought to have the contract of sale set aside and to recover the shares, on the ground that the lack of disclosure was a breach of fiduciary duty by the directors. Swinfen-Eady J, in rejecting P's claim, held that the directors did not, simply by being directors, owe a fiduciary duty to an individual shareholder; they did owe such a duty to the *company* but they had not broken it. This case remains the law in the form of **s 170(1) CA 2006**. Another example can be found in *Peskin v Anderson* (2001).

However, this rule does not preclude a director from being found to have chosen to undertake some responsibility to a shareholder on a personal level, whether fiduciary, contractual or tortious; that is, the duty arose because of an arrangement between two people who happen to be a director and shareholder (or creditor). For example, in

*Allen v Hyatt* (1914), the directors induced the shareholders to give them options to purchase shares without disclosing the possibility that the directors would be able to resell the shares at a profit. The Privy Council found that the directors had, by their words and actions, made themselves agents for each shareholder and owed the usual obligations of an agent to his principal. However, in most cases there is no question of the directors undertaking responsibility to an individual shareholder, so that *Percival v Wright* is the norm.

The fiduciary-based obligations owed to a company by a director under the **CA 2006** can be summarised as a duty to act in the best interests of the company, even if this is not in the best interests of the director. It is the fact that the directors should act in the interests of the company which has allowed some mitigation of the effect of *Percival v Wright*. The interests of the company are generally concurrent with the economic interests of current and future shareholders but not any particular shareholder. However, when the company is the subject of a takeover bid, the interests of the company have been treated as concurrent with the interests of current shareholders, so that directors have a duty to give them honest advice about the merits of the bid (first established in *Gething v Kilner* (1972)).

What, then, of creditors? There are *dicta* which suggest that directors should have regard to the interests of creditors. It should be noted, however, that the *dicta* which suggested that directors owe a duty to creditors seem incapable of support, following the decision of the Privy Council in *Kuwait Asia Bank EC v National Mutual Life Nominees Ltd* (1991). In this case, the appellant bank, which was registered in Bahrain, was a major shareholder (holding approximately 40% of the shares and nominating two out of five directors) in a New Zealand money broking company (AICS) which had gone into insolvent liquidation. The respondent company, NMLN, was, in accordance with New Zealand law, trustee for AICS's depositors and had incurred considerable liabilities and expense in connection with the insolvency. NMLN was seeking a contribution to its liabilities from a number of defendants, including the directors of AICS. The Privy Council, in considering whether the New Zealand courts had jurisdiction over the bank, advised that a director does not owe a duty to the creditors of his company simply by virtue of his office, although he may by agreement or representation undertake such a responsibility.

If the *Kuwait Asia Bank* case is construed literally, it would appear to be strongly persuasive of the view that directors cannot incur liability to corporate creditors, although they could incur liability to the company where they have failed to take into account the interests of creditors as part of their duty to act *bona fide* in a way likely to promote the success of the company (**s 172 CA 2006**).

Members and interested outsiders may find that the directors have the power to run the company and do not owe any duty to individual shareholders and creditors. A director's duty is to the company (s 170(1) CA 2006). A further difficulty facing shareholders who wish to sue directors is that, even where a wrong has been done to the company, the proper claimant is the company (a shareholder cannot sue to enforce another person's rights or remedy their wrongs), so that, as indicated above, it is the company (the operation of whose powers are vested in the board) which decides whether to sue the board or a director (*Foss v Harbottle* (1843)). However, there are a limited number of cases where a shareholder, but not a creditor, has *locus* to sue to enforce the rights of the company (a shareholder can always sue in order to enforce his own personal rights, if any) – such a claim, based on the common law, is called a derivative claim as provided for by s 260 CA 2006. For a shareholder to bring a derivative claim is somewhat unattractive; the shareholder has to pay for the litigation (although the courts have the power to order the company to indemnify the shareholder – *Wallersteiner v Moir* (1974)) and any remedy which is ordered accrues to the company and not the shareholder. Moreover, it is not easy to establish that an exception to *Foss* has arisen. To do so, the shareholder must establish a *prima facie* case under s 261 CA 2006 and, further, to obtain the permission of the court to continue with the derivative claim under s 263 CA 2006. The cause of action that can be subject to a derivative claim is one 'in respect of a cause of action arising from an actual or proposed act or omission involving negligence, default, breach of duty or breach of trust by a director of the company' (s 260(3) CA 2006). Guidance can be found by looking at common law cases that preceded the derivative claim procedure of **Part 11 CA 2006**. In *Daniels v Daniels* (1978), for example, a sale of a corporate asset to a director at a price which appeared to be substantially below its market value was held to fall within the exception.

However, even where a cause of action coming within s 260(3) CA 2006 has been established (and this can include simple negligence, thus reversing the rule in *Pavlides v Jensen* (1956)) the courts have refused *locus* where the shareholder has himself behaved improperly (*Nurcombe v Nurcombe* (1985)), the shareholders or directors who are not party to the wrongdoing have indicated that they do not wish an action to proceed (*Smith v Croft (No 2)* (1988)), the shareholder is acting for an ulterior motive rather than to enforce the company's rights (*Barrett v Duckett* (1995)), or the shareholder is claiming for relief under s 994 CA 2006, alleging substantially the same factual allegations, and the s 994 petition is a more appropriate means of dealing with the issues (*Cooke v Cooke* (1997)). The logic underpinning these cases is that, if the company is not going to benefit from the action, it is foolish to allow it to be dragged into litigation against its will. These considerations are likely to operate in the context of the statutory derivative claim (s 263 CA 2006). For instance, in *Franbar Holdings Ltd v Patel* (2008), the court refused to grant permission to a minority shareholder to continue with a derivative claim, as the same factual allegations gave rise to a cause of action that the shareholder was pursuing against the defendants under s 994 CA 2006. Further, in this case, the court considered that a hypothetical director acting in accordance with s 172 CA 2006 (duty to act in good faith in a way likely to promote the success of the company) would have attached little importance to continuing with the claim. However, in *Kiani v Cooper* (2010), the court, in granting permission to pursue the derivative claim, held that a notional director acting in accordance with his duty under s 172 CA 2006, would *wish* to continue the claim against the defendant, as the defendant had failed to adduce any corroborative evidence in support of his denial of the allegations made against him by the claimant.

As the previous paragraphs illustrate, a director can indeed assume that, while he retains the support of his fellow directors, he will be free of litigation in respect of his running of the company. However, s 994 CA 2006 is likely to prove a more troublesome provision for directors than anything else in company law. Section 994 CA 2006, which allows a shareholder to litigate if he has been unfairly prejudiced by some act or proposed act of the company, gives *locus* to a single shareholder (but not creditors), who, if successful, obtains any remedy awarded by the court, although there is no question of the company being required to fund such an action.

## QUESTION 19

Epsom is a director and employee of Ludlow Ltd and is a shareholder in another company, Aintree Ltd, in which he holds 10% of the shares. He is also owed £2,000 salary by a former employer, Fontwell Ltd. All these companies are connected with the racing industry. He seeks your advice about the following:

(a)  Fontwell Ltd is incompetently managed and is apparently moving towards insolvency.
(b)  The directors of Ludlow Ltd have proposed an allotment of shares to their employees and hope thereby to defeat a hostile takeover bid.
(c)  The board of Aintree Ltd decided that it was in no immediate need of a substantial piece of land which it owned and, being unable to sell it, leased it to the company's managing director at market rates. He intends to use the land to develop a new business unconnected with racing.

### Answer Plan

A large number of issues are raised, which allows little scope for lengthy discussion of any one issue. After general introductory comments, two issues arise in respect of each company:

❖ has Epsom (E) *locus* to bring an action in respect of these activities?;
❖ are the actions, or proposed actions, of the directors of the relevant companies a breach of their duties as directors?

# ANSWER

It can be assumed that the acts about which E seeks advice are not beyond the powers of the company (any objects must be contained in the articles – **s 31 CA 2006**). Two issues arise in respect of each company – first, has E the ability to litigate either on his own account or on behalf of the company (the *locus* point)? Second, is there a cause of action open to him?

## (A) FONTWELL

E is owed money by Fontwell ('F') Ltd – he is a creditor of the company. A creditor of a company has no right to intervene in the running of the company and has no *locus* to complain about the alleged inefficiency of the management either on his own account or on behalf of the company. E has no rights under **s 994 Companies Act (CA) 2006**, which confers rights only on shareholders. E has the usual remedy open to a creditor owed more than £750, namely to make a statutory demand for the sum and, if it is unpaid, to seek to wind up the company on the ground that it is unable to pay its debts (**s 122(1)** of the **Insolvency Act (IA) 1986**). A threat of liquidation may galvanise the company into trying to pay E's debt, although such a payment could be set aside if the company went into liquidation within six months and the payment was found to be a 'preference' (**s 239 IA 1986**). If the company was to go into liquidation before E had enforced his claim, he would, under insolvency law, be a preferred creditor for the first £800 of his debt by virtue of **s 175 IA 1986** (that is, as an employee, he would take priority over all other creditors except those with a fixed charge) and an unsecured creditor for the balance, in respect of which he would rank behind anyone holding any charge over the assets of the company. E's position does not look promising unless he moves swiftly or is confident that there will be assets available to satisfy his debt if the company goes into liquidation.

## (B) LUDLOW

As an employee of Ludlow (L) Ltd, E has no *locus* to challenge or to enforce the proposed allotment of shares, either on his own account or on behalf of the company. **Section 172 CA 2006** provides that the directors must consider the interests of the employees as part of their duty to act in a *bona fide* way that is likely to promote the success of the company, but this section confers no *locus* upon employees who wish to claim that the directors are not paying due regard to their interests (under s 170(1) CA 2006, duties are owed to the company). In addition, there is no evidence that this allotment is not in the interests of the employees. If any offer to allot shares is accepted by E, he is a party to a contract and, as such, would seem to have the usual contractual remedies if the company failed to keep its side of the bargain. However, if the allotment of shares is in some way improper, for example if it is made for an improper purpose, the contract may be unenforceable and the directors (including E), by proposing to make such an allotment, might be in breach of their codified, fiduciary duty set out in s 171 CA 2006 (*Howard Smith Ltd v Ampol Petroleum Ltd* (1974)). However, only a shareholder or the company could raise the invalidity of the allotment and such an allotment can be ratified by the company in general meeting (s 239 CA 2006), assuming the common law rules on ratification are applicable (s 239(7) CA 2006), although the disputed shares cannot be voted (*Bamford v Bamford* (1970)). There is no question of E being forced to buy the shares.

The directors should be warned that, in issuing shares, they must comply with the provisions of the CA 2006 and their own statutory obligations. Section 549 CA 2006 provides that the directors of a private company with one class of shares can allot shares, unless prohibited by the articles (s 550 CA 2006). Failure to comply with s 550 CA 2006 is a breach of s 549 CA and renders the directors liable to a fine (s 549(4) CA 2006). However, s 549 does not prohibit the allotment of shares in pursuance of an employees' share scheme (s 549(2) CA 2006) or where the directors have obtained authorisation (by the articles or company resolution) in accordance with s 551 CA 2006 (s 549(1) CA 2006). Further, to avoid the existing shareholders being entitled to a right of pre-emption (s 561 CA 2006) the company can rely on s 566 CA 2006 (securities held under an employee share scheme) or, in the case of a private company, the company's articles if they exclude the pre-emption right (s 567 CA 2006) or the directors of such a company with one class of shares, exercise a power given by the articles or by a special resolution, to disapply the pre-emption right (s 569 CA 2006). Alternatively, where the directors of a company have been given general authority to allot shares under s 551 CA 2006, the company, in accordance with any power given by the articles or by a special resolution, can disapply the pre-emption right in accordance with ss 570–571 CA 2006. If the proposed allotment to employees is at a discount (s 580 CA 2006 – shares not to be issued at a discount) or is otherwise not fully paid (s 582 CA 2006), the allotment remains valid but the allottees would be liable to make up the discount (s 588 CA 2006), although an allottee can be relieved of liability by the court (s 589 CA 2006) and the directors and L Ltd would be liable to a fine (s 590 CA 2006).

However, the most likely challenge to the allotment of shares would be the potential takeover bidder. An outsider cannot challenge the validity of the allotment but a shareholder could do so on the basis that the directors, in making the allotment, were not acting for a proper purpose in accordance with **s 171 CA 2006** (*Bamford v Bamford* (1970)); that is, they were in breach of duty. If the challenge was successful, the allotment would be invalid but capable of ratification by the shareholders in general meeting (**s 239 CA 2006**; *Bamford v Bamford* (1970)). A leading case on the improper use of directorial power is the Privy Council decision in *Howard Smith Ltd v Ampol Petroleum Ltd* (1974), which concerned the allotment of shares. In this case, the directors of HS, a company in need of further finance, issued shares to members who held a minority interest in the company but offered none to the majority shareholder (A), who had made an unwanted takeover bid, thereby reducing A's shareholding to below 50%. This allotment of shares was challenged by A as an improper use of the directorial power to issue shares.

The Privy Council ruled that, when a use of power is challenged, the court should first consider the nature of the power (that is, why was this power conferred on the directors whose exercise is in question?) and then examine the substantial purpose for which it was exercised. If the power was not exercised for the proper purpose, the exercise of the power is invalid. The court stated that the decision as to whether the power was properly exercised is determined objectively. In this case, the court ruled that the power to allot shares was given to directors to raise funds for the company and that, while the directors intended this allotment to raise capital, the primary purpose of the issue was to defeat A's bid and not to raise money. Consequently, this allotment was invalid and A, the majority shareholder, had no desire to ratify the allotment. This would seem to apply here. Thus, whether E can enforce any contractual right to the shares will depend upon whether the validity of the allotment is challenged and, if it is, whether the shareholders ratify the actions of the directors.

# (C) AINTREE

E is a minority shareholder in Aintree (A) Ltd and, as a shareholder, he can enforce any rights conferred upon him as a shareholder. Unfortunately, as a shareholder he would seem to have no individual right to complain about the conduct of the board in letting property to one of their number: even if it is a breach of statutory duty, the directors owe their duty to the company and not to individual shareholders – that is, current and future shareholders as a body (**s 170(1) CA 2006** (see *Percival v Wright* (1902) and *Peskin v Anderson* (2001))) – although a director may voluntarily undertake a fiduciary duty towards a shareholder, for example by acting as his agent (*Allen v Hyatt* (1914)). There seems no question of E being owed a statutory or fiduciary duty as an individual.

**Section 190 CA 2006** provides that, if a transaction between a director and a company is a substantial property transaction, it is voidable unless approved by the shareholders in general meeting. Approval of such a transaction can be informal, as in *Niltan Carson Ltd v Hawthorne* (1988), where knowledge and acquiescence by the majority shareholders was held to constitute approval of the activities of the director. A transaction is a substantial property transaction (**s 191 CA 2006**) if a director acquires an interest in a non-cash asset, the value of which is over £100,000 or 10% of the asset value of the company (subject to its value exceeding £5,000), which seems likely to be the case here.

However, the section provides that an unapproved substantial property transaction is voidable at the instance of the company. Thus, it seems that E has no *locus* to challenge the lease. If the lease is perceived as being in some way a device to defraud the company, E might, as an exception to *Foss v Harbottle* (1843), be able to bring a derivative claim on behalf of the company under **s 260 CA 2006**, but, since the lease is at market value, the conduct of the board seems unimpeachable. **Section 994 CA 1985** might prove a more effective statutory remedy for E if he can establish that the conduct of the directors is unfairly prejudicial to the shareholders. E would seem to have no cause of action in respect of the managing director taking up another business, either. Even if such conduct was in breach of the director's service contract, E, as a minority shareholder, would appear to have no right to litigate the matter, although he could raise it at a meeting of the company.

# QUESTION 20

The business of Whirlwind Ltd is that of a travel agency. The company's articles are based on the **Model Articles (2008)**. The managing director of the company is Liam and the company has three other directors.

Recently, Liam was approached by Boris, a director of Star plc, a customer of Whirlwind Ltd, with a view to Whirlwind Ltd providing an online travel service. A week later, Liam informed Boris that Whirlwind Ltd was interested only in developing high street agencies. However, Liam was able to inform Boris that another company, Nelly Ltd, was interested in providing an online service.

Shortly after the meeting between Liam and Boris, Nelly Ltd obtained a contract from Star plc to develop the online travel service and, subsequently, made a £1m profit from the contract. Liam is a majority shareholder and sole director of Nelly Ltd, which had no business prior to obtaining the Star plc contract.

These activities have come to light and Whirlwind Ltd seeks your advice as to what action is available to the company in respect of any breach of the duty imposed on directors to avoid a conflict of interest.

▶ Advise Whirlwind Ltd accordingly.

## Answer Plan

The question requires an analysis of directors' duties and the means by which a company can take action against a director for breach of duty in respect of the no-conflict rule. There is also a need to consider whether action can be taken against any third party who may have participated in a director's breach of duty.

# ANSWER

The codified, fiduciary (and common law) duties that directors owe are owed to the company, that is, the company's current and future shareholders as a body, and not to any individual shareholder (**s 170(1)** of the **Companies Act (CA) 2006** see *Percival v Wright* (1902) and *Peskin v Anderson* (2001)), although a director may voluntarily undertake a fiduciary duty towards a single shareholder by acting as his agent (*Allen v Hyatt* (1914)). In *Percival v Wright* (1902), the directors of a company were privy to confidential information which, once released, was likely to increase the value of the company's shares. P, a shareholder, offered to sell his shares to the directors, who accepted his offer. When the confidential information was released, P sought to have the contract of sale set aside and to recover the shares, on the ground that the lack of disclosure was a breach of fiduciary duty by the directors. Swinfen-Eady J, in rejecting P's claim, held that the directors did not, simply by being directors, owe a fiduciary duty to an individual shareholder; they did owe such a duty to the *company* but they had not broken it. In *Peskin v Anderson* (2001), the directors were held not to owe a duty to former shareholders to inform them of the disposal of a company asset, which resulted in existing members each receiving a windfall of £34,000, as there was no special factual relationship generating a fiduciary obligation such as a duty of disclosure. These codified, fiduciary duties are based on the equitable principle that a director is required to exercise his powers in a way which has regard to the interests of the person to whom the duties are owed and not to abuse his position of trust and influence within the company, so that, for instance, in common with a trustee, a director cannot, without authorisation or ratification, derive any benefit from the use of corporate property.

As Lord Porter stated in *Regal (Hastings) Ltd v Gulliver* (1942), 'Directors, no doubt, are not trustees, but they occupy a fiduciary position towards the company whose board they form'. The 'general duty' to put corporate interest above private profit is augmented in respect of corporate property; in common with a trustee, a director cannot appropriate corporate property. If he does so appropriate, he is liable as a constructive trustee (*JJ Harrison (Property) Ltd* (2003)). The duty is set out in **s 175 CA 2006**, so that a director should not benefit from his position as director, an obligation that applies after the ending of the directorship (s 170(2)(a) CA 2006). It is obvious that, if a director appropriates the company's tangible property, he will be liable to return the property to the company. The same is true of appropriation of intangible corporate assets, for example, the benefit of a contract possessed by the company. This liability for misappropriation is extended to commercial opportunities which are within the company's grasp. In *Cook v Deeks* (1916), a company, X, was about to sign a contract to build a railway line when X was persuaded by three of the four directors of X to award the contract to a new company which they had formed. The directors were held liable to hold the benefit of the contract as constructive trustees for X. Neither could the directors be excused by the subsequent shareholder ratification of their actions (the three directors held 75% of the shares in X), for misappropriation of corporate assets is an unratifiable breach of a director's duty (s 239(7) CA 2006 – the statutory procedure on ratification is subject to any common law rendering certain acts as being incapable of ratification). The duty in s 175 CA 2006, however, is not an absolute prohibition, as the duty is not infringed if the situation cannot reasonably be regarded as likely to give rise to a conflict of interest (s 175(4) CA 2006 – note the comments in *Regal (Hastings) Ltd v Gulliver* (1942)). In *Industrial Developments Consultants Ltd v Cooley* (1972), C, the managing director of the company, was party to negotiations by the company for the design and construction of a gas terminal. It became clear that the company was unlikely to obtain the contract and C feigned illness, resigned his directorship and successfully tendered for the contract on his own account. The judge held C liable to account for the profit he had made on the contract. Although the company was unlikely to get the contract, C was not entitled to use information concerning it and obtained in corporate service, for his own benefit. By contrast, in *Island Export Finance Ltd v Umunna* (1986), a former director who successfully tendered for a contract with the Cameroon postal authorities was not in breach of his fiduciary duty despite the fact that he had gained useful information and contacts with the authority while negotiating a contract with it on the company's behalf some two years before. The court noted that there was a lack of a 'maturing business opportunity' for the director to exploit. In *LC Services Ltd v Brown* (2003), however, a director delivered a copy of a company database to a rival company for whom he worked and removed company documents and company maintenance procedures. The court held that this amounted to a misuse of confidential information. And, in *Ball v Eden Project Ltd* (2002), the court held that, despite B's claim for compensation in respect of a dispute with the company over remuneration, that did not entitle the director to register the company's mark in his own name and deprive the company of the use of its property.

Judging by the cases in this area, it would appear that Liam (L) has breached the no-conflict rule by appropriating an opportunity belonging to the company. The information does not appear to be in the 'public domain' and the fact that Whirlwind

(W) Ltd might not be interested in the opportunity may not absolve L from liability, as the information might be considered to be 'worthwhile and commercially attractive' to the company (*Bhullar v Bhullar Bros Ltd* (2003)), or of a type that the director is under a duty to pass on to the company (*Industrial Developments Consultants Ltd v Cooley* (1972); *Bhullar v Bhullar Bros Ltd* (2003)). If, however, L had obtained authorisation by the directors (s 175(5) CA 2006) or approval from the shareholders (s 239 CA 2006), he might have escaped liability (*Regal (Hastings) Ltd v Regal* (1942)). In respect of authorisation under s 175(5) CA 2006, where the company is a private company, authorisation is permitted as long as it is not invalidated by anything in the articles; where a public company, the articles must provide for authorisation. For misuse of corporate property, L would be liable to account for any profit made. However, here, the profit that has been made has been made by Nelly (N) Ltd, a company controlled by L. In these circumstances, in order for W Ltd to recover the profit, the court may be prepared either to lift the veil of incorporation (*Trustor AB v Smallbone* (2000)) or to hold the third party liable as a constructive trustee. Liability can be imposed on third parties who have been involved in a director's breach of duty (*Selangor v Cradock* (1968) – third party liable as a constructive trustee). Whether such third party liability exists depends on whether N Ltd had knowingly participated in a breach of duty or trust by the director on the basis of 'knowing receipt' or 'knowing (or dishonest) assistance'; the appropriate remedy is either restoration of property misapplied and held by the third party or damages representing the value of the misapplied assets (*Royal Brunei Airlines Sdn Bhd v Tan* (1995); *Twinsectra Ltd v Yardley* (2002); *Barlow Clowes International Ltd v Eurotrust International Ltd* (2006)). In *Twinsectra*, the House of Lords held that in order to show that the defendant has been dishonest for purpose of liability as an accessory it must be shown that his conduct was dishonest by the ordinary standards of reasonable and honest people and that the defendant realised that by those standards his conduct was dishonest. It is not necessary to show dishonesty on the part of the third party in respect of knowing receipt (*Bank of Credit and Commerce International (Overseas) Ltd v Akindele* (2001)).

It should be noted that the proper claimant to address a wrong done to the company is the company itself (*Foss v Harbottle* (1843)). The power to sue on the company's behalf normally resides with the directors (art 3 of the Model Articles (2008)) but it can lie with the general meeting, either by passing of a special resolution instructing the directors to take action (art 4 of the Model Articles (2008)) or by taking action under a default power where the directors have committed the wrong to be suffered by the company. Alternatively, a shareholder, under s 260 CA 2006, can bring a derivative claim on behalf of the company against a director for breach of duty, but the shareholder would have to show a *prima facie* case in accordance with s 261 CA 2006 and to obtain the permission of the court to continue with the claim (s 263 CA 2006). Section 260 provides that the shareholder must establish that the directors are in breach of duty and the company has a cause of action arising from such a breach. Assuming that provision was satisfied, the shareholder must establish a *prima facie* case. If the court is satisfied that there is a *prima facie* case it has the power *inter alia* to give directions as the evidence to be provided by the company and, on hearing the application, to give or refuse permission to continue the claim (**s 261 CA 2006**). Under **s 263 CA 2006**, the court must refuse to give permission where the court is satisfied that a person acting in accordance with **s 172 CA 2006** (duty to promote the success of the company) would not seek to continue with the claim) (*lesini v Westrip Holdings Ltd* (2009)), or where the act has been authorised or ratified by the company (**s 263(2) CA 2006**). Where this is not the case, factors the court can take into account in deciding whether to allow the claim to proceed include whether the shareholder is acting in good faith; the importance that a person acting in accordance with **s 172 CA 2006** would attach to continuing the claim; whether the act in the circumstances would likely to be authorised or ratified by the company; whether the company has decided not to pursue the claim; whether the member could pursue an action in his own right; and the views of other members who have no personal interest (**s 263(3)(4) CA 2006**) (see *Franbar Holding Ltd v Patel* (2008); *Kiani v Cooper* (2010)). Any decision by the company to ratify the conduct of the directors amounting to a breach of duty must be taken by the members, the votes of the directors as shareholders not counting (**s 239 CA 2006**), unless the consent is unanimous (**s 239(6) CA 2006**). The common law and equitable rules on acts which are incapable of ratification are preserved by **s 239(7) CA 2006**. For example, a derivative claim did not lie at common law where the shareholder participated in the fraud or had benefited from it (*Nurcombe v Nurcombe* (1985)), was suing for an ulterior motive (*Barrett v Duckett* (1995)) or had failed to establish that it is the fraudsters who are blocking litigation by the company (*Smith v Croft (No 2)* (1987)).

## Common Pitfalls

Establishing the liability on assessment of the director is only providing 'half an answer'. The question also demands whether the breach of duty is actionable, and by whom. Therefore, your answer should be appropriately balanced between the various issues. Don't forget to mention the possibility of third party liability, either on the basis of knowing (or dishonest) assistance or receipt. Questions on directors' duties expect not only a discussion of knowing the liability of directors for breach of duty, but also, where relevant, a discussion of any third party liability, where that third party may have 'participated' in a director's breach of duty.

# QUESTION 21

The board of Kington Ltd consists of Cecil, Dot and Epsilon. The articles of the company exclude the right of pre-emption. Cecil is also a non-executive director of Pembridge Ltd, a company in the same line of business as Kington Ltd, and which owns 14% of Kington Ltd's shares. Anson plc purchased 26% of Kington Ltd's shares from the company, on the understanding that, if any further shares were created, they would be allotted to Anson plc to facilitate its eventual acquisition of the company. The remaining 60% of the shares of Kington Ltd are owned by the James family, who proposed Dot and Epsilon as directors. Kington Ltd is short of work and the board hope to sell its business to Pembridge Ltd. If the deal goes ahead, Dot and Epsilon would join the board of Pembridge Ltd, but 50% of the Kington Ltd workforce would be made redundant. The board recommended acceptance of a takeover bid by Pembridge Ltd, and members of the James family, who hold 30% of the shares of Kington Ltd, have agreed to sell their shares to Pembridge Ltd. The directors of Kington Ltd propose to create further ordinary shares and allot them to Pembridge Ltd for cash, thus giving Pembridge Ltd 53.3% of Kington's share capital; Anson plc's shareholding would be reduced to 21.6%.

▶ Advise Anson plc.

## Answer Plan

Anson plc would oppose the plan for two reasons: first, the reduction in its shareholding to a figure below that capable of blocking a special resolution; and, second, the destruction of its hopes of taking over Kington Ltd. Anson plc has a number of lines of attack. Consider:

(a) the allotment of shares – improper purpose, variation of class rights, s 994 of the **Companies Act 2006**;

(b) the role of the Kington Ltd board.

# ANSWER

Anson (A) plc has three choices open to it when faced with the proposals made by the board of Kington (K) Ltd. It could launch a rival bid to that made by Pembridge (P) Ltd, offer to sell its shares to P Ltd or try to destroy or modify the current proposals. Even if it was to launch a rival bid, there is no guarantee that it would be successful and there may be practical reasons not to proceed with such a plan, for example lack of funds. An offer to sell shares to P Ltd might be rejected and may not be in line with A plc's business plans. It should be noted that P Ltd has no right to force A plc to sell. However, if P Ltd had made an offer for all the shares in K Ltd and its offer had been accepted by holders of 90% of the shares, ss 979–987 of the Companies Act (CA) 2006 permit P Ltd to acquire the remaining shares compulsorily and these sections also give a right to the holder of the unpurchased shares to be bought out. Where shares are purchased under the provisions of ss 979–987 CA 2006, the price payable is that offered to those who have accepted the offer. Obviously, P Ltd cannot obtain 90% of the shares without A plc's agreement. If A plc does not wish to make a counter-offer or sell its shares, it may wish to oppose the proposed scheme; can it do so?

## (A) THE ALLOTMENT OF SHARES

A company which has issued its full complement of shares can increase its share capital in accordance with s 617 CA 2006. Section 617 CA 2006 permits a company to alter its share capital by either increasing its share capital, by allotting new shares in accordance with Part 17 CA 2006, or by reducing its capital in accordance with ss 641–653 CA 2006. In issuing shares, directors must comply with the provisions of the CA 2006 including the codified, fiduciary duties. Sections 549–550 CA 2006 provides that, where a private company has one class of shares, the directors have the power to allot shares of that class. Hence, the board of K Ltd have the necessary authority. Further, K Ltd has excluded the right of pre-emption, which, as a private company, it is permitted to do (s 567 CA 2006), so that shares do not have to be offered to existing shareholders. The proposed allotment is for cash at, it is assumed, a non-discounted price. The requirements of the CA 2006 appear to be satisfied.

The validity of the allotment is more likely to be questioned on the basis that the directors, in making this allotment, were not acting properly. Directors are not required to obtain the highest possible price for any shares allotted (provided that there is no discount) but, in choosing to allot shares, the directors are subject to the codified, fiduciary duty to exercise the power for a proper purpose (s 171 CA 2006; *Bamford v Bamford* (1970)). An improper allotment is invalid and capable of challenge by A plc, even though such an allotment can be ratified by ordinary resolution (s 239 CA 2006). Is the allotment by the directors of K Ltd in breach of their statutory duty? Consider the Privy Council decision in *Howard Smith Ltd v Ampol Petroleum Ltd* (1974), which concerned the allotment of shares. In *Ampol*, the directors of HS, a company in need of further finance, issued shares to members who held a minority interest in the company but offered none to the majority shareholder (A), who had made an unwanted takeover bid, thereby reducing A's shareholding to below 50%. This allotment of shares was challenged by A as an improper use of the directorial power to issue shares. The Privy Council ruled that, when a use of power is challenged, the court should first consider the nature of the power, that is, why was this power conferred on the directors whose exercise thereof is in question? It should then examine the substantial purpose for which it was exercised. If the power was not exercised for the proper purpose, the exercise of the power is invalid.

The court stated that the decision as to whether the power was properly exercised is determined objectively. In this case, the court ruled that the power to allot shares was given to directors to raise funds for the company and that while the directors intended this allotment to raise capital the primary purpose of the issue was to defeat A's bid and not to raise money. Consequently, this allotment was invalid and A, the majority shareholder, had no desire to ratify the allotment. This would seem to apply here, with the proviso that A plc, without the help of at least some of the James family, cannot block ratification. On a vote to ratify, the shareholders, whose votes are in dispute, cannot exercise the right to vote. The fact that the employees of K Ltd would be adversely affected by the takeover would tend to support the impropriety of the allotment (s 172 CA 2006), although an attempt to allot shares to preserve *bona fide* workers' jobs has been held to be improper (*Hogg v Cramphorn Ltd* (1967)). However, in *Hogg v Cramphorn* (1967), the allotment of shares was later ratified by the passing of an ordinary resolution at a general meeting of the company (see s 239 CA 2006).

If A plc cannot block the allotment of shares by raising the validity of the director's acts, it may seek to do so on the basis that it had an agreement that any new shares would be allotted to it and that failure to do so is breach of contract or a variation of its class rights. If there is a valid contract between K Ltd and A plc relating to the allotment of shares, it would seem to give A plc a contractual right to the new shares, but if it is described as an understanding, it may be difficult to enforce as a contract. The understanding might be deemed to be a class right and, where a company proposes to vary the rights attaching to a class of shares, it must comply with its own internal procedures and the provisions of ss 629–640 CA 2006.

A plc faces two difficulties. First, can its parcel of ordinary shares be regarded as a class distinct from the other ordinary shares? Secondly, is the dilution of its shareholding and the disregard of its understanding a variation of any class right? In *Cumbrian Newspapers Group Ltd v Cumberland and Westmorland Herald Ltd* (1987), Scott J postulated three situations. First, where there are rights attaching to a particular group of shares; secondly, where rights were conferred on a shareholder in his capacity as a shareholder (as in the *Cumbrian* case); and, thirdly, where rights were conferred on a particular individual. Only the first two categories create class rights. Applying this case, A plc might have class rights if the understanding could be called a right conferred on A plc in its capacity as a shareholder. If this is not the case, the mere fact that there are two opposing groups of shareholders is unlikely to be regarded as creating two classes of share (see the Court of Appeal decision in *Greenhalgh v Arderne Cinemas* (1946)). Indeed, even if A plc can be treated as constituting a separate class of ordinary shareholder, the diminution in voting strength is unlikely to be seen as a variation of class rights. In *Greenhalgh v Arderne Cinemas* (1946), G's ordinary shares had been subdivided into five, thereby quintupling his votes. The company then proposed similarly to subdivide the rest of the ordinary shares, thereby affecting the efficacy of G's votes and, as here, depriving him of negative voting control. The Court of Appeal held that, provided that the rights attaching to G's shares remained the same (they did – he was not losing votes), there was no variation of his class rights, notwithstanding the fact that the result was to alter the voting equilibrium of the shareholders.

*Greenhalgh* was distinguished by Foster J in *Clemens v Clemens Bros Ltd* (1976) on non-existent grounds. In *Clemens*, the majority shareholder (55%), who was the dominant director, authorised the allotment of shares to other directors, thereby depriving the minority shareholder (45%) of her negative voting control. The judge set the allotment aside. While this case has parallels with A plc's position, there is an important distinction. In *Clemens*, the disputed allotment was made by the majority shareholder and the judge felt able to classify the allotment as a breach of the fiduciary duty imposed on a shareholder. A plc should be warned that it is unlikely that *Clemens* will be followed here. If there is no variation of class rights, **ss 629–640 CA 2006** do not apply. A plc should argue that the understanding does create a separate class of shares and that the allotment is a variation which must be approved by the appropriate majority of the relevant class. Since A plc is the sole member of the class, the majority will not be forthcoming.

A plc will be best advised to challenge the validity of the allotment under **s 994 CA 2006**. This section provides that a shareholder can seek an order that a proposed act of the company would be unfairly prejudicial to him and, if successful, the court can make such order as it thinks fit (**s 996 CA 2006**). There has been something of a torrent of case law on this provision and it has proved a flexible tool in judicial hands for the righting of injustice to minority shareholders. **Section 994 CA 2006** provides a remedy independent of the existence of (or lack of) any other remedy, provided that there has been unfair prejudice, although any remedy is at the court's discretion. Cases have shown that an attempt to dilute the voting strength of a shareholding may be unfairly prejudicial (see *Re OC (Transport) Ltd* (1984)) even if, as in this case, that is not in breach of company law. A court would consider the basis on which A plc acquired its shares – did A plc have a legitimate expectation that it would retain negative voting control such that it would be inequitable to deny that right? If so, any dilution is likely to be unfairly prejudicial – or had A plc done anything to justify deprivation of negative voting control? If unfair prejudice is proven, the court could order A plc to be bought out at a fair price, could require shares to be allotted to A plc to preserve the voting equilibrium or could allow A plc to take K Ltd over, although the last remedy is unlikely.

# (B) THE CONDUCT OF THE DIRECTORS

A plc may feel aggrieved by the conduct of the board of K Ltd. Cecil (C) is a director of P Ltd already and Dot (D) and Epsilon (E) are to join the board of P Ltd. All three have recommended acceptance of the P Ltd bid. Surprisingly, being a director of two rival companies (P Ltd and K Ltd are in the same field) was not, at common law, a breach of director's duty (*London and Mashonaland Exploration Co Ltd v New Mashonaland Exploration Co Ltd* (1891)), but a director would have to be careful that, by having a competing directorship, he did not breach one of the codified, fiduciary duties contained in the **CA 2006**, in particular, the no-conflict rule set out in **s 175 CA 2006**. However, any breach of duty by C is actionable by the company and not by A plc (*Foss v Harbottle* (1843)), unless the circumstances are such that A plc could bring a derivative claim under **s 260 CA 2006**.

The directors of K Ltd, in recommending P Ltd's takeover bid, probably owe a duty to individual shareholders and not, as is usual, merely to the company. Whether this is because the directors, by offering advice, have voluntarily undertaken a duty towards shareholders (akin to *Allen v Hyatt* (1914)) or whether it is because directors automatically owe a duty to current shareholders as the manifestation of the company in a takeover context is not clear. The duty seems to be one of honesty and fair dealing – putting the case for the bid fairly (*Gething v Kilner* (1972)) – and there is no requirement to support the highest bid (*Dawson International plc v Coats Paton plc* (1989)), although the board should do nothing to prevent members from getting the best possible price (*Heron International v Lord Grade* (1983)). If the duty owed to the shareholders is broken, the breach is actionable by the shareholders: in *Gething*, the judge ordered the withdrawal of a misleading circular issued to shareholders, but in other cases it has been suggested, *obiter*, that damages could be awarded. If the directors of K Ltd could be said to be in a special relationship with their shareholders, it would be possible to impose liability under *Hedley Byrne v Heller* (1964), but the assessment of damages in the case of a private company would be difficult.

# QUESTION 22

Spendthrift Ltd runs a chain of letting agencies. Flogit Ltd is a subsidiary of Spendthrift Ltd and provides financial services to tenants, both residential and commercial. Jitesh is one of the directors of Spendthrift Ltd and wishes Flogit Ltd to enter into the following transactions:

(i)   to lend £95,000 to Jitesh to enable him to purchase a second home in the Lake District;

(ii)  to pay Jitesh's weekly account at a local bar (where he frequently entertains clients) on the understanding that Jitesh reimburses the company in respect of any private use of the bar; and

(iii) to guarantee a hire-purchase contract, under which Jitesh's son, Zulfi, is to acquire a van for his home gardening business.

▶ Advise the directors of Flogit Ltd as to whether the company may comply with Jitesh's requests.

## Answer Plan

The question demands an analysis of the statutory provisions on loans, etc, and whether such arrangements are prohibited, subject to approval or excepted by the legislation. It may also be necessary to consider any general points on directors' duties.

# ANSWER

The directors of the subsidiary company, Flogit (F) Ltd, have an unfettered discretion to run the company as they see fit (**art 3** of the **Model Articles (2008)**). However, they are required to comply with instructions given to them by their shareholders by special resolution (**art 4** of the **Model Articles (2008)**) and, in practice, may find it prudent to comply with the wishes of a director of their (one assumes) major or sole shareholder, Spendthrift (S) Ltd. In exercising their powers, the directors of F Ltd must comply with the usual duties imposed upon directors, particularly the obligation to act *bona fide* in a way that is likely to promote the success of the company (**s 172 Companies Act (CA) 2006**) and to exercise their powers for proper purposes (**s 171 CA 2006**). Failure to comply with these duties could result in action by F Ltd, but since F Ltd is controlled by S Ltd, this is unlikely unless Jitesh (J) was acting without the approval of S Ltd or the remainder of its board. If F Ltd were to go into liquidation, the liquidator would also have the power to sue the directors of F Ltd for breach of duty (for example, acting for an improper purpose in making these 'loans') and it would be no defence to an action that they complied with the unofficial instructions of J, although this might allow the court to relieve them from the consequences of their actions (**s 1157 CA 2006**). Indeed, these loans might be seen as wrongful trading by the directors and, if F Ltd were to go into insolvent liquidation, the liquidator could seek contribution from the directors to swell the company's assets (**s 214** of the **Insolvency Act (IA) 1986**).

In addition to the general duties imposed on directors, **ss 197–214 CA 2006** contain specific provisions dealing with loans and related transactions. These sections restrict the ability of a company to make loans (or guarantee a loan) to a director of the company, a director of a holding company or a shadow director (**s 197(1) CA 2006**). Further, where the company is a public company or a company associated with a public company, these restrictions are extended to quasi-loans and credit transactions (or guarantees thereof) and the provisions also apply to a 'connected' person (s 200 CA 2006). A connected person is defined by ss 252–256 CA 2006 and includes a spouse or civil partner and children under the age of 18 of a director of a company, so that Zulfi may be a connected person. Perhaps the purchase of a van would tend to suggest a child who may be over 18 and, consequently, not connected. J may also be deemed to be a shadow director of F Ltd since he seems to be a person on whose instructions the board of F Ltd are accustomed to act and the rules on loans, etc apply to shadow directors (s 233 CA 2006).

We must now turn to the three proposals to be considered by the board of F Ltd.

# (I) THE LOAN TO J AND M

Section 197 CA 2006 provides that a company shall not make a loan to a director of a company or its holding company unless approved by a resolution of the members of the company (and holding company if applicable) (s 197(1)(2) CA 2006) or affirmed subsequently by a resolution of the members of the company/holding company within a reasonable period (s 214 CA 2006). J is such a director, so the loan, unless approved (or affirmed), or falls within an exception to s 197 CA 2006, contravenes the section. The consequences of such a loan are that the transaction is voidable at F Ltd's behest unless restitution of money or any asset which is the subject of the transaction is impossible, the company has been indemnified or restitution would affect the rights of a *bona fide* purchaser for value (s 213 CA 2006). This would allow F Ltd to recover the money, if lent, from J. Section 213 CA 2006 also provides that a director (or connected person) who authorised the loan must account to the company making the loan for any gain made as a result of the loan and indemnify the company against loss. Thus, if the loan was made, the second home bought and then resold at a profit, the profit would be payable to F Ltd. There are exemptions from liability. For instance, s 213(6)–(7) CA 2006 exempts from liability any director or connected person who did not know the circumstances which constituted a contravention of the Act. This applies to persons who do not know the circumstances which were the contravention; not knowing about the relevant law is not a defence.

The CA 2006 provides that a loan to a director may fall within one of the exemptions in ss 204–209 CA 2006. The only section which might be relevant is s 209 CA 2006. This provides that a loan made by a money lending company may be exempted from s 197 CA 2006. Section 209(2) CA 2006 defines a money lending company as a company whose ordinary business includes the making of loans. F is a company which offers financial services to tenants and, as such, it may make loans. However, if it organises loans from third parties, for example building societies, and arranges security for loans, for example endowment policies, it would seem not to be making loans but facilitating loans; it is thus not a money lending company. Even if F Ltd is a money lending company, the loan is only exempt where (i) the loan is made in the ordinary course of business (this seems unlikely here) and the loan is on the same terms as that which would be made to an applicant of the same financial standing as J, or where (ii) the money is lent for the purchase or improvement of a house (a 'home' loan). However, the second exemption only applies to loans for the purchase, etc, of the director's only or main residence, not a second home, as in J's case.

## (II) J's WEEKLY ACCOUNT

Payment of J's weekly account is not a loan and is thus not restricted under s 197(1) CA 2006, although it may be a breach of duty by the directors of F Ltd to enter into such a transaction. In addition, there will be tax to pay on the benefit received by J. An issue might arise however as to whether the payment amounts to a quasi-loan and is caught by s 200 CA 2006 for which members' approval (or subsequent affirmation within a reasonable period – s 214 CA 2006) is required. However, s 200 CA 2006 only applies to a public company or a company associated with a public company and, although possible, it does not appear that either criteria is satisfied here. Where the criteria is satisfied, a quasi-loan is defined in s 199 CA 2006 to include an agreement whereby a person (F Ltd in this case) agrees to pay a sum to a third party (the bar) and expenditure incurred by another (J) for which the company will be reimbursed. Thus, J's private usage of the hotel, which the company pays for and which he has agreed to reimburse, is a quasi-loan. The business usage of the hotel would not be a quasi-loan, since J has not agreed, and is not liable, to reimburse F Ltd for this sum, although, in any event, s 204 CA 2006 could apply. Section 204 CA 2006 states that providing a director with funds to meet business expenses (or reimbursement thereof) does not fall within s 198 CA 2006, provided the amount does not exceed £50,000. The statutory rules on quasi-loans apart, another consideration is whether F Ltd should be paying for J to entertain clients of S Ltd. Perhaps there is an improper purpose issue here under s 171 CA 2006.

Arguably, s 209 CA 2006 could also apply if F Ltd were a money lending company (see above). Further, the quasi-loan does not require approval for a sum not exceeding £10,000 (s 207 CA 2006) – an exception that applies to loans as well. The usual civil consequences for contravention of s 200 CA 2006 apply (s 213 CA 2006).

## (III) GUARANTEE OF THE HIRE-PURCHASE CONTRACT

If Zulfi is over 18, he is not a connected person and whether the transaction should be approved by the board of F Ltd depends upon the power of F Ltd to guarantee hire purchase contracts, the ambit of the powers of the board, and whether this a proper purpose. If Zulfi is a connected person, the guarantee of a credit transaction (which includes a hire-purchase contract – s 202 CA 2006) is prohibited unless shareholder approval is obtained (s 202 CA 2006), there is shareholder affirmation (s 214 CA 2006) or an exception applies (**s 207(2), s 207(3), s 204 CA 2006**). However, as with quasi-loans, **s 202 CA 2006** only applies to a public company or a company connected to a public company. This seems improbable here but not impossible. The usual civil consequences of contravention apply in such a case (**s 213 CA 2006**) unless the guarantee is exempt. **Section 207(2) CA 2006** exempts 'small' amounts (less than £15,000), while **s 204 CA 2006** exempts transactions not exceeding £50,00 if relating to business expenditure. However, there seems to be only one section which could exempt the guarantee and that is **s 207(3) CA 2006** which exempts a transaction entered into by the company in the ordinary course of business and is made on the same terms as would be offered to an applicant who was not connected with the company. It seems unlikely, however, that F Ltd's business ordinarily includes the guaranteeing of such contracts as this.

> **Common Pitfalls**
> This question should only be tackled by a student with a good knowledge of the relevant statutory material. There is no scope for waffle, as precise statutory interpretation is all that is required.

# QUESTION 23

Certain persons, notably directors, are in a position to gain valuable information about a company. To what extent, if at all, does the law prevent such persons from using that information for their own personal profit?

> **Answer Plan**
> This is a general question, requiring an analysis of a directors' liability for misusing 'corporate' information both under the civil and the criminal law.

# ANSWER

While this question is not limited to directors, it is obvious that directors are a group well placed to acquire valuable information about their company, so directors are primarily considered. All private companies are required by law to have at least one director, public companies must have at least two (**s 154** of the **Companies Act (CA) 2006**). Limitations on the ability of a director (or others) to use information gained by virtue of his connection with the company fall into two principal categories – criminal sanctions and civil penalties – although there are other minor constraints.

## CRIMINAL LAW

Information about companies is an important factor in determining the value of company shares. Such information is available to those closely connected with the company, giving them the opportunity to deal in the shares of the company before that information is generally known. Use of inside information (insider dealing) is generally regarded as reprehensible, first, in that it lowers investor confidence in the Stock Exchange (though not all condemn insider dealing on this ground). Second, insider dealing may constitute fraud on the shareholders, for example, if they are persuaded to sell their shares to the directors or others at an undervalue relative to the value of the shares once the information known to the directors is widely known. Where fraud is provable, which is difficult, directors who defraud shareholders can be prosecuted. More importantly, the **Criminal Justice Act (CJA) 1993** (which replaces earlier legislation) makes insider dealing a criminal offence. While fraud is difficult to prove, it is wider in its scope than the **CJA 1993**, which does not apply to unlisted securities, that is, shares in private companies and shares in unquoted public companies, or face to face, as opposed to market, dealings.

The **CJA 1993** provides that, if a person deals in securities (the Act covers dealings in things other than shares, for example gilts) listed on a regulated market, for example the Stock Exchange, he is guilty of an offence if:

(a) he is an insider (or a tippee);

(b) he is privy to specific and precise information which relates to the shares themselves or the state of the company which issued them; and

(c) the information has not been made public;

(d) the information is of the sort which, if it had been made public, would be likely to have had a significant effect on the share price; and

(e) the dealing is intended to make a profit or prevent a loss.

The definition of 'insider' includes directors and a tippee is a person who has obtained information, directly or indirectly, from an insider. Liability under the **CJA 1993** is entirely criminal and no civil remedy is available to shareholders who have sold shares without knowing that the purchaser was privy to inside knowledge which might have affected the share price. Experience of the provisions concerning insider dealing suggests that so few criminal cases are brought that it is either a very effective provision (so no one breaks the law) or that it is very hard to discover if insider dealing has occurred, although the FSA, as part of a tougher approach to tackling market abuse, has, since 2009, been more willing to prosecute individuals for insider dealing. The rules requiring a director to disclose any interest in the shares of the company aid any investigation of a director's share dealing, provided, of course, proper disclosure is made.

Under the **Financial Services and Markets Act 2000**, the Secretary of State and the Financial Services Authority have a power of investigation in respect of suspected cases of insider dealing.

In addition to the criminal penalties under the **CJA 1993**, the **Stock Exchange Code for Securities Transactions**, which forms part of the Listing Rules, limits the right of a director of a company to deal in its shares and requires disclosure of all authorised dealings.

## CIVIL LAW

Directors, and possibly senior employees, have a fiduciary relationship with their company but are not to be equated with trustees. As Lord Porter put it in *Regal (Hastings) Ltd v Gulliver* (1942), 'Directors, no doubt, are not trustees, but they occupy a fiduciary position towards the company whose board they form'. As a fiduciary, each director is automatically and individually subject to equitable duties – fiduciary duties – which require him to exercise his powers in a way which has regard to the interests of the person to whom the duties are owed and not to abuse his position of trust and influence within the company. These equitable obligations have been codified as part of a director's 'general duties' by the **CA 2006**. These duties are owed to the company, that is, current and future shareholders as a body, and not to individual shareholders (**s 170(1) CA 2006**; *Percival v Wright* (1902); *Peskin v Anderson* (2001)), although it is possible for a director to have been found to have chosen to undertake some responsibility to a shareholder, as in *Allen v Hyatt* (1914).

To what extent do the duties imposed on directors and owed to the company impinge upon their ability to use information obtained by virtue of their position for their own profit? The civil law, unlike the **CJA 1993**, makes no distinction between public and private companies, nor is the law limited to market dealings in the shares of a company.

In common with a trustee, a director cannot, without the unanimous approval of the shareholders, use corporate property to make a personal profit (**s 175 CA 2006**). A director who does use corporate property to make such a profit is a constructive trustee of any benefit derived for the company (*JJ Harrison (Properties) Ltd v Harrison* (2001)). This constructive trusteeship can also be imposed on a third party who has knowingly received, or dishonestly assisted in the misuse of, corporate property (*Royal Brunei Airlines Sdn Bhd v Tan* (1995); *Twinsectra Ltd v Yardley* (2002); *Barlow Clowes International Ltd v Eurotrust International Ltd* (2006)). It is obvious that, if a director appropriates the company's tangible property, however innocently, he will be liable to return the property to the company. The same is true of appropriation of intangible corporate assets, for example the benefit of a contract entered into by the company. This liability for misappropriation has been extended to commercial opportunities which are within the company's grasp. For example, in *Cook v Deeks* (1916), a company, X, was about to sign a contract to build a railway when the railway company was persuaded by some of the directors of X to award the contract to a new company which they had formed. The directors were held liable to hold the benefit of the contract as constructive trustees for X. There seems no reason why a person other than a director should not be subject to a 'trustee' duty where the facts demand it.

As yet, there is no judicial decision that information alone can be treated as corporate property and thus subject to the 'trustee' duty imposed on a director (or others). The most important case in point is *Boardman v Phipps* (1967), in which the House of Lords considered the liability of a fiduciary (a solicitor) who had used information properly obtained by virtue of his connection with a trust to make a personal profit in dealings in the shares of a company in which the trust had a substantial minority shareholding. In his dealings, the fiduciary, B, had also benefited the trust. The House of Lords required B to account for his profits to the trust because of his breach of fiduciary duty.

A director is under a duty to act *bona fide* in a way that is likely to promote the success of the company (**s 172 CA 2006**). This responsibility has given rise to a number of areas of litigation. One obvious source of potential conflict between corporate duty and personal interest, in that the director is privy to confidential information by virtue of his office, is corporate contracts. The House of Lords in *Aberdeen Rly Co v Blaikie Bros* (1854) ruled that a director could not benefit directly or indirectly from a contract made by his company. This has been much modified when a director contracts with his company, for example when he enters into a service contract, or a director benefits indirectly from a contract between his company and a third party. Such contracts are valid if the director adequately discloses his interest in the contract (for example, in accordance with **s 177 CA 2006** (proposed transaction or arrangement)).

The position is less clear when a director benefits by the use of information obtained in his capacity as a director but there is no contract involving the company. Where a director has benefited from his position, liability can be imposed for breach of duty but the ambit of this obligation is uncertain. Some cases (see *dicta* in *Regal (Hastings) Ltd v Gulliver* (1942)) suggest that a director must account for any benefit deriving from the use or information gained in a corporate capacity, even if also available elsewhere, but the better view is that a director can benefit from information if there is no real conflict of interest between himself and his company in his use of the information (see now **s 175(4) CA 2006**). Where there is a conflict of interest, the fact that the company was unlikely to be able to use that information itself does not justify a director using it for his own benefit. For example, in *IDC v Cooley* (1972), C, the managing director of the company, was party to negotiations by the company for the design and construction of a gas terminal. It became clear that the company was unlikely to obtain the contract and C feigned illness, resigned his directorship and successfully tendered for the contract on his own account. The judge held C liable to account for the profits he had made on the contract. Even though the company was unlikely to get the contract, C was not entitled to use information concerning it and obtained in corporate service, for his own benefit. In contrast, in *Island Export Finance Ltd v Umunna* (1986), a former director who successfully tendered for a contract with the Cameroon postal authorities was not in breach of his duty despite the fact that he had gained useful information and contacts with the authority while negotiating a contract with it on the company's behalf some two years previously. The company had failed to pursue the contracts the director had made or to seek further contracts.

If a director does use information obtained in a corporate capacity and there is a conflict of interest, the profit made by the director can be retained if the company by resolution, so ratifies (**s 239 CA 2006**) or the company gives authority (**s 180 CA 2006**), unless the ratification or authorisation is declared ineffective at common law. The other directors can also authorise a conflict of interest where the conflict of interest is caught by **s 175 CA 2006**. However, this only applies where the constitution does not invalidate such authorisation (in the case of a private company) or where the constitution provides for authorisation (in the case of a public company).

In respect of a director having a competing interest, a director must be wary that by using corporate information, he does not break one of the general duties in **ss 171–177 CA 2006** (*LC Services Ltd v Brown* (2003)) or a term of his service agreement (*Thomas Marshall (Exporters) Ltd v Guinle* (1978)). Liability, however, may be subject to restraint of trade and/or whether the pursuit of a competing interest arose during the course of, or after the director left, office or whether it involved actual competing as opposed to the taking of preliminary steps (*Balston Ltd v Headline Filters Ltd* (1990); *LC Services Ltd v Brown* (2003)). A director who seeks to use confidential information to compete with the company can be restrained by an injunction. The position of employees and agents is similar to that of directors, as employees and agents are under a general duty not to compete in the course of their employment or agency relationship (*Hivac Ltd v Park Royal Scientific Instruments Ltd* (1946); *Faccenda Chicken Ltd v Fowler* (1987); *Take v BSM Marketing* (2006)).

## CONCLUSION

While there are many situations where the power of a director to use information obtained in a corporate capacity is subject to legal restraint, it is only when there is someone within the company who is willing and able to pursue the matter that any effective remedy exists.

## Common Pitfalls ✗

Select your information carefully. Do not repeat vast chunks of statutory material even if relevant. The key is to use your own words in condensing the relevant provisions and applying them to the question.

# QUESTION 24

A friend of yours has been approached by a relative and asked to join the board of the family company. You have no doubts as to your friend's honesty and feel he would never act improperly, but he lacks any business sense and has no financial expertise. He seeks your advice about such issues as disqualification and the possibility of an action for wrongful trading in the event of the company going into insolvent liquidation.

▶ Advise him accordingly.

## Answer Plan

This straightforward question divides neatly into two sections:

(a)   a discussion of disqualification; and
(b)   a discussion of wrongful trading.

# ANSWER

Since your friend is honest, discussion of his liability, if any, in the event of the company going into insolvent liquidation can exclude breach of fiduciary duty, which tends to involve a want of probity or fair dealing. He has raised two specific concerns – disqualification and wrongful trading.

## (A) DISQUALIFICATION

**Section 1** of the **Company Directors Disqualification Act (CDDA) 1986** permits a court to disqualify a person from being a director, or being directly or indirectly concerned in the management of a company, in a number of prescribed circumstances. **Sections 2–6, 8 and 10 CDDA 1986** set out the grounds for disqualification; **ss 2–5, 8 and 10 CDDA 1986** give specific grounds – namely, conviction of *indictable* offence in connection with the management of a company, persistent breaches of company legislation, fraud in relation to the running of a company, adverse report by a company inspector, etc – but the majority of reported cases involve **s 6 CDDA 1986**. **Section 6 CDDA 1986** provides that a person shall be disqualified (for a minimum of two years) from corporate management where he is or has been a director of a company which has become insolvent *and* his conduct as a director of that, or any other company, makes him unfit to be concerned in company management (this second condition also applies to **s 8 CDDA 1986** – adverse report by inspector). An application for disqualification under any section can be sought by the Secretary of State for Trade and Industry and some sections also confer the ability to disqualify under that section on specified persons. An application under **s 6 CDDA 1986** cannot be heard, unless the court gives leave, more than two years after the company has first become insolvent (as defined in **s 6 CDDA 1986**). Acting as a director, etc, while disqualified is a criminal offence, punishable on indictment, by a fine and/or imprisonment for up to two years under **s 13 CDDA 1986**.

The crucial question for your friend is whether any incompetence he might display could result in him being disqualified. In determining cases on the **CDDA 1986**, especially **s 6 CDDA 1986**, the courts have stressed that the Act, while designed to protect the public and while not a purely penal statute, can result in penal consequences for a disqualified person, in that a person may be precluded from trading through a limited company. Indeed, even to be the subject of an application for disqualification could have a serious effect on a person's reputation. Consequently, it is not surprising that judges, in interpreting the provisions of the **CDDA 1986**, have recognised these possible practical consequences whilst also seeking to give effect to Parliament's intention to limit the activities of unfit directors. Leaving aside the procedural aspects of the **CDDA 1986**, in what circumstances have the courts exercised their powers of disqualification and what is the courts' view of the appropriate period of disqualification? Guidance is provided by **Sched 1** to the Act – factors to take into account include breach of fiduciary duty, misuse of assets, responsibility for breaches of mandatory requirements and, where the company is insolvent (necessary for **s 6 CDDA 1986**), the extent of the director's responsibility for the insolvency.

The leading case on **s 6 CDDA 1986** is *Re Sevenoaks Stationery (Retail) Ltd* (1990). In this case, C, a chartered accountant with an MBA and experience in the City as a merchant banker, had been a director of five companies which had gone into insolvent liquidation between 1983 and 1986, with a total deficit in excess of £650,000. C admitted that he had failed to keep proper books of account, prepare profit and loss accounts or make annual returns; one of the companies had, to his knowledge, traded while insolvent. The Court of Appeal held that the words 'unfit to be concerned in the management of a company' should be treated as ordinary English words, which should be simple to apply in most cases. Each case turned on its own facts, said the court, but a director need not display total incompetence to be unfit. The court approved earlier cases which had held that simple commercial misjudgment should not merit disqualification while a lack of commercial probity and an appropriate degree of incompetence could do so (see, for example, *Re Lo-Line Electric Motors Ltd* (1988)).

Since each case turns on its own facts, your friend cannot be given definite advice about the type of conduct, or lack of action, likely to lead to disqualification, but other cases make it clear that leaving everything to others who turn out to have defrauded the company may be enough to render a person 'unfit'. In *Re City Investment Centres Ltd* (1992), the Official Receiver was seeking an order for the disqualification of the three directors, S, D and B, under **s 6 CDDA 1986**, based upon the conduct of the directors in connection with City Investment Centres (CIC) and other companies of which they were or had been directors. All the companies were concerned with the 'over the counter' market in shares. There was little doubt that S (who was the moving spirit in all these companies) was liable to disqualification and he was duly disqualified for ten years. D and B sought to escape disqualification by saying that they left all relevant matters to S. D had had 35 years' experience as an employee of the Council of the Stock Exchange, which included knowledge of disciplinary proceedings – he was called the compliance director. Morritt J had no doubt that D's conduct in allowing CIC to take over the assets and liabilities of other companies controlled by S without proper valuation of the assets (the assets proved illusory, the liabilities were not), allied to the failure of CIC to deliver shares which had been paid for because S had removed funds from the client account without any check by D and his failure to prevent or question CIC lending money to other ailing companies controlled by S, compounded by his inadequate supervision of the unqualified accounts staff, justified disqualification. The fact that D did not realise that CIC was trading while insolvent and that he relied upon S did not avail him – six years' disqualification were ordered. B's previous experience had been in connection with marketing and he had no relevant financial experience. He, too, simply relied upon S's word: when S took money from CIC's accounts, he believed S's statement that it was profit to which S was entitled. While it was agreed that B did not know that CIC or other companies in the group were trading while insolvent, he should, said the judge, have known. B was disqualified for six years.

But this case can be contrasted with *Re Polly Peck International plc (No 2)* (1994) and *Secretary of State for Trade and Industry v Taylor* (1997), where directors, forming a minority, were able to escape a disqualification order. However, in *Re Westmid Packing Services Ltd* (1998) the Court of Appeal considered that former directors of a company could not be excused from performing their obligations just because they may have been 'dazzled, manipulated and deceived' by a dominant member of the board who controlled the company. In *Re Barings plc* (2000), the Court of Appeal upheld a six year period of disqualification imposed on a senior director of three companies of the Barings Group, which had collapsed owing millions of pounds to creditors and members following the unauthorised activities of one of Baring's employees, Nick Leeson. The conduct of the director concerned had involved a serious abdication of responsibility in connection with supervising the employee and his activities.

# (B) WRONGFUL TRADING

While disqualification would prevent your friend from being a director, it would not have direct financial consequences; a finding that a director had engaged in wrongful trading would do so. The concept of wrongful trading was introduced by s 214 of the **Insolvency Act (IA) 1986** and it allows a court to declare a director liable to contribute to the assets of the company if the director knew, or ought to have concluded, that there was no reasonable prospect of the company avoiding insolvent liquidation, and he did not take every step he ought to have taken to minimise the potential loss to the company's creditors. Thus, on insolvent liquidation, the liquidator can seek a court order for one or more directors of the company to contribute to the assets of the company which will be available to creditors. **Section 214 IA 1986** does not authorise an order requiring a director to contribute towards the costs of liquidation or post-liquidation debts. An order is to contribute to the assets of the company and the section does not authorise an order that a particular creditor be paid, nor only those creditors whose debts were incurred after the director should have known that the company would go into insolvent liquidation (*Re Purpoint Ltd* (1991)).

A director cannot be liable under **s 214 IA 1986** unless he both knew, or ought to have concluded, that insolvency could not be avoided *and* he failed to take every step which he ought to have taken to minimise loss to creditors. The section only envisages the imposition of liability on a director who has not realised what he should have done and has not done what he should have done. In determining whether a director has met the standard expected of him, **s 214 IA 1986** provides guidance as to the setting of the standard. **Section 214(4) IA 1986** states that a director is to be judged by what a reasonably diligent person with the 'general knowledge, skill and experience that may reasonably be expected of a person carrying out the same functions as are carried out by that director' (that is, the director potentially subject to an order) and the 'general knowledge, skill and experience' of the director whom it is sought to make liable. This somewhat obscure provision seems to mean that what a director should have known or done is to be judged by reference to a theoretical director who possesses those skills that may 'reasonably be expected' of a director, unless the director is better qualified than this theoretical director, when he is to be judged by reference to his own qualifications. The Act is silent as to what qualifications one can reasonably expect from a director. Given that there is neither a minimum age for a director nor a test of competence, it could be argued that one cannot reasonably expect a great deal.

There is one case which should be drawn to the attention of your friend – *Re Produce Marketing Consortium Ltd* (1989) *(PMC)*. In *PMC*, the company was engaged in the import of fruit. It traded successfully for some 9–10 years and remained profitable until 1980. Thereafter, between 1980 and 1984 the company built up an overdraft and in 1984 had an excess of liabilities over assets and a trading loss. Between 1984 and 1987, when insolvent liquidation ensued, the trading loss continued, as did the excess of liabilities over assets, but the overdraft approximately halved, due to an increase in indebtedness to the company's principal supplier. By February 1987, one of the directors realised that liquidation was inevitable, but the company was allowed to trade until October – this decision being justified as allowing disposal of the company's supplies of perishable goods which were held in cold-store. The judge found that the directors should have concluded by July 1986 that liquidation was inevitable because, although accounts were not available until January 1987, their knowledge of the business was such that they must have realised that turnover was down and that the gap between assets and liabilities must have increased. Since the **IA 1986** provides that the directors are to be judged by reference to what they know and what they ought to know, Knox J held that they ought to have known the financial results for the year ending 1985 in July 1986 at the latest, so that the fact that these results were not known until 1987 was no excuse. Moreover, the directors had failed to take all steps to minimise loss – they had not limited their dealings to running down the company's stocks in cold-store, even if this was a justified step. Knox J held that both directors must contribute £75,000 to the assets of the company, this being the loss which could have been averted by speedy liquidation. In contrast, in *Re Hawkes Hill Publishing Ltd* (2007), the court held that the defendants were not liable for wrongful trading as they had not known or concluded that there was no reasonable prospect that the company could have avoided going into insolvent liquidation. They were entitled to take the view that the company could trade its way out of its difficulties and, although mistaken in holding this view, it was inevitable that, in cases such as these, directors would attempt to keep the company afloat.

While an action for wrongful trading may be a remote possibility, it is potentially extremely disadvantageous. A well-advised friend should check the regularity and accuracy of the management accounts before consenting to be a director. Presumably, non-executive directors are less vulnerable for action under **s 214 IA 1986**.

# QUESTION 25

The rules pertaining to the ability of a director to enter into an enforceable contract with the company of which he is a director give shareholders no effective control over such contracts.

▶ Comment on this view.

## Answer Plan

A relatively straightforward question, requiring a summary of the existing rules relating to contracts between a director and his company, the extent to which there is, or is not, effective control and a comment on the desirability of the present situation.

# ANSWER

'Directors, no doubt, are not trustees, but they occupy a fiduciary position towards the company whose board they form' (*Regal (Hastings) Ltd v Gulliver* (1942)). Since a director is not (except when dealing with corporate property) to be treated as a trustee, he is not debarred from deriving some benefit from his directorship – most directors are remunerated for their efforts – but, as a fiduciary, a director does not have an unfettered right to profit from his position. A director is subject to a number of statutory duties, based on equitable principles. These require him to exercise his powers in a way which has regard to the interests of the person to whom the duties are owed and not to abuse his position of trust and influence within the company. These duties are owed to the company, that is, current and future shareholders as a body, and not to individual shareholders (**s 170(1) Companies Act (CA) 2006** – *Percival v Wright* (1902); *Peskin v Anderson* (2001)). Consequently, one difficulty faced by a minority shareholder who is unhappy with contracts between the company and a director is the lack of ability to litigate other than in exceptional circumstances (*Foss v Harbottle* (1843)). The minority shareholder's inability to litigate will not matter if there is appropriate control over a director's contracts at an earlier stage, that is, when the contract is made. Nor will it matter if the company chooses to take action against a director when it discovers a secret contractual benefit at a later stage.

The reason for the imposition of the general, fiduciary duties is that they are essentially duties of fair dealing, in respect of the director – company relationship. Consequently, a director has a duty to put the interests of the company before his own interests. Obviously, this impinges upon his ability to contract with the company he serves. For example, a director who wishes to sell his own property to the company wishes, as vendor, to obtain the highest possible price, while his duty as a director is to negotiate the lowest possible price on behalf of the company. The potential for conflict between private interest and directorial duty has led to the formulation by the judges of various principles which have been codified by the **CA 2006** in the form of 'general duties'.

These 'general duties' are based largely on equitable principles. An early case in point is the House of Lords' decision in *Aberdeen Railway Co v Blaikie Bros* (1854). In *Blaikie*, the company wished to purchase iron chairs for use on railway stations. The contract was awarded to Blaikie Bros, a partnership in which a director of the company was a partner. The company repudiated the contract and its repudiation was upheld. The Lord Chancellor, Lord Cranworth, said: 'no one having [fiduciary] duties to discharge shall be allowed to enter into engagements in which he has or can have a personal interest conflicting, or which possibly may conflict, with the interests of those he is bound to protect.' Later cases have modified this view where any possible conflict of interest is 'so small that it can as a practical matter be disregarded' (*Movitex v Bulfield Ltd* (1988)) and have stressed that a potential conflict can arise only where there is 'a real sensible possibility of conflict' (*Boardman v Phipps* (1967); *Re Allied Business & Financial Consultants Ltd* (2008)). Where a director enters into a contract in circumstances where there is a conflict of interest or there is a sensible risk of such a conflict, the contract is voidable at the company's option, even if the contract is entirely fair and reasonable (**s 178 CA 2006**). Thus, a company can rescind a contract from which a director benefits, directly or indirectly, if he has entered into it in breach of duty even if the contract terms are fair and are no less favourable to the company than those obtainable from non-directors. This would not appear to be fair to directors. However, a company, while a company, can rescind a contract entered into by a director when he is in breach of his duty; the law does not say that a director can never benefit from a contract with a company of which he is a director (**s 180 CA 2006** – authorisation; **s 239 CA 2006** – ratification).

A director can benefit from a contract between himself and the company he serves provided that he makes adequate disclosure of his own interest before the contract is entered into (**s 177 CA 2006** – proposed transactions or arrangements). Originally, disclosure to the shareholders was required to remove any issue of conflict, but companies soon began to adopt articles which provided that disclosure to the directors would suffice (e.g. **art 85, Table A**). The current model articles for public and private companies do not contain such a provision but, where appropriate, the **CA 2006** deals with the matter through ratification or authorisation. **Section 182 CA 2006** bolsters the civil law by providing rules for the nature and degree of disclosure in respect of a director having an interest in an existing transaction or arrangement. The failure to comply with **s 182 CA 2006** constitutes a criminal offence (**s 183 CA 2006**).

There are a number of additional statutory provisions which could be described as designed to ensure fair dealing by directors. **Section 188 CA 2006** places restrictions upon the service contract which a director can make, **s 190 CA 2006** affects 'substantial property transactions' and **s 197 CA 2006** imposes restrictions on loans to directors. The general thrust of these provisions is not to prohibit contracts between directors and their companies but, rather, to ensure that such contracts are valid only if affirmed by the shareholders in general meeting. By virtue of **s 231 CA 2006**, these provisions extend to shadow directors (that is, those 'in accordance with whose directions or instructions the directors of the company are accustomed to act', but this does not include those giving advice to the directors 'in a professional capacity' (**s 251 CA 2006**).

**Section 188 CA 2006** prohibits any term in a contract with a director whereby he is to be employed as an executive or non-executive director for a period of more than two years (previously five years under the **CA 1985**) without provision for termination (or where termination is possible only in specified circumstances), unless the term is first approved by the company in general meeting (see *Atlas Wright (Europe) Ltd v Wright* (1999)). One consequence of **s 188 CA 2006** is that directors tend to have contracts for less than two years, thus removing the necessity of exposing the contract to the shareholders for their approval, but which contain a provision for reappointment for a similar period on the same terms, that is, including a reappointment term. Certain large investors have expressed disapproval of 'rolling' contracts or contracts whereby the directors are appointed for too lengthy a period. The Combined Code, which sets out best practice in the corporate governance of listed companies, says that 'there is a strong case for setting notice periods at, or reducing them to, one year or less'.

**Sections 190–195 CA 2006** provide that if a transaction between a director and a company is a 'substantial property transaction', it is voidable unless approved in advance by the members (**s 190(1) CA 2006**) or affirmed subsequently by the members within a reasonable period (**s 196 CA 2006**). A transaction is a substantial property transaction if a director acquires an interest in a non-cash asset from the company, or the company acquires an interest in a non-cash asset from a director, where the value of the asset is over £100,000 or 10% of the asset value of the company (subject to its value exceeding £5,000) (**s 191 CA 2006**). As **s 190 CA 2006** states that an unapproved substantial property transaction is voidable at the instance of the company, it would seem that a shareholder has no *locus* to challenge an unapproved transaction. A transaction entered into in breach of these sections ceases to be voidable by the company if it is too late to avoid it or the company in general meeting has affirmed it or another limit to rescission set out in **s 195 CA 2006** applies. Where there is breach of **s 190 CA 2006**, the consequences can be harsh. In *Re Duckwari plc (No 2)* (1998), a director who, without proper disclosure, sold property to the company at a fair market price was required to compensate the company when the land was resold at a substantial loss. The loss was due to the fall in the property market and not any fraud or malpractice by the director. It should be noted that, where a board lacks the authority to enter into a transaction, for example a substantial property transaction, the provisions of s 40 CA 2006, which would normally confer authority on the directors and thus validate the contract, do not apply and the transaction remains voidable (s 41 CA 2006).

Sections 197–214 CA 2006 provide a highly elaborate set of provisions affecting the ability of a company to make loans to, or enter into related transactions with, directors. These sections restrict the ability of a company to make loans (or guarantee a loan) to a director of the company, or a director of a holding company, or to a shadow director (s 197(1) and s 231 CA 2006).

Further, where the company is a public company or a company associated with a public company the restriction is extended to quasi-loans and credit transactions (or guarantees thereof) to the same people or to a person 'connected' to such a person (ss 198–202 CA 2006). A connected person includes a spouse or partner and children under the age of 18 (ss 252–253 CA 2006) of a director of a company. The CA 2006 provides a number of exceptions to the basic restrictions on loans, etc. For example, s 204 CA 2006 allows a company to provide a director with funds (limited to £50,000) to meet expenditure incurred for the purposes of the company or to carry out his duties on behalf of the company. Section 205 CA 2006 contains a similar exception in respect of expenditure incurred in defending proceedings, as does s 206 CA 2006 in respect of regulatory action or investigation. Failure to obtain the necessary approval will result in the director having to repay the sums provided (s 213 CA 2006), unless an excepted transaction. As with substantial property transactions, the loan transaction, etc is voidable unless one of the limits to rescission applies (s 213 CA 2006).

## Common Pitfalls

The major difficulties with such a question are sticking to the point and not discussing all aspects of the duties imposed on directors. Further, you may have to gather together information that has arisen at different points in the course.

# 5

# Shareholders and their Rights

## INTRODUCTION

In considering the shareholders and their rights, three issues arise – who is a shareholder, what rights do shareholders have and against whom these rights are exercisable. The first issue concerns the validity of the allotment, or transfer of shares, and is addressed primarily in Chapter 6, although it has been touched on in Chapter 4. Thus, in this chapter, the question of whether a person *is* a shareholder will not be central to any question.

The other issues, the nature of rights of shareholders and their enforcement, can arise in many contexts. Such matters have already formed part of questions in previous chapters, for example when considering corporate capacity and the division of powers within a company, and will arise in later chapters, for example when appraising rights to dividends and the variation of class rights. In this chapter, it is the ability of shareholders (generally a minority shareholder) to do something either when dissatisfied with corporate management or when generally unhappy with the way the company is operating, which may involve the board and/or the majority shareholder, or when unable to co-exist happily with their fellow shareholders. A majority shareholder is able to dismiss the board (**s 168** of the **Companies Act (CA) 2006**) and may be able to give the board instructions on how the company is to be run (**art 4** of the **Model Articles (2008)**) or even change the articles (**s 21 CA 2006**), and so has less need, but may still wish, to use the remedies discussed in this chapter. Since it is the company who generally has the sole right to challenge the actions of the board, any question which demands advice for a shareholder is necessarily asking you to consider not merely the cause of action open to a shareholder, but also how, if at all, the shareholder can enforce his rights (a *locus* question, which issue also played a prominent role in Chapter 4, above).

Where, as is common, the company is the only potential claimant, you should necessarily appraise alternative remedies. Possible general alternative remedies being just and equitable winding up (**s 122(1)(g)** of the **Insolvency Act 1986**) and an 'unfair prejudice' action (**s 994 CA 2006**). Both statutory provisions have generated considerable case law, much of it recent. In rare cases, a shareholder may also be able to persuade the Department of Business Skills and Innovation – formerly the Department of Trade and Industry (DTI) – to initiate an investigation into a company. These remedies can also apply to situations where a shareholder wishes to challenge the actions of fellow shareholders in the limited cases where shareholders owe duties to fellow shareholders.

As with questions on the directors, it is possible to combine questions on shareholder remedies with almost any other part of a company law syllabus.

# QUESTION 26

Despite the wide interpretation given by judges to s 994 of the **Companies Act 2006**, it is unlikely to be applied to a complaint about the mismanagement of a company. In such cases, the rule in *Foss v Harbottle* (1843) still represents a substantial, unjustifiable barrier to litigation by minority shareholders.

▶ Comment on this view.

## Answer Plan

This requires a general introduction to the problem of *locus*, then discussion of the two main issues:

(a) what is the rule in *Foss v Harbottle* (1843) and does it have the effect claimed?; and

(b) the width of the interpretation of s 994 of the **Companies Act (CA) 2006** and the likelihood of it being applied to private and public companies, ending with a conclusion as to the validity of the view expressed in the question.

# ANSWER

What courses of action are open to a minority shareholder who is unhappy with the way a company is being operated? The simplest remedy available to a shareholder in a public company is to sell his shares and seek a better investment, although if others are equally unhappy the sale price may represent a loss. However, it is unlikely that a shareholder will find a ready market for a minority shareholding in a private company unless the directors or other shareholders wish to buy the shares (or it is a company running a football club where people buy shares for non-investment reasons). Further, the price of shares in a private company may well not represent the asset value or earnings potential of the company, therefore, making a sale, even where possible, an unattractive option. If the shareholder wishes to stay with the company but improve its operation, he could seek to change the directors of the company (s 168 CA 2006 – ordinary resolution required) or to instruct the board how to operate (art 4 of the Model Articles (2008) or s 21 CA 2006 – both requiring a special resolution) but both require the support of others. Assuming that the unhappy shareholder cannot persuade others to join him, he can consider two approaches. First, he could seek to initiate litigation on his own account, or, second, he could attempt to sue on behalf of the company. In respect of both approaches, the courts have been greatly influenced by the view that a company is a democracy, that a shareholder who is outvoted should abide by the result of a vote and that a court should intervene only when the interests of justice clearly demand it. As Lord Wilberforce put it, 'Those who take interests in companies limited by shares have to accept majority rule'.

A person can sue on his own account when a wrong has been done to him. Such a wrong would arise in respect of mismanagement, if such was a breach of a common law or statutory duty owed to the shareholder. Unfortunately, at common law, a shareholder is unlikely to be able to establish such a wrong if his complaint relates to simple mismanagement. The reason is twofold. First, mismanagement may not be a breach of directors' duty, since the standard of care and skill required of honest directors is traditionally very modest. Second, the duty of care and skill is owed to the company and *not* to an individual shareholder (s 170(1) CA 2006, see *Percival v Wright* (1902) and *Peskin v Anderson* (2001)). **Section 214 of the Insolvency Act (IA) 1986** may impose a higher standard of care on directors, but the section does not give shareholders a right to sue to restrain incompetence; rather, it imposes personal liability to creditors on directors when the company has gone into insolvent liquidation and there has been 'wrongful trading'. Even where the alleged mismanagement consists of irregularity in conducting the affairs of the company, a shareholder may find that a wrong has not been done to him but only to the company. For example, an internal irregularity which is capable of ratification by ordinary resolution is not regarded as a wrong done to a member and, hence, an individual shareholder cannot sue those responsible for the irregularity (*MacDougall v Gardiner* (1875)). In contrast, where the wrong complained of consists of breach of a personal right vested in a member, the member can sue, but there is no clear test of what is a personal right (breach cannot be ratified so an individual member can sue) as opposed to a right to have the business of the company carried out properly, breach of which may be ratifiable (where a wrong is ratifiable, a member cannot sue).

The justification given for denying a shareholder the right to sue, other than when a personal right is breached, is twofold. First, where there is a mere irregularity, there is little point in allowing litigation where the majority can ratify, and, second, to allow litigation on every procedural irregularity would open the famous floodgates of litigation. Where there is no common law right to initiate litigation about mismanagement, a shareholder may find a remedy by using s 994 CA 2006 (see below).

The circumstances in which a member can sue to enforce the rights of the company are even more limited. In *Foss v Harbottle* (1843), Wigram VC laid down the basic principle that a shareholder could not sue in respect of wrongs done to a company (by insiders or outsiders); this remains the basis of the modern law – the wrong has been done to the company, so the proper claimant is the company. This decision was approved by the Court of Appeal and the Privy Council in *Burland v Earle* (1902). *Foss v Harbottle* (1843) itself, and later cases, confirmed that there are limited exceptions to this basic principle, as modified by the CA 2006. Most of the so called exceptions are cases where *Foss v Harbottle* (1843) does not apply, for example where the company acts *ultra vires*, or where a shareholder's personal rights are breached (the common law rules on acts that cannot be authorised or ratified are preserved by the CA 2006 – s 180(4)(a) and s 239(7) respectively). The principal exception to *Foss v Harbottle* (1843), however, is where a shareholder can bring a derivative claim to enforce the company's rights in accordance with Part 11 of the CA 2006; Part 11 replaces what was known at common law as a 'fraud on the minority' as perpetrated by those in control of the company. If mismanagement falls into the provisions of Part 11, a minority shareholder can sue on behalf of the company.

However, bringing a derivative claim under Part 11 CA 2006 imposes a not insignificant burden on the complaining shareholder. First, he must establish that the director's conduct is caught by s 260 CA 2006 (breach of duty, breach of trust etc, although, unlike at common law, negligence is covered) and secondly, he must seek permission of the court to continue with the derivative claim in accordance with ss 261 and 263 CA 2006. In some cases, s 263 CA 2006 states that the court must refuse to give permission (s 263(2) CA 2006 – see *Iesini v Westrip Holdings Ltd* (2009)) and even where s 263(2) CA 2006 is not a bar to a claim, the court can consider a wide range of factors before determining whether to exercise its discretion in favour of the shareholder (s 263(3)(4) CA 2006), including those factors which were identified at common law. For example, a derivative claim did not lie at common law where the shareholder had participated in the wrongdoing or had benefited from it (*Nurcombe v Nurcombe* (1985)), where the shareholder was seeking to sue for an ulterior motive (*Barrett v Duckett* (1995)) or where the shareholder had failed to establish that it was the wrongdoers who were blocking litigation by the company (*Smith v Croft (No 2)* (1988)). In *Kiani v Cooper* (2010), the court, in granting permission to persue the derivative claim, held that the claimant was acting in good faith and that a notional director, acting in accordance with his duty under s 172 CA 2006, would wish to continue with the claim against the defendant, as the defendant had failed to provide any corroborative evidence in support of his denial of the allegations made against him.

While a difficult test to apply, it clearly militates against action by a minority shareholder in a case of mismanagement. Assuming that the votes of the directors are disregarded, it would be a bold decision for a court to rule that the remainder of the shareholders had rejected litigation for an improper purpose, particularly in a public company, where shareholding is widespread. Even where a shareholder has *locus* and sues successfully on behalf of his company, the benefits accrue to the company and not the shareholder.

Does s 994 CA 2006 provide the answer for a shareholder who regards the management as incompetent? There is no *locus* problem with the section, since 'A member of a company may apply to the court' and the definition of a 'member' includes 'a person who is not a member of a company but to whom shares in the company have been transferred or transmitted by operation of law'.

However, merely because that court will hear an application does not mean that a member has been unfairly prejudiced. Two cases are pertinent. In *Re Elgindata Ltd* (1991), the petitioner had joined the company on the basis of detailed written agreements which were reflected in the articles. The court accepted that it could find, but refused so to do on the facts, that the petitioner had interests other than those set out in the agreements. The courts are unlikely to do so unless there are clear reasons why the legal agreement between company and shareholder should not prevail. Hence, a shareholder who is unhappy with the management of the company may simply find that, provided that the incompetent directors are complying with the constitution of the company, he can expect no more. While it is unlikely to be a specific provision in the articles, a member of a company could claim that he, in common with all shareholders, legitimately expects the company to be properly managed and that mismanagement is unfairly prejudicial.

In *Re Elgindata Ltd* (1991), the petitioner alleged, *inter alia*, that incompetence by management was unfairly prejudicial. In a lengthy judgment, Warner J held that in an appropriate case a court could find that serious mismanagement might be unfairly prejudicial but that courts would be extremely reluctant to accept that managerial decisions could be so (but see *Re Macro (Ipswich) Ltd* (1994)). A more recent case in point is that of *Re Saul Harrison and Sons plc* (1995), in which the holder of non-voting shares claimed that the directors of the company were keeping the company running purely to earn substantial salaries when a reasonable board would, given the company's prospects, have liquidated the company and distributed its assets. The action was based partly on an allegation of fraud and partly on an allegation of incompetence. The company was a long established, family owned and run company, dealing mainly in paper and textile wiping cloths, which had in recent years suffered declining profitability. In support of her claim for unfair prejudice, the petitioner claimed that when, in 1990, the company negotiated a sale of its premises prior to the passage of a Bill which would have authorised compulsory acquisition, it was the ideal time to wind up the company and distribute its assets rather than, as had happened, acquire new premises. She also claimed that the directors had failed to wind up the company in order to continue to receive large salaries as directors. The Court of Appeal upheld the judge's decision to strike out the petition. In deciding what is fair or unfair for the purposes of **s 994 CA 2006**, one judge held that 'it is important to bear in mind that fairness is being used in the context of a commercial relationship'. The relationship of shareholders is primarily governed by the constitution of the company, which, in the light of the **CA 2006**, means essentially the articles of association and commercial fairness can be seen as predominantly a question of complying with the constitution. The approach in *Re Saul Harrison* was approved by the House of Lords in *O'Neill v Phillips* (1999), where the House stressed that compliance with the rules of company law cannot be unfairly prejudicial unless the company was 'using the rules in a manner which equity would regard as contrary to good faith'. Even if conduct is not in accordance with the constitution and the powers thereby conferred, it is not necessarily unfair. For example, trivial and technical infringements of the articles will not attract the statutory remedy.

In conclusion, a shareholder who regards a company as incompetently managed is unlikely to have a remedy under **s 994 CA 2006**. Nor is an action for breach of personal rights likely to be attended by success, and so he will continue to find *Foss v Harbottle* (1843) a barrier to litigation on behalf of the company.

## Common Pitfalls

The crucial thing to beware of is writing an answer that is simply a discussion of **s 994 CA 2006** followed by a discussion of *Foss v Harbottle* (1843). It is important to use material selectively, so that it is tailored to the question.

# QUESTION 27

In 1995, Albert began a book selling business with two of his children, Ben and Connie. In 1998, a company, Bookit Ltd, was formed and the business was sold to the company in exchange for shares in the company. Albert, Ben and Connie had equal shareholdings and were directors of the company; most of the profits of the company were paid to the directors in salaries. In 2005, Albert died, leaving his shares to his wife, Anna, who was appointed to the board and draws a salary as a director although she takes no part in running the business and rarely attends meetings. On Albert's death, Ben took over as managing director and his wife, Diana, was appointed as a director.

In 2009, Ben proposed that the company specialise in books relating to sport and begin selling sporting memorabilia. Connie disagreed with this change of policy but Anna and Diana supported Ben and the plan went ahead. During the next financial year, the company made a loss. Consequently, Ben proposed to sell the company's premises to raise working capital. Connie objected to the sale but was voted off the board and the sale went ahead. The company is now beginning to prosper and Ben has suggested that the company should lend money to a company controlled by Diana which manufactures china models of sporting figures, to enable that company to expand. Anna wishes to sell her shares to the company and emigrate to Spain but the company has refused to purchase them.

▶ Advise Anna and Connie.

## Answer Plan

The main issues are:

❖ Anna – refusal to buy shares and consequent inability to realise value of shares;
❖ Connie as a director – removal from the board;
❖ Connie as shareholder – lack of dividends, change of policy, sale of premises, loan to Diana's company.

# ANSWER

Bookit (B) Ltd is a company which is beginning to prosper financially but is facing boardroom turmoil. Assuming that the parties cannot be reconciled with each other, what does the law provide? Anna, Ben and Connie have equal shareholdings, so that any one of them can block a special resolution and any two in combination can pass an ordinary resolution. Anna and Connie, two of the three shareholders, are unhappy with aspects of the company's operation, but unless they combine to form a majority they have a limited ability to influence the affairs of the company.

Anna, who plays little part in operating the company, would like to realise the value of the shares and emigrate. Since B Ltd is a private company, there is no ready market in the shares and an outsider is unlikely to be interested in purchasing a minority shareholding in a family company. This is a common problem for those holding shares in private companies and wishing to retire, and is indeed one of the reasons that the law was changed to allow a company to purchase its own shares (**s 690 CA 2006**). However, while a company is permitted to purchase its own shares (subject to any restriction or prohibition in the articles) in accordance with the statutory provisions, that does not mean that it is required to do so at the behest of a shareholder and the board can legitimately decline to purchase Anna's shares. On her own, Anna cannot change the board, nor can she issue instructions to the board as to how they are to operate the company; nor can she change the articles and take the power to run the company away from the board. However, in combination with Connie, she could pass an ordinary resolution sacking Ben and Diana as directors (**s 168 CA 2006**) and then run the company herself. Assuming that Anna does not have Connie's support, she could consider an action for unfair prejudice under **s 994 CA 2006** or seek a just and equitable winding up under **s 122(1)(g)** of the **Insolvency Act (IA) 1986**. A successful application under **s 122(1)(g) IA 1986** would result in an order to wind up the company, thus releasing its asset value to the shareholders. It is of little use to Anna if the company has no assets and it destroys what appears to be a viable business. There is an important statutory restriction on a court's ability to wind up a company on the basis that it is just and equitable so to do – **s 125(2) IA 1986**. This provides that, where the petitioner is a contributory (**s 79 IA 1986**), which Anna is, and it would be just and equitable to wind the company up, the court will *not* order winding up if there is some other remedy open to the petitioner *and* they are acting unreasonably in seeking winding up rather than pursuing that other remedy.

Consider whether it would be just and equitable to wind this company up. The courts have used this provision where there is deadlock within a company so that it cannot operate (*Re Yenidje Tobacco* (1916)), or where the shareholders have justifiably lost confidence in the management, who appear to be lacking in probity (*Loch v John Blackwood Ltd* (1924)), neither of which appear to be applicable. The courts also use **s 122(1)(g)** when the company is a quasi-partnership company and relations within the company are such that, had the company been a partnership, it would have justified dissolution, that is, where there is a mutual justifiable loss of confidence in one's fellow shareholders. It is probable that B Ltd would be a quasi-partnership company, since it bears many of the hallmarks listed by Lord Wilberforce in the leading case of *Ebrahimi v Westbourne Galleries* (1973). The fact that the company is small or private is not enough. In addition, the company should display all or some of the following factors: First, it will be an association formed or continued on the basis of a personal relationship involving mutual confidence – this may not apply, since Anna is not one of the founders of the company and has taken little part in its operation. Secondly, the company is one in which it has been agreed that all, or some, of the shareholders would participate in management – this seems to apply. Thirdly, the shares of the company will not be freely marketable, thus locking a disappointed shareholder into the company. If B Ltd is within the ambit of the section, it is unlikely that simple failure to buy Anna's shares would be sufficient to justify winding up. Moreover, the change of direction and sale of the premises were supported by Anna and cannot form the basis of her complaint. The possible loan to Diana's company might be regarded as a breach of directors' duty by Ben (and Diana), but again seems unlikely by itself to justify just and equitable winding up. Arguably, Connie has a better case for winding up than Anna, in that she has been excluded from management. Even if winding up is possible, the court would not order it if Anna (or Connie) has an alternative remedy which she is rejecting unreasonably. Is there such a remedy?

**Section 994 CA 2006** allows any member of a company to petition the court for an order that the affairs of the company are being, have been or will be conducted in a manner which is unfairly prejudicial to the petitioner's interests. Extensive case law since 1980, when the section was introduced as **s 75 CA 1980** (later replaced by **s 459 CA 1985**, as amended by the **CA 1989**), has led to the formulation of several principles in determining applications under this section. First, a shareholder can be unfairly prejudiced, whether that was the intention of the company or not, that is, *mala fides* is not required although lack of *mala fides* may render prejudicial conduct 'fair' (*Re A Company (No 007623 of 1984)* (1986)). Secondly, misconduct on the part of the petitioner does not preclude a remedy (*Re RA Noble Ltd* (1983)). Thirdly, a member must be unfairly prejudiced in their capacity as a member, for example, failure to buy goods from a shareholder would not affect a member in a shareholder capacity (*Re A Company (No 004475 of 1982)* (1983)). Fourthly, what constitutes unfair prejudice depends on the facts, but inability to work together leading to the exclusion of a director is not necessarily unfair (*Re A Company (No 007623 of 1984)* (1986)). What is needed is a lack of fairness in the circumstances.

Fairness has been considered by the House of Lords in *O'Neill v Phillips* (1999). In *O'Neill* a minority shareholder, O, had effectively run the business and the majority shareholder, P, had allowed O to keep 50% of the profits and had indicated that he might consider transferring some of his shares to O. Subsequently, P decided to return to management and not to transfer shares to O. P's conduct did not breach company law, the constitution or any concluded agreement between the parties. O argued that the disappointment of his legitimate expectation that he would continue in management and obtain more shares was unfairly prejudicial. The House of Lords rejected O's claim. Lord Hoffmann ruled that where there is no breach of company law or any agreement between the parties on the running of the company, there is no unfair prejudice unless equitable considerations make it unfair for those running the company to rely on their strict legal powers.

Failure by the management to pursue the course desired by the petitioner is unlikely by itself to be sufficient (*Re A Company (No 004475 of 1982)* (1983)) and this seems likely to apply to Anna. In *Re A Company (No 004475 of 1982)* (1983), a shareholder alleged unfair prejudice on the basis that the company had failed to purchase the member's shares at the price he wanted and the company was expanding into new fields (a wine bar) which might prove unsuccessful. The court rejected both arguments: failure to buy the shares did not prejudice the petitioner as a member, and the court was reluctant to intervene in a commercial decision by the board to expand the company's business, even if there was no risk of loss to the company. Her final complaint, the proposed loan, might be sufficient for an action to proceed, in that any loan may be a breach of directors' duty, but an appropriate remedy is unlikely to include an order to buy her shares. Anna is unlikely to have any legal remedy for her complaint.

Connie could seek just and equitable winding up as well, with a greater chance of success. She was a founder member of the company and had been part of the business from its foundation, so that she might well argue that her exclusion from management, with its consequent loss of income, justified winding up the company. The facts of the case are similar to those in *Ebrahimi*, where a founder member who was legally excluded from the company which had taken over his business was able to obtain a winding up order. However, unlike Anna, Connie may be more concerned with regaining a place in the company and the court might regard such a remedy as a better alternative than winding up a profitable company. Has Connie a **s 994** case?

There is no doubt that exclusion from management has been accepted as unfairly prejudicial to the interests of a *member*, where the member's interests included a legitimate expectation that the member would be entitled to participate in management, in other words, equitable considerations limited the exercise of strict legal rights to dismiss a director. In such cases, to dismiss a director could found a successful petition (*Re A Company, ex p Holden* (1991) is an example). However, to dismiss a director, even a founder director, is not necessarily unfairly prejudicial; each case turns on its facts. The lack of attention paid to the business by Anna might form part of an unfair prejudice claim (even if unlikely to be a breach of director's duty, given the modest level of attendance required of non-executive directors), as could any gross over-payments to the directors (*Re Cumana* (1986)), especially where the company pays only small, or no, dividends (*Re Sam Weller Ltd* (1990)). Allied to the exclusion from management, the lacklustre attendance record of Anna and the lack of dividends, Connie could also raise the proposed loan. Loans to directors, or persons connected to directors (Diana's company), are prohibited unless approved by a resolution of the members (**s 197 CA 2006**) and, as such, are voidable at the company's option (s 213 CA 2006). While the company is *prima facie* the proper claimant to pursue recovery of such a loan (unlikely here), so that Connie might not be able to succeed in an action for breach of director's duty, even under ss 260–261 and s 263 CA 2006 in respect of a derivative claim, the loan could form part of the s 994 CA 2006 claim (breach of company law does not necessarily trigger s 994 CA 2006 but it is a factor – *O'Neill v Phillips* (1999)). There are exceptions to s 197 CA 2006 (for example, s 207 CA 2006 (small loans in the course of business) and s 204 CA 2006 (loans for business expenditure not exceeding £50,000)), but it is not obvious that any of these exceptions would apply to Diana. In addition, any loan authorised by the directors must be for a 'proper purpose' (s 171 CA 2006) and, if such is not the case with this loan, the directors' conduct would strengthen Connie's unfair prejudice claim.

The change in the business and sale of the premises are not likely to be regarded as matters for the courts (as with the wine bar case of *Re A Company (No 004475 of 1982)* (1983)) unless the directors have acted improperly, for example if the sale was to a director who failed to declare an interest. If Connie succeeds in claiming unfair prejudice on the part of the company, the court has an unfettered discretion as to the remedy (s 996 CA 2006). The court could order her to be bought out at a fair price, or that she be restored to the board, or it may even require the other shareholders to sell their shares to her (as in *Re A Company (No 00789 of 1987) ex p Shooter* (1990)), or award any other remedy it considers. It is likely that any loan would be declared invalid at the very least and, if she remained a shareholder but was not reinstated as a director, the court might order the payment of dividends to protect her income.

Perhaps Annie and Connie should combine their votes to become majority shareholders and achieve their aims without going to court.

## Aim Higher ★

Credit can be given for mentioning other cases on s 994 CA 2006, although care must be taken with cases decided before the decision of the House of Lords in *O'Neill v Phillips* (1999).

# QUESTION 28

In 2001, Tilda, Neil and Charles formed Parliament Ltd, a company providing advice to people lobbying Members of Parliament. Each of them became a director and was allotted one-third of the issued share capital. The articles of the company provide that any shareholder who wishes to sell his or her shares must first offer them to the other shareholders at a price calculated by the company's auditors, in accordance with a stated formula. The articles also provide that if any person ceases, for any reason, to be a director he or she must, if asked to do so, transfer his or her shares to a remaining director or directors at a price calculated in accordance with the same formula.

The company has generated a large income but, in order to develop the business, all profits, except for directors' remuneration, have been reinvested in the company. In 2010, Tilda died and her husband John inherited her shares; he now needs funds to develop his own business and wishes either to sell his shares to Fred, who runs a similar business in Brussels, or persuade the company to pay dividends. Charles, who is extremely short tempered, has fallen out with Neil and would like to remove him from the board, purchase his shares and replace him with his (Charles's) wife, Glenys. Neil is refusing to resign from the board and has said that he will not sell his shares if asked to do so because, he claims, the price-fixing formula for the shares is unfair.

## Answer Plan

Careful consideration must be given to the particular needs of the parties:

(a)   John wants to sell his shares to an outsider. Can he do so? Alternatively, can he force the company to pay dividends?

(b)   Neil does not wish to be forced out of the company or to sell his shares.

## ANSWER

The relations between the shareholders seem so unhappy that they might be best advised to wind up the company; if they cannot agree to a voluntary winding up, perhaps Neil should petition for a just and equitable winding up under **s 122(1)(g)** of the **Insolvency Act (IA) 1986**, since it seems plain that there is a mutual loss of confidence between the three shareholders. However, the difficulty with a business of this type (people and skills based) is that its break up value is not likely to be large. A company may be capable of generating large profits but have little in the way of assets, so that winding up is killing the (potential) golden goose, but there may be no other solution to the shareholder antipathy. Assuming that the shareholders do not seek voluntary winding up, what course of action is open to John and Neil?

## (A) JOHN

John (J) wishes to sell his shares to an outsider, so it can be assumed that Fred (F) is willing to pay a higher price than that generated by the price-fixing formula in the articles, perhaps because, being in the same line of business, he intends to try to merge the companies. However, J is not totally unhappy with Parliament Ltd, since he would be willing to remain a shareholder if the company paid dividends. Obviously, J sees his shares as a means of generating revenue, so that he is neutral as to how this arises, but selling to F would produce a capital sum and would, it is assumed, be preferred by J. A shareholder, however he acquired his shares, is bound by the articles of the company and **s 33** of the **Companies Act (CA) 2006** provides that the articles constitute a contract between the shareholder and the company (and vice versa), and also between each and every shareholder *inter se*. It is not clear how a shareholder enforces this contractual right; *dicta* in the House of Lords suggested that it could only be enforced through the company (*Welton v Saffery* (1897)) but, in *Rayfield v Hands* (1960), Vaisey J held that a shareholder could enforce relevant articles directly, without joining the company. Thus, in *Rayfield v Hands* (1960) the directors were able, as members, to enforce a provision which required a shareholder wishing to sell shares to offer them first to the directors – similar to the provision in this case.

While criticism has been levelled at *Rayfield*, particularly in allowing *directors* to enforce the articles, it seems likely to be applicable here. Consequently, any attempt to sell shares without giving first refusal to the existing shareholders could be restrained by injunction and J should be so advised. However, J cannot force the existing shareholders to buy the shares: the articles require him to offer; he is not required to purchase. Should the other shareholders decide to purchase J's shares, **s 33 CA 2006** would render the price-fixing formula enforceable against him. For a consideration of whether the price-fixing formula could be ignored, see (b) below.

J cannot require the company to pay dividends; the dividend policy is for the directors to determine, so he cannot guarantee an income from his shareholding. There are, however, a limited number of cases in which the courts have ruled that failure to pay an adequate dividend could constitute unfair prejudice to the interests of a member, that is, **s 994 CA 2006**, and have used their power under **s 996 CA 2006** to instruct the directors to reconsider their dividend policy. A degree of caution should be exercised in advising J of these cases, since any application under **s 994 CA 2006** necessarily turns on its own facts and simple non-payment of dividend may not be sufficient to constitute unfair prejudice. Moreover, these cases pre-date *O'Neill v Phillips* (1999), in which the House of Lords stressed that where a company is complying with company law and the constitution (and failing to pay dividends is not a breach of the law or the constitution), it will find unfair prejudice only where equitable considerations require intervention.

In *Re Sam Weller Ltd* (1990), the company had substantial net assets (including cash) and, in 1985, made net profits of £36,330. The sole director, W, who was a minority shareholder, proposed a dividend of 14 p per share absorbing £2,520, the same dividend as had been paid for the previous 37 years, and the petitioner alleged that the director was running the company for the exclusive benefit of himself and his two sons, who were employees of the company. In a preliminary action to strike out the petition, Peter Gibson J, in refusing to do so, held that it was arguable that failure to pay dividends at anything other than a very modest level, where profits were substantial, which decision was made by those who derived their income from the company, was unfairly prejudicial. He firmly rejected the idea that low dividends would be unfairly prejudicial in all cases and was influenced by the apparent use of company money by W to buy a holiday home for his sons and W's refusal to register the petitioners as holders of shares which they had inherited. While the directors of this company are not paying dividends and are taking directors' fees, the situation is different from *Weller*: the company is relatively new and unlikely to have substantial reserves; retaining funds to develop the business seems only prudent; and there is no allegation that the directors are effectively preferring themselves at the expense of shareholders in their use of profits. J's action for unfair prejudice is unlikely to succeed.

## (B) NEIL

Between them, Charles (C) and J could vote Neil (N) off the board (by the passing of an ordinary resolution under **s 168 CA 2006**), although, if this also has the effect of terminating a service contract, substantial damages might be payable to N. If C is determined to sack N, J could use this as a bargaining chip to get what he wants in return for his votes. If N ceases to be a director, the articles provide that he may be required to transfer his shares to C (the only director left) and he is bound by this provision (see the argument above regarding J and the article on share transfer). If N is dismissed, can he complain, and is there any way he can evade either the requirement to sell shares or the price-fixing formula?

**Section 994 CA 2006** permits a shareholder to petition the court, alleging that the affairs of the company are being, have been or will be conducted in such a way as to be unfairly prejudicial to his interests. Interests in this context have been held to be interests as a member only (see *Re JE Cade Ltd* (1991) for a reaffirmation), but interests extend beyond rights. Consequently, even where rights under the articles have not been infringed, an action for unfair prejudice may lie. Interests of a member can include a legitimate expectation that, where he has ventured capital on the understanding that he would participate in management, he would continue as a director (*Re A Company (No 00477 of 1986)* (1987)). The wider equitable considerations, that the wording of the section has been held to permit, would allow a court to rule that reliance by the company on its legal rights, for example use of **s 168 CA 2006**, could be unfairly prejudicial. However, where the articles accurately reflect the intentions of the members, a court would be unlikely to treat reliance on the articles as unfairly prejudicial.

N could argue that attempts to dismiss him, particularly where his conduct does not seem to justify it, would be unfairly prejudicial. If such is the case, a court could order any dismissal to be invalid, but the powers of the court under s 996 CA 2006 are not limited to any particular remedy. Since it seems unlikely that N and C can continue working together, a court might think it apt that one or other of them should be ordered to purchase the shares of the other (or perhaps s 122(1)(g) IA 1986 should be used). If such an order is made, the question arises as to how the shares should be valued. If C is allowed to exercise his right to purchase (contained in the articles), will the court simply adopt the formula in the articles? Early cases on s 994 CA 2006 held that, where the articles contained, as here, a price-fixing formula which the majority proposed to use, the court would not intervene, but this has been modified in later decisions. In *Re A Company (No 00330 of 1991) ex p Holden* (1991), the majority shareholders (who were also the directors) argued that, since the articles provided for expert valuation by the auditor, Holden was assured of a fair price and, consequently, the court had no need to usurp the function of the articles in substituting its own price-fixing formula. Harman J accepted that, where the articles provided an adequate price-fixing formula for the compulsory purchase of the shares of the minority, the court would not usually intervene (see *Re A Company (No 006834 of 1988) ex p Kremer* (1989)), but that this issue must be adjudged in the light of the Court of Appeal decision in *Virdi v Abbey Leisure Ltd* (1990).

In *Virdi*, the Court of Appeal accepted that a petitioner could reasonably refuse to accept a valuation conducted in accordance with the articles, and the court should not follow it if there was a risk that that method of valuation would depreciate the value of the interest. For example, in *Holden*, the judge found that such a risk arose, in that the auditor/valuer was not required to explain how he reached his valuation, leaving H no basis to attack it, and also in that there was no machinery for H to put relevant matters to the valuer, particularly those relating to any other legal claims against the company (the effect of which might considerably affect the value of shares), and the potential capital gains tax liability that the company's valuation procedure would impose on H. N could argue that any attempt to use the formula was itself unfairly prejudicial, and the court should not use it, if the price-fixing formula did not accurately reflect the value of his interest. Situations where a court has rejected the valuation machinery in the articles (apart from *Holden*) have included cases where the conduct of those prejudicing the petitioner has depressed the value of the shares (*Re A Company (No 006834 of 1988)* (1989)) or where the valuation machinery is arbitrary and unfair on its face (*Re A Company (No 00477 of 1986)* (1987)). Where a court substitutes its own valuation machinery for shares, it can also fix its own valuation date: for example the date of the judgment or petition or a date preceding the unfairly prejudicial conduct, whichever it thinks most appropriate (for some guidance (see *Profinance Trust SA v Gladstone* (2001) where the Court of Appeal endorsed the view of Nourse J in, *Re London School of Electronics* (1985) that the 'usual' evaluation date is the date of the order of the court, subject to the overriding requirement that the valuation should be fair on the facts of the particular case).

Since N has not yet been dismissed or requested to sell his shares, he should present an interim petition to the court, asking that the affairs of the company be frozen until a full hearing. It must be said that N might be well advised to try to buy J's shares (although J might challenge the price-fixing formula and he is not compelled to sell) and put himself in a majority, or sell his shares and go (if the price is right), or seek a just and equitable winding up, since it is plain that there is a loss of confidence between the remaining directors of what is plainly a quasi-partnership (noting as with J the probable lack of break up value).

## Common Pitfalls

Do not be tempted to think that, as there is a falling out amongst members of a small private company, the solution to the problem lies with a petition for a winding up order on the just and equitable ground in accordance with **s 122 IA 1986**. Although **s 122 IA 1986** is touched on, a winding up order is a drastic remedy and the question is more appropriately answered by looking, first, at the effect of the articles and, secondly, at the viability of a petition for relief under **s 994 CA 2006**.

# Share Capital

## 6

## INTRODUCTION

Questions about shares and share capital can cover a wide variety of issues, many of them dependent upon statutory provisions of immense complexity. Few questions are likely to be in the form of essays on the power to allot shares or reduce share capital, etc, but such issues could arise in the context of other questions, particularly ones involving directors, variation of class rights and shareholder remedies.

General questions arising in this area are on such matters as the power of the company and/or the board to issue or rearrange share capital (including schemes of arrangement under ss 895–901 of the **Companies Act (CA) 2006**) and the capital maintenance doctrine. This doctrine covers the issue of shares (including the nature of the consideration and valuation procedures), as well as dealings in respect of shares, such as the payment of dividends out of capital and the ability of the company to buy (or assist others to buy) its shares. In addition to questions on the issue of shares, this chapter includes questions on doing things with shares, for example, the transfer of shares, variation of class rights and issues relating to takeovers may arise in this context.

Some courses consider the Stock Exchange listing requirements, but this is more a matter for a course on financial services.

## QUESTION 29

Sandy, Laura and Mark are the directors of Bombay Ltd; each of them holds 15% of the company's shares. Of the remaining shares, 50% are split between a number of smaller shareholders, none of whom has more than 10%, and 5% remain unissued. The articles of the company depart from the **Model Articles (2008)** in that they include a provision which requires any shareholder who wishes to dispose of his shares to offer them first to existing shareholders who will buy them at a fair price. One shareholder has recently died and his widow is anxious to sell his shares. The directors would like to increase their total shareholding so that, between them, they hold at least 51% of the shares. A significant minority of shareholders are reluctant to allow the directors voting control of the company.

▶ Advise the directors as to how they might achieve their aim, including, if relevant, how a scheme might be funded.

## Answer Plan

An open ended question which points you in no particular direction. There are two obvious ways of increasing a shareholding – buying issued shares from existing shareholders (or their representatives) or obtaining the allotment of unissued shares. Where this does not achieve the necessary majority, the creation and allotment of further share capital is a possibility. If the directors are seeking to obtain a voting majority, they could also seek to insert a weighted voting clause in the articles or to subdivide their shareholding whilst keeping one vote per share. You should consider these possibilities, and any other schemes, bearing in mind potential opposition.

# ANSWER

The directors of Bombay (B) Ltd wish to acquire at least 51% of the shares in the company. This may mean that they wish to obtain voting control rather than being concerned about the number of shares they own. If this is so, they could attempt to achieve their objective without altering the size of their shareholding or reorganising the company's share structure. For example, it is possible to alter voting rights of existing shares by the insertion in the articles of a weighted voting clause. Unfortunately for the directors, amendment of the articles requires a special resolution (**s 33** of the **Companies Act (CA) 2006**) and obtaining a majority of three-quarters of the votes cast, given the likely opposition of existing shareholders, seems doubtful. Alternatively, the directors could seek to subdivide their shares into two or more shares, each of which carries a vote. **Sections 617–618 CA 2006** permits a company, subject to any restriction or prohibition in the articles, to subdivide shares into shares of smaller nominal value than its existing shares. The decision to subdivide must be made by the company in general meeting, that is, an ordinary resolution is required (**s 618(3) CA 2006**). An ordinary resolution cannot be passed by the votes of the directors alone (unless some shareholders fail to vote), but they may be able to persuade holders of some shares to side with them and allow the subdivision. A subdivision will decrease the voting strength of the non-director shareholders, but, since their rights (one vote per share) remain unaltered, a subdivision is not treated as a variation of their class rights (*Greenhalgh v Arderne Cinemas Ltd* (1950)) and the requirements for the variation of class rights are not relevant.

The literal approach to class rights taken by the Court of Appeal in *Arderne*, where no regard was paid to the fact that A's shares, each carrying one vote per share, were rendered less valuable in voting terms when the shares of others were divided into five (thus quintupling their voting efficacy), was rejected by Foster J in *Clemens v Clemens Bros* (1976). In *Clemens*, where the shares of the minority shareholder were reduced in voting value from 45% to less than 25%, the judge, for no very clear reason, struck down the scheme. While the directors could be advised that *Clemens* may not be followed, they should note that an attempt to dilute the voting strength of the majority has been held to be unfairly prejudicial and subject to s **994 CA 2006** (see *Re OC Transport Ltd* (1984) for an example). If attempts to alter the weight of the two voting blocks are unlikely to succeed, the directors might wish to consider the acquisition of further shares.

The simplest solution open to the directors is to purchase shares from existing shareholders. In seeking to purchase shares, the directors do not owe a fiduciary duty to shareholders (*Percival v Wright* (1902)); nor are they at risk from the rules on insider dealing, which apply only to public companies. However, purchase of shares depends upon the existence of a willing seller and, fortunately, there is one available. Nevertheless, the articles of B Ltd provide that shares must be offered to existing shareholders. **Section 33 CA 2006** determines that the articles of the company create contractual rights between members and, while there is doubt about the precise effect of s **33 CA 2006**, there is no doubt that this provision in the articles is enforceable by the members (see *Rayfield v Hands* (1958)). The difficulty is that the article merely requires the shares to be sold to existing members without specifying how to resolve a situation where more than one member wishes to purchase the shares. The attitude of the courts is to treat the articles as a business document and construe them so as to give them reasonable business efficacy (*Holmes v Keyes* (1959)), so that it would seem appropriate to regard this provision as offering shares to all shareholders. Whether the offer is accepted by the first person to reply is doubtful – it would be more appropriate to hold that the vendor offers the shares to existing shareholders in proportion to their existing holding. If the directors acquire further shares, they are required to report the addition to their existing holdings to the company in writing; this information would be entered in the register of directors' interests. Failure to disclose renders the directors liable to a fine and/or imprisonment. The price payable for any shares purchased from existing shareholders is fixed by the contracting parties, but in this case the articles require it to be a fair price.

If shares cannot be purchased to bring the directors up to their desired holding, they could seek to allot the unissued 5% to themselves (bringing their holding to 50%). In addition, or in substitution, they might try to increase the company's share capital and then allocate the new shares to themselves. To make their position impregnable, any new shares could have a weighted voting provision from the outset, since it is unlikely that the court will treat the articles of the company as unfair and contrary to s **994 CA 2006**. Subject to any prohibition in the articles, the directors have the power to allot shares under s **550 CA 2006** (which is a permitted form of increase in share capital under s **617 CA 2006**), where the company, as here, is a private company with one class of shares. But the directors may be well advised not to try to create shares with weighted voting rights, which may well arouse suspicion in the minds of the non-director shareholders.

Further, the articles of B Ltd provide a right of pre-emption for existing shareholders. Section **561 CA 2006** states that, where a company is proposing to allot equity securities (defined in s **560 CA 2006** and including ordinary shares) wholly for cash, the shares must first be offered to existing shareholders in proportion to their existing shareholding. Thus, s **561 CA 2006** allows the directors to offer only 45% of any increase in share capital (or of the unissued 5% of existing shares), which they are allotting, to themselves. A private company, such as B Ltd, can exempt itself from s **561 CA 2006** under s **567 CA 2006**, but it appears not to have done so. However, if the directors breach s **561 CA 2006** and allot all the shares to themselves, the allotment remains valid, although the directors are liable to compensate shareholders to whom shares were not offered for any loss suffered thereby (under s **563 CA 2006**, there is a two year limitation period). The directors can avoid any difficulties with s **561 CA 2006** by allotting the shares other than wholly for cash (see below).

The directors might think that, if they comply with (or avoid) all the statutory regulations, any allotment made by them would be unimpeachable. They would be wrong. The greatest hurdle to any scheme by the directors to allot shares (old or new) to themselves is the imposition on them of the statutory, fiduciary duties to exercise any power of allotment *bona fide* in a way that is likely to promote the success of the company (s **172 CA 2006**) and for a proper purpose (s **171 CA 2006**). The obligation to act *bona fide* is subjective, so that, provided that the directors honestly believe that they are acting properly in allotting themselves shares, they are not in breach of this duty. However, the directors must exercise their powers not only honestly, but also for a purpose consistent with that for which the powers were conferred on them, that is, for a 'proper purpose'.

A leading case is the Privy Council decision in *Howard Smith Ltd v Ampol Petroleum Ltd* (1974). In *Ampol*, the directors of HS, a company in need of further finance, issued shares to members who held a minority interest in the company but offered none to the majority shareholder (A), who had made an unwanted takeover bid. This allotment of shares reduced A's shareholding to below 50% and was challenged as an improper use of the directorial power to issue shares. The Privy Council ruled that, when a use of power is challenged, the court should first consider the nature of the power (that is, why was this power conferred on the directors whose exercise thereof is in question?) and then examine the substantial purpose for which it was exercised. If the power was not exercised for the proper purpose, the exercise of the power was void. The court stated that the decision as to whether the power was properly exercised is determined objectively. In this case, the court ruled that the power to allot shares is given to directors to raise funds for the company, and that, while the directors intended this allotment to raise capital, the primary purpose of the issue was to defeat A's bid and not to raise money. Consequently, this allotment was void.

Other cases on this area have held that an improper use of directorial power can be ratified by ordinary resolution under **s 239 CA 2006** (see *Bamford v Bamford* (1970); *Hogg v Cramphorn* (1967)), but the directors of B Ltd cannot guarantee that they will be able, without shareholder support, to pass such a resolution. Whether the directors can convince the court that a proposal to increase their own shareholding is a proper use of directorial power depends upon why they were given the power to allot shares. Perhaps if the directors proposed to allot shares to themselves in return for an agreement to work for the company, this could be seen as beneficial to the company (even though no cash was raised, which is what the cases seem to say is the only proper purpose underlying an allotment) and, hence, an allotment for a proper purpose. Note that the power to raise the proper purpose point is technically a matter for the company (that is, *Foss v Harbottle* (1843) applies), but the courts have been prepared to allow a minority shareholder to raise the issue (*Hogg v Cramphorn* (1967)) unless and until the impropriety is ratified by the company in general meeting. The matter would now be dealt with by the derivative claim procedure provided for by **Part 11 CA 2006**, in particular **ss 260–261 and 263 CA 2006**).

Finally, the directors should consider how they are going to pay for any shares they decide to allot to themselves. They could pay in cash. There is no requirement that the shares be issued at a price in excess of their nominal value (*Hilder v Dexter* (1902)), but the price which the directors agree to pay cannot be less than the nominal value (**s 580 CA 2006**). If shares are allotted at a discount, the allotment is valid but the allottee (and, in some cases, any subsequent holder) is liable to pay the amount of the discount, with interest, to the company (**ss 580 and 588 CA 2006**). The directors might prefer to pay other than in cash and **s 582 CA 2006** provides that shares can be paid for in money or money's worth. This may be an attractive proposition, in that the directors do not have to pay cash and it evades the pre-emption rule. Since B Ltd is a private company, there is no requirement that the non-cash consideration be professionally valued, and it is common practice in private companies for directors to pay for shares by agreeing to work for the company. Provided that the non-cash consideration is not wholly illusory (for example, when the agreement to work is given by a director who is incapable of work) and the company (manifested by the directors) honestly regards the consideration as approximating in value to the nominal value of the shares allotted, the court will not examine too closely the valuation of non-cash consideration (*Re Wragg Ltd* (1897)).

# QUESTION 30

You have recently become company secretary of Glitz Ltd, a moderately successful company owned and run by various members of the Sparkle family. The board has decided to undertake a major acquisition of new machinery, which cannot be financed from the company's reserves. The machinery is likely to enhance production efficiency and capacity for a number of years. The directors do not wish to dilute their voting strength within the company and are uncertain whether the shareholders will support this major purchase. The board is keen to ensure that whatever means of financing is adopted will attract the necessary funds.

▶ Outline the possible sources of finance and the extent to which these methods meet the requirements of the board.

## Answer Plan

First, analyse the requirements of the board, then consider possible sources of finance – particularly loans and shares (ordinary and preference) – in light of them.

# ANSWER

The board wishes to raise finance for a long term project designed to increase the profitability of the company. It wishes to ensure that the money is raised, so the proposed source of funding must be sufficiently attractive to potential investors. However, the directors do not wish their voting strength to be diluted and, given the possible disquiet among existing shareholders, the board will need to ensure that its shareholdings and benefits are not diminished.

What are the relative merits of shares and loans in this context?

## (A) SHARES AND LOANS

The issue of further shares may be attractive to a company from a financial point of view, in that dividends must be paid only if the company has made a distributable profit and the directors have declared a dividend (**s 289 CA 2006**; **art 30** (private companies) and **art 70** (public companies) of the **Model Articles (2008)**). Thus, shares provide a means of raising capital without any continuing payment obligation on the part of the company. Nor is a company required to repay the capital acquired by means of an allotment of shares (unless they are redeemable shares), so the funds raised for the machinery need not be repaid by the company. Consequently, to an investor, the purchase of shares can be seen as a risky investment. There is no guarantee of income and the capital invested is, at best, recoverable on winding up. Indeed, on winding up, a shareholder has claims on the assets of the company only when the creditors have been paid in full. While the company is a going concern, and particularly if the machinery is as useful as suggested, there is the possibility of capital growth within the shares, but in a private company this growth is hard to realise, the shares are not freely marketable and the attitude of the Sparkle family to new shareholders may not be accommodating if the allottee wishes to sell out subsequently. Hence, seeking new shareholders (even if the practical problems of issue can be overcome – see below) from outside the company may not be successful. Of course, the board can always offer shares to existing shareholders to raise further funds. Indeed, a further issue of shares to outside investors may be unattractive to existing shareholders who see the pool of money available for the payment of dividends being available to a greater number of participants than previously. Further, extra shareholders would diminish the proportion of shares held by existing shareholders, including the directors, which the board wishes to avoid if this dilutes its voting strength. Of course the pre-emption rules, if applicable, could prevent dilution of the voting strength of a shareholder or group of shareholders.

Loans, on the other hand, do not dilute existing shareholdings but do carry a continuing financial commitment. The interest payable on the loan must be paid even if the company has not made any profits, although interest payments can be deducted from income to determine the company's net profits. In addition, the loan will have to be repaid in accordance with the loan particulars and failure to meet repayments could lead to the lender initiating action against the company. A loan may be secured or unsecured. The latter will carry a higher rate of interest, and for a potential investor the secured loan is more attractive. A lender may have power to intervene in the affairs of the company if the loan contract so authorises, but a secured lender has statutory and common law powers to seize the charged asset or appoint a receiver to act on his behalf if his security is at risk. The obvious lenders whom the company should consider approaching if this is the preferred route are the existing shareholders, especially in a family owned company, and the company's bankers.

One way of reconciling some of the advantages of shares and those of loans could be to attract investment into a new class of shares which do not have voting rights and, thus, do not affect the current voting position within the company. However, non-voting ordinary shares would not be very appealing to an investor and it might be necessary to consider the creation and allotment of preference shares.

# (B) PREFERENCE SHARES AND LOANS

Preference shares (voting or non-voting) have the attraction from the company's point of view that the financial commitment to pay the preference dividend is, like interest on a loan, a predetermined sum – assuming that the company has profits to sustain any dividend. As with ordinary shares, there is no obligation to repay capital while the company is a going concern, although many preference shares are created as redeemable shares and the company will have to redeem them at some future date. Unlike loans, preference shares cannot be issued at a discount (**s 580 CA 2006**) so that the contracted purchase price cannot be below the nominal value of the shares; thus, there can be no question of investors buying preference shares of £100 nominal value for £70 and obtaining £100 on redemption. However, Glitz Ltd could sell loan notes with a face value of £100 for £70 with the contract providing that, when the loan is discharged, the loan notes would be redeemed in full so that the holder would receive back £100. Glitz Ltd should be told that it is possible to redeem shares at a premium if the articles so permit and a person buying a share from an existing shareholder may be able to pay a price below the nominal value of the shares, although this is hardly a hopeful sign.

Preference shares might be unattractive to Glitz Ltd for several reasons. First, the shares may be issued at a time of high interest rates, thus requiring the company to issue them with a relatively high fixed dividend which remains a continuing commitment even when interest rates fall; this problem is obviated by the use of redeemable shares. Second, a preference shareholder is a member of the company and has, unless the articles provide otherwise, the right to vote and otherwise participate in the running of the company; this is easily overcome by issuing the shares without any or with limited voting rights, but, unless this is done, the directors may find their voting strength diminished. Third, extra classes of shares complicate the share structure of the company and can give rise to problems if the company wishes to vary class rights. Again, in common with ordinary shares, preference dividends are paid out of taxable profit and cannot be set against profits. While a lender is not a member of the company and has no direct influence over its affairs, which might be attractive to the company, Glitz Ltd might still feel the necessity to listen to a major creditor and the documents creating the loan might confer rights on a lender, for example to appoint a director. A lender who seeks to influence the company from outside runs the risk of being classified as a 'shadow director' with consequent directors' duties, but the same could apply to an influential shareholder. However, the courts have been very cautious about treating shareholders as shadow directors, and even more cautious about non-shareholders (see, for example, *Secretary of State for Trade and Industry v Laing* (1996)).

# (C) PRACTICAL ISSUES

The board might be able to retain voting control, even if further shares are issued, without using non-voting shares. For example, it is possible to alter voting rights of existing shares by the insertion into the articles of a weighted voting clause. Unfortunately for the directors, amendment of the articles requires at least a special resolution (s 21 CA 2006) and obtaining a majority of three-quarters of those present and voting, given the likely opposition of existing shareholders, seems doubtful. Alternatively, the directors could seek to subdivide their shares into two or more shares, each of which carries a vote. Sections 617–618 CA 2006 permit a company, by resolution, subject to any restriction or exclusion in the articles, to subdivide shares into shares of smaller nominal value than that fixed in the memorandum. The decision to subdivide must be made by the company in general meeting; that is, an ordinary resolution is required. If the directors decide to raise the necessary capital by allotting shares, they can allot further shares. Under s 550 CA 2006, the directors have the power to allot further shares where the company is a private company with one class of shares, unless prohibited by the articles. In all other cases, authorisation (by the articles or by a company resolution) is required (s 551 CA 2006). Assuming the latter, the directors may need support from other members of the Sparkle family to achieve a majority and, in the absence of such authorisation, which can be general or specific and for a period up to five years, the directors can be advised that, if they breach s 549 CA 2006 and allot shares without authority, they are liable to a fine but the allotment is valid.

Whether the directors have the power to allot shares or are willing to contravene s 549 CA 2006, they must still be wary of s 561 CA 2006, which provides a right of pre-emption for existing shareholders. Section 561 CA 2006 states that, where a company is proposing to allot equity securities (defined in s 560 CA 2006 and including ordinary but not preference shares) wholly for cash, the shares must first be offered to existing shareholders in proportion to their existing shareholding. Thus, s 561 CA 2006 would require the directors to offer any new issue of shares to members of the Sparkle family before seeking outside investment, but the section also provides that breach of it does not invalidate the allotment. Breach does, however, expose the directors to liability. The power to organise loans falls within the remit of the board and there is no need to involve the shareholders in any way, so there are practical advantages for a board with sceptical shareholders using loans to raise funds for expansion. Further, the allotment of shares, but probably not the raising of loans, is subject to the duty to exercise any power of allotment *bona fide* in a way likely to promote the success of the company (s 172 CA 2006) and/or for a proper purpose (s 171 CA 2006).

The obligation to act *bona fide* in the interests of the company is subjective, so, provided that the directors honestly believe that they are acting properly in allotting shares to raise funds for the machinery, they are not in breach of this duty.

# QUESTION 31

Krisp Ltd was incorporated in 1997. Its share capital is divided into 5,000 £1 shares – 2,000 preference shares and 3,000 ordinary shares. The articles provide that the preference shares confer on the holders thereof:

(a) the right to a dividend of 6% on the paid up value of the shares held; and
(b) the right on winding up to secure the paid up value of the shares in priority to any payment to the ordinary shareholders.

On incorporation, Mr Crunch became the sole director of the company, the shares of which were all allotted, fully paid, as follows:

❖ 2,999 ordinary shares to Mr Crunch in consideration of his transferring to the company his existing business;
❖ one ordinary share to Mrs Crunch for cash; and
❖ the preference shares to Mrs Crunch's elderly mother, Mrs Brittle, for cash.

Crunch is paid a generous salary by the company and Mrs Crunch is also paid handsomely for acting as company secretary. The company has made modest profits every year since it commenced trading but has never declared a dividend on either the ordinary or preference shares. Mr and Mrs Crunch have recently separated and there are rumours that Mr Crunch will appoint as company secretary Ms Toffee, his new partner. Mrs Crunch would like to bring an action in Krisp Ltd's name to restrain alleged transfers of assets from Krisp Ltd to a new company founded by Mr Crunch and Ms Toffee.

▶ Advise Mrs Crunch and Mrs Brittle as to their entitlements as shareholders while the company is a going concern and on winding up.

**Answer Plan**

You are asked to deal with the entitlements of ordinary and preference shareholders while the company is a going concern and the rights of these shareholders if the company is wound up.

# ANSWER

Before considering the position of the shareholders (other than Mr Crunch), it may be noted that the allotment of shares to Mr Crunch in return for the transfer of his existing business to the company is valid. **Section 582** of the **Companies Act (CA) 2006** permits shares to be paid for in money or money's worth and there is no requirement that the non-cash consideration be professionally valued (as would be the case if Krisp Ltd was a public company). A court has the power to treat shares issued for non-cash consideration as shares issued at a discount (allotment still valid, but shares must be paid for), but it is exercised very rarely and only when the alleged consideration is manifestly illusory – that is not the case here. Even if the shares had been issued at a discount, the allotment would be valid and Mr Crunch would be liable to make good the shortfall. Thus, there is no doubt that Mr Crunch is the majority shareholder in the company. The extent of his majority depends upon whether the preference shares carry the right to vote at general meetings of the company. Let us consider the position of the minority shareholders.

# SHAREHOLDER RIGHTS

## (A) MRS CRUNCH

While the company is a going concern, Mrs Crunch has the usual rights of a member; for example, in relation to the **Model Articles (2008)**, for a private company, she can attend meetings (**art 38**) and vote (**art 43**) and she is entitled to a dividend, if one is declared (**art 31**). As a minority shareholder with only one share, she has no influence within the company, although she would be entitled (subject to permission of the court – **ss 261** and **263 CA 2006**) to bring a derivative claim action on behalf of the company if Mr Crunch was in breach of directors' duty (**s 260 CA 2006**).

However, even with one share, she could petition under **s 994 CA 2006** if the affairs of the company were being conducted in a way that was unfairly prejudicial to her interests as a member. Unfortunately, even if that is the case, the remedy most likely to be awarded is that the company or the respondent shareholder(s) should buy her share at a fair price, which is unlikely to yield a large return. Has she a **s 994** claim?

While Mrs Crunch might object to the absence of dividends, she has been paid 'handsomely' for acting as company secretary. Exclusion from the post of company secretary (should it arise) would not by itself be unfairly prejudicial, but, if she had a legitimate expectation based upon a legal agreement or equitable considerations that she would participate in some way in the corporate governance of the enterprise, albeit not as a director, she might have a remedy, but this seems improbable. Further, if the allegations about the asset-stripping are proved, this breach of duty by Mr Crunch would be grounds in itself for a s 994 action. In addition, she could seek just and equitable winding up (s 122(1)(g) of the **Insolvency Act (IA) 1986**) but she would have to establish some basis for the winding up, which seems unlikely on the facts given. Even if just and equitable winding up was a possibility, under s 125(2) IA 1986, the court could deny her this remedy if she had an alternative remedy which she unreasonably failed to pursue (s 994 CA 2006 is the obvious one). Arguably, to destroy a viable company where her likely entitlement on winding up is small (£1 being the nominal value of her share, plus a percentage of any surplus assets after the claims of the company creditors and her mother have been satisfied) and, where she can be adequately compensated for any wrongs in some other way, is unreasonable and unlikely to be awarded by a court.

Mr Crunch may be equally keen to disengage himself from any business connection with his estranged wife. He could achieve this by offering to buy her out, which preserves the company as a going concern, or he could choose to initiate a voluntary winding up of the company. A voluntary winding up requires the passing of a special resolution (s 84 IA 1986) and his ability to achieve such a resolution depends upon whether Mrs Brittle can vote.

### (B) MRS BRITTLE

Mrs Brittle's position is very different. In determining her rights, the courts have regard to two canons of construction (presumptions drawn in the absence of evidence to the contrary). First, the House of Lords in *Birch v Cropper* (1889), in which the issue was whether the ordinary and preference shareholders had equal rights to the surplus assets of a company on winding up, ruled that all shares of whatever class are presumed to carry equal rights unless this presumption is rebutted by words indicating an inequality. Thus, where the articles are silent, all shareholders have the right to attend all company meetings and vote on all resolutions. The courts have tended to find words sufficient to rebut the presumption of equality with relative ease. However, on the facts of this case, there seems no reason why Mrs Brittle should not be entitled to vote; she (with Mrs Crunch) controls two-fifths of the votes at a general meeting and has the power to block a special resolution, but not an ordinary resolution. The second presumption applied by the courts is that, where the articles (or other relevant documents) specify that preference shares carry particular rights, that is, a statement of maximum entitlement, this presumption is extremely difficult to rebut. Consequently, where, as here, the articles of the company provide that the preference shares carry a right to a preferential dividend (6% in this case), the preference shareholder must be paid her dividend (if the company has made profits and declares a dividend) in full before the ordinary shareholders are entitled to a penny. However, having received her 6% (£120 per annum), that exhausts her right to dividend and she has no further entitlement to dividend on those shares.

Does this mean that where, as in this case, a company has declared no dividends for some years, the company continues to roll up profits and at some point in the future decides to pay a dividend of 6% to Mrs Brittle for that year and then distribute the balance to the ordinary shareholders (this sounds very tax inefficient)? In other words, is a preference dividend, once missed, lost for ever, or does the unpaid dividend roll up year on year so that the accumulated sum must be paid before the ordinary shareholders can receive anything? In *Webb v Earle* (1875), the court held that preference dividend is presumed to be cumulative (that is, unpaid dividend rolls up) unless there is evidence to rebut the presumption – the articles of Krisp Ltd do not appear to render preference shares non-cumulative (but note the position if the company is wound up – see below). Non-payment of dividend, particularly if Mr Crunch could be said to be using the company's profits unfairly to enhance his own position (the generous salary), might justify a finding of unfair prejudice (**s 994 CA 2006**, *Re Sam Weller Ltd* (1989)), which would allow the court, if it wished, to order that the dividend be paid or to alter the articles to strengthen Mrs Brittle's rights (**s 996 CA 2006**).

Mrs Brittle appears to have the power to block a voluntary winding up of the company (Mr Crunch cannot pass a special resolution if she votes against it), but she could not prevent an unpaid creditor petitioning. It might be argued that Mrs Brittle should seek a just and equitable winding up of the company (**s 122(1)(g) IA 1986**) on the ground that this company was a family company, that she invested in the company to support her son-in-law and that, if the Crunches divorce, the relationship of the members is such that, had they been partners, a dissolution of the partnership would have been ordered (*Ebrahimi v Westbourne Galleries Ltd* (1973)).

If there is a voluntary winding up (on whatever basis) and, after payment of the liquidator and the creditors, there are surplus assets, what are Mrs Brittle's rights? The articles plainly displace the presumption of equality – she is entitled to £1 per share (£2,000) if the assets are sufficient, but to no more (*Scottish Insurance Corp v Wilson and Clyde Coal Co Ltd* (1949)), whatever the size of the surplus. Thus, if Krisp Ltd has surplus assets of £2,000, it all goes to Mrs Brittle; if £5,000, then each shareholder receives £1 per share; but if £11,000 then Mrs Brittle gets £2,000 and the ordinary shareholders share the remainder (£3 per share). One further point – suppose that, at the date of any winding up, Mrs Brittle is owed arrears of preference dividend, are these arrears a debt which must be paid off before the shareholders receive anything, or are arrears not paid off prior to winding up lost? It appears that, unless the presumption can be rebutted, arrears of preference dividend are lost once winding up commences. This would allow an unscrupulous board to miss dividends for many years, build up surplus funds from profits which could have been paid as dividends, put the company into liquidation and pay the accumulated surplus (less any prior claim to return of capital vested in the preference shareholders) to the ordinary shareholders alone. Not surprisingly, the courts have tended to find words to rebut the presumption that the unpaid dividend is lost on winding up if at all possible (*Re Wharfedale Brewery Co Ltd* (1952)). In this case, the wording of the articles might, surprisingly, suffice – 'in priority to any payment to the ordinary shareholders' could be the straw to which a court would cling to avoid the unfairness of denying arrears to Mrs Brittle.

Mrs Crunch and Mrs Brittle would be well advised to pursue the statutory remedies (**ss 994 CA 2006** and **122(1)(g) IA 1986**) open to them as members, rather than rely on their contractual rights as shareholders. Alternatively, they might seek to sell their shares to Mr Crunch, but they cannot force him to buy them.

# QUESTION 32

Surplus plc was once a large trading concern and has substantial cash assets. Over recent years it has hived off the majority of its activities into new companies, over which it retains control, leaving itself with little in the way of direct trading operations, but it continues to generate substantial profits.

The articles of the company provide that rights attaching to any class of shares can be varied, provided that holders of three-quarters of the nominal value of the issued shares of that class approve, in writing or at a meeting, the proposed variation. The preference shareholders have no right to vote at general meetings of the company.

The company proposes the following:

(a)  To reduce share capital by paying off at par the 'A' preference shares, which carry a right to a 10% preference dividend, are preferential as to return of capital and have a right further to participate on winding up to a maximum of £1 per share.

(b)  To redeem immediately at £2 over par the 'B' preference shares, which carry a right to a 15% dividend and which are redeemable at par next year.

(c)  To reduce the preference dividend payable on the 'C' preference shares (which carry rights of equal participation on winding up) from 12% to 10%.

Amy, who owns 'A', 'B' and 'C' preference shares, objects to these proposals. She believes that the majority of the A and B preference shareholders would accept the proposals.

▶ Advise her on the legitimacy of these proposals.

### Answer Plan

The first two proposals involve a reduction of share capital and Amy may also allege that they are a variation of her class rights. The third proposal is not a reduction but may be a variation.

# ANSWER

Amy is faced with proposals for massive restructuring of the share capital of the company. She is unhappy with the scheme put forward by the management, but believes that she will be in a minority in objecting to it. The **Companies Act (CA) 2006** allows a company to alter its share capital (**s 617 CA 2006**) but provides special rules for the reduction of capital and the variation of rights attaching to any class of shares. Can Amy avail herself of any of these provisions? The **CA 2006** provides that a reduction of capital by a public company, as here, needs to be supported by a special resolution of the company and the resolution needs to be confirmed by the court (**s 641(1) CA 2006**). The provision is subject to any restriction or prohibition contained in the articles (**s 641(6) CA 2006**).

## REDUCTION OF CAPITAL

The proposals concerning the A and B preference shares both involve a reduction of share capital. Reduction of share capital has an adverse effect on the creditors' buffer and may also, as here, be opposed by shareholders whose shares will be abolished. Reduction is possible if it is done in compliance with the **CA 2006**. **Section 641(1)(a) CA 2006** states that a private company can reduce its share capital provided that (**s 641(6)** and **ss 642–644 CA 2006**):

❖ it passes a special resolution to do so;
❖ the resolution is supported by a solvency statement; and
❖ a reduction of share capital is not restricted or prohibited by the company's articles.

In all other instances, e.g. a public company, subject to any restriction or prohibition in the articles (**s 641(6) CA 2006**), a special resolution which is confirmed by the court is required (**ss 641(1)(b)** and **645–651 CA 2006**). The creditors of Surplus plc are given *locus* to object to any reduction in respect of a public company (**s 646 CA 2006**), but it seems that none is doing so. It is assumed that the proposed reduction will not reduce the share capital of the company below the minimum specified in the Act (s 650 CA 2006). There are no specific provisions in the CA 2006 dealing with the rights of shareholders when a reduction is proposed, but the House of Lords determined in the nineteenth century that the courts have a discretion to confirm or reject a proposed reduction of capital. The definitive view of when the discretion should be exercised was given in *Scottish Insurance Corp Ltd v Wilsons and Clyde Coal Co* (1949), in which the House of Lords held that the jurisdiction of the courts was not limited to ensuring the technical accuracy of a petition to reduce but was extended to ensuring that the reduction was fair and reasonable. However, despite the existence of a broad jurisdiction to reject an application to reduce, the courts have exercised that power very infrequently. In *Re Ratners Group plc* (1988), Harman J ruled that, assuming that the reduction was not a 'hollow and pointless act', the court would confirm a reduction where three principles had been satisfied. First, all shareholders should be treated equitably (which generally, but not necessarily, means equally, unless some shareholders have agreed to being treated differently). Secondly, the proposals should have been properly explained to the shareholders so that they could exercise an informed judgment on them. Thirdly, creditors must be adequately protected. As a gloss on Harman's view, it must be added that, where a scheme is supported by the company, creditors and the majority of shareholders, it is unlikely to be rejected by the court. Consequently, Amy should be advised that the procedures for reduction of capital may be satisfied. What may cause a court to pause before confirming the proposals for the A and B shares is the fact that the preference and ordinary shareholders are being treated differently *and* there is perhaps a variation of class rights.

## REDUCTION AND VARIATION OF CLASS RIGHTS

In determining whether to confirm the reduction of share capital, the courts will decide whether the proposal treats the preference shareholders equitably. Where the reduction involves a variation of the class rights of the relevant shareholders, the court will not treat the proposal as fair and equitable unless the relevant class have consented to the proposal. The court will ascertain whether there is a variation of class rights by comparing the rights of the preference shareholders on winding up (or redemption in the case of the redeemable shares) with their rights under the proposed reduction. This literal approach has been much criticised but remains the norm for variation of class rights cases. An extreme example of the literal approach is *Re Mackenzie* (1916), discussed below.

In this case, Surplus plc is seeking to repay the preference shareholders the par value of their shares with, in the case of the B shares, a £2 bonus. The B shareholders are being deprived of their income (the dividend) but are receiving that which they would get on redemption plus a bonus. The A shareholders are obtaining a preferential right to return of capital but are losing their right to dividend and the right to participate on winding up to the extent of a further £1 per share. What will the courts do in such cases? Amy should be advised that the courts have generally been reluctant to treat the abolition of preference shareholders (with consequent loss of an assured income) as a variation of class rights. In *Re Saltdean Estate Co Ltd* (1968), Buckley J said that, where a company wished to pay off capital as surplus to its requirements, *prima facie*, it should repay first those shareholders who would be repaid first on winding up. The A and B shareholders would appear to have rights which would require them to be repaid before the ordinary shareholders, and thus to pay them off would not be regarded as unfair. In the same case, Buckley J said that no doubt the preference shareholders hope to retain their interest in the company, but this expectation is always vulnerable to a future winding up or reduction of capital. The decision in *Saltdean* was approved by the House of Lords in *House of Fraser v ACGE Investments Ltd* (1987), but these cases left open the problem of the preference shareholder whose rights on winding up extended beyond a preferential right to return of capital.

The A shares have a limited participatory right on winding up (£1 per share over par – assuming sufficient surplus assets), which abolition will destroy. In *Re William Jones and Sons Ltd* (1969), the court confirmed a reduction by which the preference shareholders with such a participatory right were abolished. However, the preference shareholders made no objection to the scheme, which involved them being paid off at par when the market value of the shares was below par. The judge, Buckley J again, treated the right of participation as ephemeral given that there was no prospect of the company being wound up. Whether the lack of an immediate prospect of winding up justifies the refusal to treat the abolition of the preference shareholders' rights as unfair seems doubtful. Clearly, when winding up is imminent, an attempt to implement a reduction of capital which abolishes preference shareholders with participatory rights is a variation which could lead to a rejection of a capital reduction proposal (*Re Old Silkstone Collieries Ltd* (1954)).

It seems probable that these proposals will be confirmed by the court. However, if the reduction of the A shares is a variation of class rights, it is likely that the company would be required to comply with its own variation clause in order to obtain confirmation of the reduction. It is possible that the articles of the company provide that *any* reduction of share capital is a variation of the rights of a class of shares which is subject to the reduction. If this is so, then the usual rules for variation apply (see *Re Northern Engineering Industries plc* (1994), where the articles were so construed). Where the company has to consult its shareholders about a proposal because it is a variation, **s 633 CA 2006** provides an unhappy shareholder with a further line of attack.

## VARIATION WITHOUT REDUCTION

Is the proposal to reduce the C preference dividend a variation of the class rights of holders of those shares? The courts adopt a narrow view of variation, in that a comparison is drawn between the right which would attach to a share before and after the proposed amendment of the class right and the right which would arise – if the right is literally the same, there is no variation. Hence, in *Re Mackenzie and Co Ltd* (1916), the company had 4% preference shares with a nominal value of £20, thus paying a dividend of 80p per share. The company amended its articles to reduce the nominal value of the preference shares to £12, thus reducing the preference dividend to 48p per share. The court held that, since the preference shareholders had the same right both before and after the amendment (4% dividend), their class rights had not been varied. However, in this case, the proposed amendment is a variation (reduction of dividend from 12% to 10%). That being the case, the company must comply with the appropriate procedures for the variation of class rights.

Class rights can be varied if the company has a class rights variation clause in the articles and complies with it, or where no such provision exists, holders of that class consent to the variation in accordance with **s 633 CA 2006** – namely, a special resolution by the class at a separate general meeting (or written consent of three quarters in nominal value of the issued shares of the class). There is no such provision in the **Model Articles (2008)**. Consequently, the C shareholders should be consulted to see if they support the proposal and, if they do not approve by the necessary majority (consent seems improbable), the variation cannot take effect. Even if the relevant shareholders do approve the variation, **s 633 CA 2006** allows (a) dissentient shareholder(s) who hold(s) 15% of the relevant class of shares and who did not vote for the variation to apply to the court to have the variation set aside. The application must be within 21 days of the vote unless and until the court confirms that the variation has no effect. The court can refuse to confirm a variation if it would unfairly prejudice the shareholders of the class represented by the applicant. There are very few cases on this provision, so it is difficult to advise Amy as to what might constitute unfair prejudice. Where the company proposes to hold a class meeting to vote on the variation, the **CA 2006** lays down rules for the amount of notice, etc required.

Given that Amy believes that the majority of preference shareholders will support these proposals, she is unlikely to be successful in her applications to court, even where she has *locus*.

# QUESTION 33

Teddy has recently taken over as company secretary of Bear plc, an unlisted public company, and has been investigating the administration of the company. He has discovered the following and seeks your advice:

(a) Six months ago, Rupert purchased shares in the company and applied to be registered as a shareholder. The directors have just decided to refuse to register Rupert but have given no reasons. The articles of the company provide that 'The directors may choose to refuse to register as a member any person to whom shares have been transferred'.

(b) Paddington, the Registered holder of 1,000 shares, claims that his share certificate was stolen and that a forged transfer of shares was made in favour of Bungle. Bungle is seeking registration as a shareholder.

(c) Bear plc has recently paid a dividend and it has come to light that payment was made to six members who had sold their shares in the previous year. This occurred because the names of these members had not been removed from the Register.

(d) It has just emerged that the previous company secretary, X, forged a share transfer from a member, Yogi, and issued a share certificate in respect of the shares so 'transferred' to his wife. Winnie innocently purchased shares from X's wife, was registered as a shareholder and was issued with a share certificate by X. Yogi wishes to be reinstated on the Register of members.

All the shares in Bear plc are fully paid up.

## Answer Plan

The question, on various aspects of share transfer, is broken down into four single issue parts. The issues raised are: the right (if any) of the directors to refuse to register a transferee of shares; the effect of a forged share transfer; the effect of non-removal from the Register of members; and whether the company is bound by an act of forgery committed internally.

# ANSWER

Public companies are required to have a company secretary (s 271 of the **Companies Act (CA) 2006**), who may be a natural legal person or a company and who may also be a director of the company. Private companies are not required to have a secretary (s 270 CA 2006). Public companies, like Bear plc, are required to take reasonable steps to appoint as company secretary a person of appropriate qualification and experience (s 273 CA 2006). Teddy, as company secretary, is likely to carry out many of the administrative tasks imposed on companies by the **CA 2006** and supervise the general administration of the company, including the maintenance of the company's registers. One register which is required to be kept is a register of members (s 113 CA 2006), which must be kept at the company's registered office or at a place specified by regulation in accordance with s 113 CA 2006 (s 114 CA 2006). In this case, Teddy appears to have discovered some problems in respect of the Register of members and seeks your advice about four particular cases.

## (A) RUPERT

Shares in a company are freely transferable (s 541 CA 2006). The basic transfer procedure is that the Registered holder completes and signs an instrument of transfer and delivers it with his share certificate to the transferee (Rupert), who completes the instrument of transfer, has it stamped, and then delivers it with the share certificate to the company. However, agreeing to a transfer does not make Rupert a member of the company. He must be registered as a shareholder if he is to be a member of Bear plc and, until registration, the company will not issue a share certificate in his name. **Sched 3, art 63** to the **Model Articles for Public Companies (2008)**, entitles the directors to refuse to register *partly* paid shares, but gives them no discretion to refuse to register fully paid shares unless the articles so provide. The articles of this company do so provide. A shareholder is entitled to be registered under s 771 CA 2006. However, where the directors, as in this case, are given a discretion to refuse to register and they choose to refuse to register, they must notify the shareholder of their decision within two months of an application to be registered and they must give reasons for the refusal (s 771(1)(b) and (2) CA 2006). Failure so to do renders the company and the directors liable to a fine (s 771 CA 2006). It appears that Bear plc seems to have exceeded the time limit and so Rupert can apply to the court for rectification of the Register (s 125 CA 2006) and the issue of a share certificate. Another possible course of action is that a refusal to register could be challenged if the directors were not acting *bona fide* in a way likely to promote the success of the company for the benefit of the members as a whole (s 172 CA 2006) or were not using their powers for a proper purpose (s 171 CA 2006 – *Re Smith and Fawcett Ltd* (1942)). However, the burden of proving a lack of *bona fides* falls on those challenging the refusal to register and this may be a heavy burden.

# (B)  PADDINGTON

Shares in a company are transferable (s 541 CA 2006), but in this case it is alleged that the share transfer was forged – who is entitled to be registered as a member of Bear plc. Paddington or Bungle? A share certificate is *prima facie* evidence that the named member has title to the shares (s 768 CA 2006), so that Paddington should be regarded as having title unless the shares have been validly transferred to another person. Thus, Bungle bears the burden of proving his entitlement to be registered as a shareholder. **Section 770 CA 1985** requires a transfer of shares to be made by a proper instrument of transfer. The **Stock Transfer Act 1963** sets out forms of transfer document for fully paid shares and it is assumed that an appropriate form was used. If the signature of the holder is forged on an instrument of transfer of those shares, then the instrument is void (*Dixon v Kennaway and Co* (1900)). Consequently, the shares are not transferred and Paddington remains the holder of the shares. Bungle's remedy is against the person who purported to transfer the shares to him – if he can be found. Indeed, even if Bungle succeeded in being registered, the company could remove him from the Register because the only basis for registration is the forged transfer (*Sheffield Corp v Barclay* (1905)).

# (C)  THE SIX MEMBERS

**Section 127 CA 2006** states that the Register of Members is *prima facie* evidence of its contents. Thus, the six members to whom dividends were paid were *prima facie* members and entitled to the payment. However, the Register is not conclusive evidence and s 125 CA 2006 provides that it can be rectified and s 125(1) CA 2006 states that, if there is any unnecessary delay in entering on the Register the fact that a person has ceased to be a member, the person aggrieved or any member of the company can apply for rectification. While rectification of the Register would correct the Register for the future, it does not determine the fate of the past dividend payment. It is assumed that the transferees of the shares were also paid a dividend and, if they were not, they are entitled to a payment from the company, whether the company can recover the money from the former shareholders or not. **Section 125(3) CA 2006** authorises the court to decide any question necessary or expedient to be decided for rectification of the Register. The ability of the company to recover dividends wrongly paid is arguably not a question 'necessary or expedient to be decided for rectification of the Register', so the court would not have the power to order the return of the money under this section. It is assumed that the quasi-contractual (restitutionary) rules on money paid by mistake operate and the dividends may be recoverable by reference to the general law.

Whether rectification can be arranged by agreement between all relevant parties, that is, the company and transferors and transferees, is as yet unsettled, with cases both supporting and denying the efficacy of informal rectification.

## (D) WINNIE

Winnie has been issued with a share certificate. A share certificate is *prima facie* evidence of title (s 186 CA 1985). However, the presumption raised by the share certificate, that Winnie owns the shares, can be rebutted. Where there is evidence in rebuttal, the presumption will still prevail if the company is estopped from relying on that evidence. Thus, in Winnie's case, there are three issues. First, can the company disclaim the share certificate altogether? Secondly, can it produce evidence to rebut the presumption that the person in possession of the share certificate is the rightful owner of the shares? Finally, is the company estopped from relying on that evidence?

The company might seek to disclaim all liability for the share certificate on the basis that the person who had issued it on behalf of the company, X, was not authorised so to do. For example, in *Ruben v Great Fingall Consolidated* (1906), the company secretary forged a share transfer and issued to Ruben a share certificate, which was signed by the secretary and bore the names of two other directors of the company. The signatures of the directors had been forged by the company secretary. The issue for the House of Lords was whether the company could deny the validity of the certificate. The House of Lords stated that the forged certificate was a complete nullity and could not bind the company. It was held that a company secretary had no authority to guarantee on the company's behalf the genuineness or validity of a document. While this decision may have been appropriate in 1906, it is surely the case nowadays that the company secretary does have authority (actual or ostensible) to guarantee the validity of a document such as a share certificate. However, if X was not so authorised, the company can deny the validity of the share certificate issued to X's wife. That being so, it could be argued that the wife had nothing to transfer and the subsequent transfer to Winnie was a nullity. It seems very odd that Bear plc should be able to deny liability for the acts of its employee, and it can be hazarded that *Ruben* would not now be followed, particularly since the role and authority of a company secretary has been greatly enhanced since 1906 (see, for example, *Panorama Development Ltd v Fidelis Furnishing Fabrics Ltd* (1971)).

The evidence that the transfer to X's wife was forged is evidence on which the company could rely to rebut the presumption of title raised by the share certificate. However, it appears that, since Winnie has paid for the shares on the faith of a share certificate, albeit one issued as the result of a forged transfer (to the wife), the company is estopped from denying the genuineness of its own issued certificate (subject to the previous paragraph). Winnie is entitled to say: you issued a certificate, I believed what it said (that X's wife was the owner), so I am entitled to rely on it (*Re Bahia and San Francisco Rly Co Ltd* (1868)). If the company is estopped from denying Winnie's right to be a member and has to reinstate Fred, it can seek compensation from X's wife, even if she was not party to the fraud (*Royal Bank of Scotland plc v Sandstone Properties Ltd* (1998)). Should X's wife be found liable, she can seek a contribution from the company if it was negligent in registering the transfer, although this seems unlikely unless it should have spotted and curtailed X's fraudulent activities earlier. Estoppel allows Winnie to assert her rights against the company, but it does not affect the validity of Fred's title, unless perhaps he knew of the original forged transfer and failed to denounce it with reasonable speed. If Fred was tardy once he discovered the truth in asserting his rights, he would be estopped from raising the forgery and might not be able to demand reinstatement on the Register of members.

Public companies generally insure themselves against the consequences of acting on a forged transfer. If Bear plc was a listed company, it could have uncertificated shares and use the computer-based system which records title to shares and enables title to be transferred.

# QUESTION 34

Answer *both* parts:

(a) **Section 658(1)** of the **Companies Act 2006** provides that '[a] company limited by shares shall not acquire its own shares, whether by purchase, subscription or otherwise, except in accordance with [**Part 18** of the Act]'.

▶ In what circumstances, might a company wish to acquire its own shares?

(b) College Ltd was formed as result of a joint venture by Baljit and Shazia. Baljit is looking forward to early retirement and wishes to reduce her involvement in the company. It has been suggested to her that College Ltd acquires 150,000 of its own £1 shares at par from Baljit. It is further suggested that the purchase will not be accompanied by a fresh issue of shares, but will involve the use of all the company's distributable profits of £100,000 and a permissible capital payment of £50,000.

▶ Comment on the legal issues arising in respect of the company's proposal.

## Answer Plan

Part (a) requires a consideration of when, and why, the rule in s 658(1) of the Companies Act 2006 does or does not apply. Part (b) requires consideration of whether the proposed payment to Baljit is valid. You might also want to consider the consequences where there is an insolvent liquidation within 12 months of a payment out of capital.

# ANSWER

## (A) THE ACQUISITION BY A COMPANY OF ITS OWN SHARES

The rule contained in s 658 of the **Companies Act (CA) 2006**, that a company may not acquire its own shares, restates the common law decision in *Trevor v Whitworth* (1887). The House of Lords in that case showed the courts' concern for the interests of creditors and held that, since a creditor effectively 'lent' money to the company (by allowing credit), he has a right to expect that the company will retain its capital and not use it improperly (including not returning it to the shareholders). The share capital (plus undistributable reserves) can be called the 'creditors' buffer'. Consequently, s 658 (1) CA 2006 provides that a company cannot reduce its share capital (nominal value of shares subscribed by shareholders) by buying its own shares (no new capital provided and existing capital used). This does not mean that the money subscribed for shares cannot be used and must be locked away in the bank – the money can be used in the course of the business. All that a creditor is entitled to expect is that the money subscribed for shares has been used in the legitimate course of business. There are, however, a number of exceptions to s 658 CA 2006.

Section s 659 (1) CA 2006 provides that a company can acquire its own shares where:

(i)    a redemption or purchase of shares in accordance with ss 684–723 CA 2006;
(ii)   a reduction of capital duly made.

Other circumstances, which are not strictly necessary for consideration here, are where the acquisition is ordered by the court pursuant to its powers under s 721(6) CA 2006 (objection to redemption or purchase of shares out of capital), s 98 CA 2006 (application to cancel resolution for re-registration of public company as a private company), s 759 CA 2006 (remedial order in case of breach of public offers by private company) or s 996 CA 2006 (remedy for unfair prejudice), or where the shares are forfeited by the company because the acquirer has not paid for them.

The exception in (i) was introduced by the **CA 1980** and, along with exception (ii), demonstrates the circumstances in which a company might wish to acquire its shares. Exception (ii), although of much earlier origin, has been modified by the **CA 2006**.

### (I) REDEMPTION OR PURCHASE OF SHARES

Both public and private companies may redeem or purchase their own shares, provided that the company maintains the creditors' buffer. Indeed, private companies can reduce the creditors' buffer and make a permissible capital payment provided that they act in accordance with ss 709–723 CA 2006. This exception was part of a package of measures introduced in the early 1980s to help companies, particularly private companies, raise money. Prior to 1980, a private company wishing to raise outside investment faced two difficulties – issuing new shares diluted existing shareholdings, thus affecting the control of the company (unattractive to current shareholders, particularly in a family company), and new investors would obtain a minority shareholding which would be, effectively, unmarketable. The provisions allowing a company to issue redeemable shares or to buy back its own shares were designed to provide sufficient flexibility to permit existing shareholders to retain control whilst increasing the marketability of shares and continuing to protect creditors. The ability to issue redeemable shares means that a company increases its capital and the investor knows that he will be locked in only for a determinable period. The ability to re-purchase shares allows a company to reorganise its share structure as and when (and if) required and gives an investor some possibility of releasing his investment even if the company does not go public. The facility to re-purchase allows a company to buy out a founder-shareholder when he wishes to retire (assuming that other shareholders lack the funds or the desire to purchase the shares), or to buy out a troublesome shareholder. Alternatively, re-purchase may have financial benefits, for example to enhance the earnings value of the remaining shares (this has been the principal reason why public companies have used the re-purchase provisions) or reduce future dividend payments (by abolishing preference shares, for example).

A public company might also seek to purchase its own shares to preclude a takeover bid, but directors may have to be mindful that this might involve a breach of the directors' duty to use the powers conferred on them for a proper purpose (s 171 CA 2006).

Where a company wishes to redeem redeemable shares or purchase its own shares, there are procedural requirements designed to ensure that only certain funds are used for these purposes and that an appropriate amount of publicity for the proposed scheme is provided. Any attempt to redeem or re-purchase other than in compliance with the CA 2006 leaves the company open to a fine and every officer of the company in default liable to a fine and/or imprisonment. Further, the acquisition will be void (s 658(2)–(3) CA 2006).

## (II)  REDUCTION OF CAPITAL DULY MADE

Section 641(1)(a) CA 2006 permits a private company to reduce its share capital by a special resolution of its members, supported by an insolvency statement in accordance with ss 642–644 CA 2006. In any case, s 641(1)(b) CA 2006 permits a company to reduce its capital by special resolution confirmed by the court in accordance with ss 645–651 CA 2006. However, these provisions are subject to any restriction or prohibition on a reduction of share capital contained in the company's articles. **Section 641 CA 2006** does not limit the circumstances in which a company may seek to reduce capital, but it does specify three possible grounds for so doing, as follows:

- ❖ the extinction or reduction of unpaid share capital (no self-acquisition by company);
- ❖ cancellation of paid up share capital which is lost or unrepresented by available assets; and
- ❖ payment of any paid up share capital in excess of the company's wants.

Where one of these three grounds is the basis of an application, and court confirmation is required, a court is likely to approve the reduction, provided that the position of the company's creditors is secured.

Cancellation of paid up share capital is designed to reflect reality. There is little point in a company having a high nominal capital when trading losses have reduced its net assets to a lower figure. Reduction of capital here would allow a company to resume dividend payments; this might be regarded as a sensible basis for reduction. In all cases of reduction, for which court confirmation is required, the court has to be satisfied that the creditors of the company are adequately protected before confirming the reduction.

The provision for private companies set out in s 641(1)(a) CA 2006 reflects the views of the Company Law Review Steering Group in allowing private companies to avoid what was regarded as an unnecessarily strict regime for private companies contained in the **CA 1985**. However, in acting in accordance with s 641(1)(a) CA 2006, a reduction of capital is not allowed if, as a result of the reduction, there would no longer be any member holding shares other than redeemable shares (s 641(2) CA 2006).

## (B) THE PROPOSAL TO ACQUIRE BALJIT'S SHARES

The proposed share acquisition must be approved by the board of College Ltd, which must exercise its decision whether or not to purchase Baljit's shares *bona fide* in a way likely to promote the success of the company for the benefit of the members as a whole (s 172 CA 2006). Breach of duty would render the directors liable to reimburse the company for any loss and the recipient of corporate funds (Baljit) might also be liable to refund the money under the principles of constructive trusteeship. If the scheme is acceptable, the shares must be paid for. Obviously, existing shareholders may be prevailed upon to buy the shares, but this does not seem likely in this case.

Perhaps the shareholders have no funds and no desire or ability to borrow the necessary sums. However, the company is willing to buy the shares. A new share issue has been rejected; perhaps because it would dilute the ownership of the company, and it is proposed to fund the acquisition partly by a payment out of income (£100,000 from distributable profits) and partly from capital (£58,000). Private companies are permitted to purchase their own shares, provided that certain statutory conditions are complied with, and may use the funds proposed in appropriate cases.

These provisions are complex but are designed to ensure that the shareholders approve the purchase, that only appropriate funds are used for the purchase and that there is adequate publicity for the purchase. First, there must not be any restriction or prohibition in the company's articles (**ss 690** and **709 CA 2006**). **Sections 691–708 CA 2006** then set out conditions for the purchase out of distributable profits, while **ss 710–720 CA 2006** set out the conditions for a private company where payment is out of capital. In the case of the use of the distributable profits of £58,000, the conditions for payment are that the contract to purchase was approved in advance by special resolution (and Baljit must not have voted on the resolution (**ss 694–695 CA 2006**)) and that the purchase so authorised was paid for out of the company's distributable profits or a fresh issue of shares made for the purpose. Thus the payment of £100,000 would appear to be acceptable as it is made out of distributable profits (defined in **ss 829–830 CA 2006**). Further, **s 733 CA 2006** requires a transfer of a sum representing the share purchase price from distributable profits to the capital redemption reserve. This also appears to have been satisfied. However, a purchase must also be given appropriate publicity for the purchase – notice to the Registrar of Companies, copy of contract at registered office, etc. In respect of the payment of £50,000, **s 709 CA 2006** allows private companies to purchase their own shares out of capital. Such a payment is called a 'permissible capital payment' and it may represent all or part of the purchase price. There are strict rules for the use of a permissible capital payment. **Section 716 CA 2006** provides that the payment must have been approved by special resolution (at a meeting or by written resolution) which has been obtained after the directors of the company have made a solvency statement (**s 714 CA 2006**). This statement must (i) specify the amount of the permissible capital payment and (ii) state that the directors, having made full inquiries into the affairs and prospects of the company and taking into account all the company's liabilities, are of the opinion that the company will be able to meet its debts immediately after the permissible capital payment, will continue as a going concern for the next 12 months after the permissible capital payment and be able to pay its debts as they fall due. The auditors must have commented on the directors' statement to the effect that, having inquired into the company's affairs, they were not aware of anything which would render the directors' opinion unreasonable (**s 714(6) CA 2006**). After a special resolution approving a permissible capital payment has been passed, the decision must be publicised (**s 719 CA 2006**). The publicity must mention the power of members and creditors to object. If College Ltd complies with these conditions, the payment of £50,000 will also be valid.

However, even if a permissible capital payment is valid at the time that it is made, the directors can incur liability to any subsequent liquidator of College Ltd. **Section 76 IA 1986** provides that, where a company goes into insolvent liquidation within 12 months of the payment out of capital being made, the directors who signed the s 714 statement are liable to contribute to the company's assets. The directors can escape liability if they can establish that they had reasonable grounds for their opinions; it seems probable that the auditors' approval would be a 'reasonable ground', provided that the directors had not concealed any information from the auditors. **Section 76 IA 1986** would also render the directors liable to contribute to the assets of the company to the extent of the permissible capital payment.

> ## Common Pitfalls
>
> As with any two- or multi-part question, time management is important and, unless there are different marks allocated to each part of the question, try to allow equal time for each part.

# QUESTION 35

It is a fundamental rule of company law that a company cannot provide financial assistance to a purchaser of the company's own shares.

▶ Discuss this statement.

## Answer Plan

An answer requires an analysis of the general rule against financial assistance, the rationale for the rule, the relaxation of the rule, particularly in respect of private companies, and the changes introduced by the **Companies Act 2006**.

# ANSWER

The general rule prohibiting companies from providing financial assistance in respect of the purchase of their own shares is part of a fundamental principle in company law that, in order to protect the interests of creditors, a company must maintain its capital. The overall purpose of these rules was explained by Lord Watson in *Trevor v Whitworth* (1877): 'The capital may, no doubt, be diminished by expenditure upon and reasonably incidental to all the objects specified. A part of it may be lost in carrying on the business operations authorised. Of this, all persons trusting the company are aware, and take the risk. But I think [those dealing with the company] have a right to rely, and were intended by the legislature to have a right to rely, on the capital remaining undiminished by any expenditure outside these limits, or by the return of any part of it to the shareholders.'

Some of the other significant rules on the maintenance of capital can be summarised as follows:

❖ Subject to certain exceptions, companies are prohibited from redeeming or purchasing their own shares. Public companies can only redeem or purchase their own shares out of profits or out of the proceeds of a fresh issue of shares. Private companies may purchase their own shares out of capital subject to certain safeguards.

❖ Companies can only reduce their capital by passing a special resolution to this effect and obtaining the consent of the court to the reduction, although a private company can do so by the passing of a special resolution, supported by a solvency statement.

❖ Distributions, for the purpose of any dividend, can only be made out of accumulated realised profits less accumulated realised losses. If a dividend is wrongly paid, a member may be liable to repay it under **CA 2006**. Directors who are responsible for unlawful distributions can be held liable for breach of duty (*Flitcroft's Case* (1882); *Bairstow v Queens' Moat Houses plc* (2001)) and if the directors have relied upon the auditors in recommending a dividend, the auditors may be liable (*Dovey v Cory* (1901)).

**Section 582** of the **Companies Act (CA) 2006** provides that the consideration for shares may be provided in money or money's worth. **Section 580 CA 2006** states that shares must not be issued at a discount, but, where the consideration for shares is not in the form of cash, it is unlikely that the shares would be treated as anything other than fully paid. There is no statutory requirement that the consideration for shares in a private company be valued and the courts will not treat consideration such as this as other than full payment unless it is manifestly inadequate or illusory (*Re Wragg* (1897)). Indeed, in the classic case of *Salomon v Salomon & Co Ltd* (1895), where the promoter transferred his boot business to the company, the House of Lords refused to investigate too closely the value of the business transferred by S in return for shares and a secured loan, even though the value appeared to have been, at best, a wildly optimistic figure. There can be no objection to a shareholder selling his shares in a company, since shares are supposed to be transferable (s 541 CA 2006). However, the method of payment may cause problems.

Section 678(1) CA 2006 provides that, where a person is acquiring shares in a public company, it is not lawful for that company to give financial assistance directly or indirectly for the purposes of the acquisition before, during or after the acquisition (note also s 679(1) CA 2006 – public company acquiring shares in a private holding company). There are however exceptions to s 678(1) CA 2006 (and s 679(1) CA 2006). These include where the company lends money in the ordinary course of business, for example where a bank customer borrows money to buy shares in the bank, or where the financial assistance is authorised by some other provision of company law (e.g. for the purpose of an employee share scheme).

The most significant exception, however, is contained in s 678(2) CA 2006 which states that a *public* company can give assistance if its principal purpose in doing so is not to give financial assistance to facilitate the acquisition or to reduce or discharge any liability incurred by a person for the purpose of the acquisition of the shares but is an incidental part of some larger purpose of the company and the assistance is given in good faith in the interests of the company. The ambit of this exception is uncertain, but it is designed largely to ensure that the broad scope of the prohibition does not unintentionally ensnare genuine commercial transactions which are of benefit to the company.

What constitutes a larger purpose was discussed by the House of Lords in *Brady v Brady* (1989), which was a case concerned with s 153 CA 1985, a provision which related to both public and private companies (under the CA 2006 the rule no longer applies to private companies). In this case, the facts of which are complicated, two brothers, who had fallen out, sought to split a family business, which operated through a series of interlinked, private companies, into two main spheres (haulage and soft drinks). A plan was evolved which was designed to leave one brother with the haulage-based business and the other brother with the soft drinks-based business. The plan required M to purchase all the shares in Brady (the holding company) from O, leaving M with a debt due to O. This debt was partly paid by the transfer to O of assets belonging to Brady. Clearly, Brady was contributing financial assistance to the purchase of its own shares. It was argued that the assistance was simply incidental to a larger purpose – the reorganisation of the family business – and that it was in the interests of Brady, since the only alternative, given the rancour between the brothers, was to wind up Brady. The House of Lords accepted that the plan was in the best interests of the company. However, the Lords, reversing the Court of Appeal, found no larger purpose to which the financial assistance was merely incidental. It ruled that the financial assistance in this case was driven by a more important reason than the provision of the assistance – the reorganisation plan – but said that purpose and reason were different. Simply because there was an important reason underpinning the scheme did not make it incidental to a larger purpose. On the facts, the scheme was designed to facilitate the purchase of shares in Brady, even if the reason was to split the family businesses, and there was no larger purpose to which it was incidental.

The issue of the effect of breach on the transaction for which the assistance was given arose in a number of cases concerning the forerunners of s 678 CA 2006. In *Victor Battery Co Ltd v Curry's Ltd* (1946), it was said that the granting of a debenture could not, in law, be financial assistance unless the debenture was valid, and consequently concluded that breach of the CA did not invalidate the financial assistance. Later cases, while not overruling *Victor Battery*, have looked at the commercial realities and concluded that, where the financial assistance has the effect in fact of underpinning the acquisition, it is financial assistance (whether it is legal or not) and is void (*Heald v O'Connor* (1971) and *Carney v Herbert* (1985) are two examples). In *Carney v Herbert* (1985), the Privy Council determined that where the unlawful assistance was ancillary to the overall transaction *and* its elimination would leave unchanged the subject matter of the transaction, it could be severed, leaving the remainder of the transaction enforceable. In *Carney*, the court felt able to sever from a contract for the sale of shares a guarantee of the purchaser's debt given by the company whose shares were being sold. Breach of the provision may also trigger criminal liability. Under s 680 CA 2006, the company is liable to a fine and officers of the company in default are liable to a fine and/or imprisonment.

The narrow interpretation of s 678(2) CA 2006, ignoring the commercial context and focusing on the disputed transaction, suggests that it may be difficult for *public* companies and their advisers to devise schemes that do not infringe CA 2006. It should be noted in passing that, in *Brady*, the House of Lords held, further, that the exception contained in s 155 CA 1985 (the 'whitewash' procedure), which only applied to private companies, could have operated to resolve the conflict. There is little doubt that had s 155 CA 1985 been relied on earlier, the company would have saved an enormous amount of money on professional and legal fees. Section 155 CA 1985, of course, has been abolished by the CA 2006, as private companies are no longer prohibited from providing financial assistance.

It was not surprising that the difficulties faced by businesses in respect of the financial assistance rules were recognised by the Department of Trade and Industry (DTI) as part of its review of modern company law. The DTI suggested that the rules on financial assistance for the purchase of shares were causing unnecessary, substantial professional fees to be incurred by companies in their attempts to ensure that innocent and worthwhile transactions did not breach the rules (*Modern Company Law for a Competitive Economy* (DTI, 1998)) and, in a later consultation document, the Company Law Review Steering Group proposed that the best way forward in dealing with this problem was for the financial assistance rule to be abolished completely in relation to private companies (*Modern Company Law for a Competitive Economy: Developing the Framework* (DTI, 2000)).

The recommendation of the Company Law Review Steering Group was later incorporated into the **CA 2006**. The **CA 2006** abolishes the rule against a private company providing financial assistance, but the rule remains in place for public companies. The abolition of the rule for private companies should avoid the expense associated with cases like *Brady* coming before the courts; *Brady* itself went to the House of Lords. The amount of money saved in terms of avoiding substantial professional and/or legal fees should be of real benefit to private companies.

## Aim Higher ★

Credit can be expected for a student examining in depth the reasons for reform of company law in this area and the views of the Department of Business Skills and Innovation (formerly the DTI) in response to the recommendations for change.

# QUESTION 36

Christie, James, Rendell and Sayers hold all the issued share capital of Detective Ltd, of which they are the executive directors. Christie has indicated that she would like to retire from the business and sell her shareholding. James, Rendell and Sayers would like the company, which is highly profitable, to pay Christie £100,000 for her past services (she has received a salary and has a company pension). The articles of the company do not restrict the company from making gratuitous payments, nor do the articles containing restrictions on the transfer of shares.

Christie is willing to sell her shares in the company when she retires; the remaining directors would prefer these shares to be retained within the company.

## Answer Plan

Two issues arise: first, the payment to Christie – is it legal, and if so, how can it be achieved? Secondly, keeping the shares in the company. In respect of the purchase, can it be by the company or existing shareholders and how is it to be funded? None of the remaining shareholders has sufficient funds of their own to purchase all Christie's shares. Advise the directors how to proceed in order to achieve their aims.

# ANSWER

## PAYMENT TO CHRISTIE

The need for a company to have an objects clause has been abolished by the **Companies Act (CA) 2006**, so, unless any restriction as to the company's objects is contained in the articles (**s 31 CA 2006**), the company has the power to make the proposed payment to Christie on her retirement and the board, it can be assumed, is authorised to make such payments since the board has the power to run the company (**art 3 Model Articles (2008)**, or equivalent article). Indeed, since the directors are also the shareholders, there is no one to object to the proposal. Thus, the payment would seem to be valid provided that the directors were not in breach of their statutory, fiduciary duties in authorising it and **ss 215–217 CA 2006** (payment to directors on retirement) has been complied with. There should be no difficulty in complying with **ss 215–217 CA 2006**, since all that is required is approval in advance by the shareholders, and the remaining directors are also the shareholders of Detective Ltd. There is still some doubt as to the ability of the directors to give away the company's money, even where the company is authorised to make gratuitous payments, but where some benefit, however elusive, to the company can be discerned, such payments are valid (*Re Horsley and Weight Ltd* (1982) took a more generous view and did not require any benefit to the company). Certainly, a gratuitous transaction decided on by the directors other than *bona fide* in a way likely to promote the success of the company for its members as a whole (**s 172 CA 2006**) would presumably be invalid as well as being a breach of duty by the directors (see *Aveling Barford Ltd v Perion Ltd* (1989) – sale of asset to company controlled by a director at gross undervalue was breach of director's duty and an attempt to defraud the company). If Detective Ltd remained solvent, this transaction is unlikely to be challenged, since all the shareholders were party to the decision. However, if the company went into insolvent liquidation, the liquidator might wish to challenge its validity. If the company failed to make the payment, it is unlikely that Christie would have a contractual claim to the money, since she has not provided any consideration for the agreement. Perhaps she should suggest that the price of the shares is augmented by £100,000 and she forgoes the retirement gift.

## SALE OF SHARES

Although the remaining directors do not wish Christie's shares to be sold to an outsider, Christie is not debarred from selling her shares to anyone who wants to buy them, unless the articles of the company limit their transferability. The **Model Articles for a Private Company (2008)**, contain no such restriction (but note **art 24(5)** below) and Detective Ltd has no such provision, although an attempt could be made to insert such a clause since the remaining shareholders could change the articles (**s 21 CA 2006**) by special resolution (they control three-quarters of the votes). On the facts, however, as it appears that the remaining shareholders and Christie are on good terms, the insertion of such an article is unlikely to be sought. The board of Detective Ltd does not have a power to refuse to register a new fully paid up shareholder under **art 24(5)** of the **Model Articles for a Private Company (2008)**, so indirect pressure cannot be put on Christie by a threat to refuse to register any transferee. However, an outsider who purchased the shares would not be a director, unless appointed by the board (to fill a casual vacancy). Consequently, an outsider would be unlikely to wish to purchase a minority shareholding unless this was a scheme acceptable to the remaining shareholders. Christie might prefer, as the remainder of the board would, to sell her shares to the company or to the existing shareholders.

**Section 658 CA 2006** appears to preclude the simple solution that the company purchase the shares. The inability of a director-shareholder to retire and sell his shares to the company was one of the reasons put forward to permit, in prescribed cases, a company buying its own shares. There are two ways of approaching the issue: Detective Ltd could seek to buy the shares either out of income or out of capital (only private companies can purchase shares out of capital). The statutory provisions are complex but are designed to ensure that the shareholders approve the purchase, that only appropriate funds are used for the purchase and that there is adequate publicity for the purchase. On any vote to approve a purchase, the shareholder who is intending to sell to the company cannot vote. If Detective Ltd does purchase the shares, they are cancelled thereby, reducing the issued share capital (and reducing capital if the purchase is made out of capital). Consider, first, purchase with payment out of income. **Section 690 CA 2006** allows a company to buy its own shares if not restricted or prohibited to do so by its articles and the conditions set out in the **CA 2006** are complied with. The conditions are that the contract to purchase is approved in advance by special resolution (**s 694 CA 2006**) and any purchase so authorised to be made must be paid for out of the company's distributable profits or a fresh issue of shares made for the purpose (**s 692 CA 2006**). The distributable profits of a company are determined by reference to **s 830 CA 2006** and are, in essence, the company's accumulated, realised profits (not previously distributed or capitalised) less its accumulated, realised losses (not previously written off in an authorised reduction or reorganisation of capital). Effectively, the fund used to pay for the shares must be money which could have been paid to the shareholders or constitute new capital. Since Detective Ltd is 'highly profitable', it seems likely that the directors could decide to pursue this method of purchase and have the funds to do so. If a purchase is made in compliance with s 694 CA 2006, s 702 CA 2006 requires appropriate publicity for the purchase (notice to registrar, copy of contract at registered office, etc) and s 733 CA 2006 requires a transfer of a sum representing the share purchase price from distributable profits to the capital redemption reserve. The capital redemption reserve forms part of the share capital of the company and can be reduced only by compliance with the usual rules (s 641 CA 2006) for the reduction of share capital. There is one exception to the rules on reduction in respect of the capital redemption reserve – it can be used to pay up unissued shares to be allotted to members as fully paid up bonus shares.

The board of Detective Ltd could be advised that, if the company has insufficient distributable profits to apply for the purchase of Christie's shares, the company might still be able to buy the shares. Section 709 CA 2006, which applies only to private companies, allows companies to purchase their own shares out of capital – such a payment (which may represent all or part of the purchase price) is known as a permissible capital payment (PCP). Needless to say, there are rules for the use of a PCP. Section 713 CA 2006 requires the payment out of capital to be approved by special resolution after the directors of Detective Ltd have made a solvency statement. This statement must specify:

- the amount of the PCP;
- that they have inquired into the financial situation of the company; and
- that, in their opinion, after the company has purchased the shares, it will be able to pay its debts and the company will continue business as a going concern for a full year.

The auditors must comment on the solvency statement to the effect that, having Inquired into the company's affairs, they are not aware of anything which would render the directors' opinion unreasonable (s 714(6) CA 2006). After the special resolution approving the PCP has been passed, the decision must be duly publicised (s 719 CA 2006), and this notification must inform the creditors of their right to object to the payment. Section 721 CA 2006 allows a member or creditor to object to a PCP (five week time limit from date of resolution) and s 721 CA 2006 sets out the court's powers when an objection has been lodged; the court can, among other things, affirm, reject or modify the special resolution and can order the objectors to be paid off. In this case, all three shareholders would have to vote for the proposal, so only creditors would be able to object. The directors might prefer not to use a PCP because, if the company goes into insolvent liquidation within 12 months of the payment out of capital being made, s 76 of the **Insolvency Act (IA) 1986** provides that the directors who signed the statutory declaration are liable to contribute to the company's assets unless they can establish that they had reasonable grounds for their opinion. Christie would also incur liability to the extent of the PCP.

If the company seeks to purchase Christie's shares other than in accordance with the **CA 2006**, the purchase is unlawful and the directors are in breach of duty (there are also criminal penalties – contained in **Part 18** of the **CA 2006**).

While no single shareholder may be able to afford Christie's shares, the shareholders might be able to afford a block each or purchase the total block jointly. Either scheme could preserve the existing share balance between the remaining shareholders and not allow any one of them to obtain a dominant position within the company. However, even if one shareholder purchased all Christie's shares, she would still have only 50% of the votes, and this amount is insufficient on its own to pass a resolution. Alternatively, all or some of the directors could seek to borrow money from the company to allow them to purchase Christie's shares. However, although a loan by a company to a person to enable him to purchase shares in the company is no longer prohibited in respect of a private company by virtue of the **CA 2006**, a company cannot make loans to a director unless approved by a resolution of the members of the company (**s 197 CA 2006**). Without such approval, the loan made is voidable at the company's option (**s 213 CA 2006**). However, since the directors are the shareholders, they are unlikely to seek to avoid the loan. In any event, there are exceptions to **s 197**, for example, small loans up to £10,000.

There seems little doubt that, one way or another, the remaining shareholders will be able to purchase Christie's shares if she is willing to sell them either to them or to the company.

# Loan Capital

## INTRODUCTION

Loan capital is the rather grand name attached to a company's borrowings (so remember that your overdraft is your loan capital); borrowing is an important method of financing for many companies. Loan capital can be divided into two categories. First, sums owed by the company as a specific debt, for example a loan from X, the most common example of which is the company's overdraft; and, second, marketable loans. Marketable loans are in essence potential debts which may be issued (sold) to investors. These loans will be issued on strict terms and conditions relating to date when the interest is due, date of redemption and other rights attaching. A company could create £1 million of marketable debt divided into £1 units bearing interest at X%, which it can sell as and when required and for whatever price it will fetch (there is no prohibition on issuing a loan at a discounted price unless it is convertible into shares). If £1 of redeemable debt is sold at a discount, the owner at redemption, who receives the face value of the debt and not the issue price, will make a capital profit. Marketable loans are frequently known as bonds. Individual loans or marketable loans may be secured by a charge or unsecured; much of the law in this area concerns company charges. Fashions in marketable loans vary. The highly specialised rules relating to international or euro bonds fall outside the scope of a company law syllabus.

Any document which states the terms on which a company has borrowed money may be called a debenture (s 738 of the **Companies Act (CA) 2006**) whether or not it carries security, but in the business world an unsecured loan is likely to be called an unsecured loan note rather than a debenture. Charges have to be registered to be valid against other creditors of the company, but the position on registration is presently something of a mess. The registration of company charges is determined by the **CA 2006**. The provisions of the **CA 2006** restake the provisions of the **CA 1985**. These provisions were subject to changes introduced by the **CA 1989**. However, the **CA 1989** changes were not implemented and have been repealed by the **CA 2006**. Instead, the Law Commission in a Working Paper *Company Charges, Registration of Security Interests: Company Charges and Property other than Land* (2002) proposed a fundamental change in this area of the law.

Loan capital raises general issues – the ability of the company to borrow, the powers of the directors to borrow and the issue of marketable loans – and specific provisions relating to company charges. Questions on loan capital often involve a company which has gone into insolvent liquidation and requires the liquidator to be advised on the validity and priority of certain debts. In all questions of this type, two issues arise: how can the liquidator maximise the company's assets (for example, sue the directors for wrongful trading, or have some charges set aside); and how should the liquidator determine priorities between competing creditors?

# QUESTION 37

Answer both parts:

(a)  What is the distinction between a fixed and floating charge? Why is the distinction important?

(b)  In 2004, Lo Cost Loans plc lent £600,000 to Finger Foods Ltd. The loan was secured by a charge, which was termed 'fixed', over book debts. As customers paid Finger Foods, the amount was paid into a special account. Finger Foods was able to draw on this special account unless and until Lo Cost Loans told it to stop, but was not able to assign its book debts to a third party.

Lo Cost Loans has become uneasy about the loan to Finger Foods and seeks your advice on the nature of the charge and its position should Finger Foods become insolvent.

## Answer Plan

The question falls into two parts. The first part is relatively straightforward. What is needed is a comparison of fixed and floating charges and a clear explanation of why the distinction matters.

In the second part, there is a need to give an analysis of the nature of the charge and why it is important in the event of Finger Foods' insolvency.

# ANSWER

## (A) DISTINGUISHING FIXED AND FLOATING CHARGES

If a company decides to borrow to expand its business, any creditor is likely to require security. Companies can deploy two forms of security – fixed charges, that is, a charge over a specific, identifiable asset or property, or floating charges, that is, a charge over a class of asset. Shareholders are largely unaffected by the type preferred. Both types of charge are subject to registration and if not registered are void (**s 874** of the **Companies Act (CA) 2006**), although the underlying debt is unaffected by non-registration. Both **ss 238 and 239** of the **Insolvency Act (IA) 1986** allow a liquidator (or administrator if the company is in administration) to apply to the court to have certain transactions, entered into by a company within the statutory period prior to the commencement of the winding up (or administration), set aside and the position of the company restored to what it would have been but for the disputed transaction. These transactions could include the granting of a charge.

## FIXED CHARGE

A fixed charge may be legal or equitable. For example, if a company charges its real property to its bank by means of a mortgage, the bank has a fixed legal charge over that property. The bank will obtain the title deeds to the property, which effectively precludes the company from dealing with the property without the knowledge and consent of the bank. A fixed equitable charge is less formal and can be achieved by the deposit of title deeds. The holder of a fixed charge can, on winding up or if the security is at risk, seize the charged property and sell it to discharge the indebtedness, thereafter accounting for any surplus to the company. A fixed charge holder does not claim against the general assets of the company on winding up, he simply claims against the asset that is the subject matter of the charge, and provided he has ensured that it is of adequate value he is not in competition with the other creditors for the assets of the company unless the same asset has been used as security for a further loan – when a question of priority will arise. A fixed charge generally prevents the company from dealing with the charged asset without the consent of the charge holder and is, it would seem, an inappropriate form of security for assets which are constantly changing, for example stock or book debts.

## FLOATING CHARGE

There is no statutory definition of a floating charge, and what the parties call the charge is not conclusive evidence of its status (*Re New Bullas Trading Ltd* (1994)). While the decision in *Bullas* was doubted by the Privy Council in *Re Brumark Investments Ltd* (2001) and overruled by the House of Lords in *Re Spectrum Plus Ltd* (2005), it was approved on this point. Judicial pronouncements have isolated certain factors which are likely to be present if a charge is to be classified as floating. These factors, derived from *Re Yorkshire Woolcombers' Association Ltd* (1903), are:

❖ that the charge is over a class of assets both present and future;
❖ which assets are constantly changing, for example book debts; and
❖ that the charge leaves the company free to use and deal with those assets.

While it is tempting to see fixed charges as relating to permanent assets and floating charges as attaching to changing assets, this is not the case. In the decision of *Siebe Gorman and Co Ltd v Barclays Bank Ltd* (1979), where it was held that the company had created a fixed charge over book debts, the judge stressed that the courts will not regard any single factor as crucial in seeking to classify a charge as fixed or floating. However, as authority, *Siebe Gorman* was doubted by the Privy Council in *Re Brumark* and overruled by the House of Lords in *Re Spectrum Plus*, and freedom to deal with the assets without consulting the chargee has generally been regarded as close to conclusive evidence that the charge is floating, irrespective of the wording adopted by the parties to the charge (*Re Cimex Tissues Ltd* (1995); *Re Cosslett (Contractors) Ltd* (1998)). Thus, in *Re Brumark*, where a company had created a charge over uncollected book debts which left it free to collect and use the proceeds in the ordinary course of business (subject to certain conditions imposed by the lender), the Privy Council held that the company had not created a fixed charge, whatever the contract of charge provided. *Re Brumark* was approved by the House of Lords in *Spectrum Plus*.

## DIFFERENCES BETWEEN FIXED AND FLOATING CHARGES

Since a floating charge is over a class of assets, the charge holder is uncertain as to the value of his security at any moment before the charge crystallises (i.e., it becomes a fixed charge on the happening of a certain event, for example receivership, liquidation or the giving of notice by the charge holder). If there is a fixed and floating charge over the same asset – the fixed charge (being fixed and legal) will generally have priority over the floating charge, even if created later than the floating charge. Floating charge holders, to protect themselves, may include in their charge notification that they take priority over later charge holders (even if fixed), that is, a negative pledge clause, but such a clause is effective only if the later charge holder has actual notice of the clause. It can be argued that this restriction on the company's ability to deal with its asset – by double charging – is contrary to the whole nature of a floating charge, which supposedly allows a company freedom to deal with the charged asset. Floating chargees are also experimenting with automatic crystallisation clauses, which seek to provide that if a company attempts to charge an asset subject to a floating charge, the charge automatically crystallises (without any intervention on the part of the charge holder) and becomes fixed, thus retaining its priority over the new charge. The efficacy of such clauses is not yet settled.

There are three further drawbacks of a floating charge as compared to a fixed charge. First, a floating charge ranks behind preferential debts on winding up. Secondly, it attaches only to assets of the relevant class which belong to the company. Consequently, where a floating chargee has a charge over raw materials to be used in production, he may find that the supplier of the goods has retained title to them until he is paid (a retention of title clause), thus allowing him to remove them, if not paid, from the company's premises and out of the grasp of the floating charge (*Aluminium Industries BV v Romalpa Aluminium Ltd* (1976); *Clough Mill Ltd v Martin* (1985); *Hendy Lennox Ltd v Grahame Puttick Ltd* (1984)). Similarly, goods are not company assets susceptible to the clutch of a floating charge if they are subject to a lien or a trust or have been leased. Thirdly, a floating charge created within 12 months of winding up (or two years if the charge holder is a connected person) is invalid (**s 245 IA 1986**) unless the company was solvent at the time the charge was granted. If a charge is *prima facie* invalidated by **s 245 IA 1986**, it will remain valid to the extent of any consideration provided for the charge.

## (B)  LO COST LOANS (LL) AND FINGER FOODS (FF)

Assuming that LL's charge is properly registered, LL has a charge, which is expressed to be fixed, over the book debts of FF which provides security for the loan. If the charge is indeed fixed, LL could require FF's creditors to pay it directly and would not suffer any of the disadvantages of floating charges outlined above. The critical issue is whether it is possible to create a fixed charge over book debts and, if it is, whether LL has successfully created a fixed charge.

In *Siebe Gorman and Co Ltd v Barclays Bank Ltd* (1979), it was accepted that it was possible to create a fixed charge over book debts. However, as indicated above, the fact that the parties have called the charge 'fixed' is not conclusive of the status of the charge. Thus, both in this case and in *Re Brightlife Ltd* (1987) it was held that if the company granting the charge was free to collect the debts and use the proceeds without restriction, then the charge was floating. In *Re New Bullas Trading Ltd* (1994), the court had been willing to distinguish between the book debts prior to collection (which could be subject to a fixed charge) and the debts once collected, at which point the sums received were subject only to a floating charge. *Re New Bullas*, however, was disapproved in *Agnew v Commissioner of Inland Revenue* (2001) and overruled by the House of Lords in *Re Spectrum Plus Ltd* (2005). The current view is that the courts must seek to determine what the parties intended but not necessarily give effect to that intention; ultimately it is a question of categorisation by reference to the law. The courts should apply the 'tests' set out in *Re Yorkshire Woolcombers Ltd*, as set out above. Hence, it seems that where the contract of charge contemplates that the company will be able to deal with the assets covered by the charge without reference to the chargee, then the charge is likely to be floating. In contrast, where the assets can be dealt with only after being released from the charge by the chargee, then it is probably a fixed charge. In *Agnew v Commissioner of Inland Revenue*, the charge purported to be fixed in respect of uncollected book debts and floating once the sums were collected. The Privy Council was not willing to treat uncollected book debts as subject to a fixed charge unless the party having the benefit of the security had placed one of two possible restrictions on the chargor. To be fixed, either:

❖ the chargor must be prohibited from collecting the book debt itself or realising it by assignment without the consent of the secured party; or

❖ the chargor must pay the proceeds of book debts it collects into a blocked account that is controlled by the secured party and actually operated as a blocked account.

It was argued in *Agnew v Commissioner of Inland Revenue* and *Re Spectrum Plus* that (as in *Re New Bullas*) it was possible to split the book debts into uncollected debts and proceeds and have different charges over the two. However, the Privy Council in *Agnew v Commissioner of Inland Revenue* and the House of Lords in *Re Spectrum Plus* held that a restriction on sale or transfer of the book debt would not be sufficient to create a fixed charge if the chargor remained free to collect the book debts and use the proceeds without any restriction.

Given these cases, has LL done enough to ensure that the charge is indeed fixed? The money collected when book debts were paid was to be paid into a special account and FF was not able to assign the proceeds of book debts – this would tend to support the view that the charge was fixed. However, FF had freedom to deal with the sums collected until given instructions to the contrary by LL. Given the weight placed upon freedom to deal with the charged asset expressed in *Agnew v Commissioner of Inland Revenue* and *Re Spectrum Plus*, it may well be that this freedom is fatal to LL's case and the charge would be treated as floating, with all the disadvantages which follow if FF were to become insolvent.

## Common Pitfalls

As with all two-part questions, effective time management is critical, since roughly equal time should be devoted to both parts of the question (unless it is clear that the mark allocation is not equal).

# QUESTION 38

Conservative Ltd had been experiencing severe financial difficulties since early 2009 but its directors, John and Kenneth, continued to trade, hoping that the company's trading position would improve, although they thought it unlikely that the company would be able to pay its debts unless there was a massive upturn in business. They gave up the struggle and called a meeting on 1 June 2010 to wind up the company.

Conservative Ltd has assets of £34,000. Additionally, its plant and machinery has an estimated value of £22,000. The company's liabilities are:

(a)  £25,000 loan owed to Big Bank plc secured by a fixed charge, created in March 2001 and duly registered, over plant and machinery;
(b)  £15,000 overdraft owed to Small Bank Ltd secured by a floating charge over the company's assets and undertaking, created in August 2001 and duly registered;
(c)  £20,000 owing to employees (one month's salary for 20 workers); and
(d)  £21,000 owed to sundry trade creditors.

In November 2009, Kenneth negotiated the sale of property to the company, for which he was paid a commission by the vendor, thereby making a profit of £8,000; he has not, so far, disclosed this profit to John or the shareholders.

Liquidation costs are likely to be around £5,000.

▶ Advise the liquidator on any relevant issues of company law and indicate which creditors will be paid.

### Answer Plan
The usual issues arise – how can the assets of the company be augmented (actions against directors, etc) and how should the assets be distributed? Consider each debt in turn to determine its validity and conclude with a rank order for payment.

# ANSWER
On the appointment of a liquidator, the powers of the directors of a company cease, except insofar as they are permitted to act either by the company in general meeting or the liquidator. The liquidator has to comply with a complex web of procedures, but his principal obligation can be summarised by reference to s 143 of the **Insolvency Act (IA) 1986** (albeit that this section only applies to companies being wound up by the court), namely, to secure the company's assets and to realise and distribute them to the company's creditors.

## SWELLING THE ASSETS
In addition to seeking contributions from shareholders who hold partly paid shares and pursuing legal actions against third parties, the liquidator of Conservative Ltd might wish to consider whether he can recover any sums from the directors of the

company. Consider first the contract negotiated by Kenneth. The House of Lords in *Aberdeen Rly Co v Blaikie Bros* (1854) ruled that a director could not benefit directly or indirectly from a contract made by his company. This has been codified by the **Companies Act (CA) 2006** so that a director cannot benefit from a contract between himself and his company or between his company and a third party without making *adequate disclosure* of his own interest (**ss 177** and **182 CA 2006**). Disclosure in this company could have been achieved under **s 177 CA 2006** (proposed contracts) or **s 182 CA 2006** (existing contracts). If there has been inadequate disclosure and the members of the company do not approve or authorise the breach of duty, the company can rescind the contract (where the director has received a direct benefit and rescission is still possible) or make the director liable to account for any indirect benefits (as in this case); the equitable rules are preserved by **s 178 CA 2006**. In this case, the liquidator should seek to recover the £8,000 from Kenneth.

Another possibility which the liquidator might pursue is an action against the directors for wrongful trading. The concept of wrongful trading was introduced by **s 214 IA 1986** and it allows a court to declare a director liable to contribute to the assets of the company if the director knew, or ought to have concluded, that there was no reasonable prospect of the company avoiding insolvent liquidation and he did not take every step he ought to have taken to minimise the potential loss to the company's creditors. Thus, if this is an insolvent liquidation, the liquidator can seek a court order for one or more directors of the company to contribute to the assets of the company (*Re Purpoint Ltd* (1991)). John and/or Kenneth cannot be liable under **s 214 IA 1986** unless they knew or ought to have concluded that insolvency could not be avoided *and* they failed to take every step to minimise loss to creditors which they ought to have taken. The section only envisages the imposition of liability on a director who has both not realised what he should have done and has not done what he should have done.

In determining whether a director has met the standard expected of him, **s 214 IA 1986** provides guidance. **Sub-section (4)** says that a director is to be judged by what a reasonably diligent person with the 'general knowledge, skill and experience that may reasonably be expected of a person carrying out the same functions as are carried out by that director' (that is, the director potentially subject to an order) and the 'general knowledge, skill and experience' of the director whom it is sought to make liable. This somewhat obscure provision seems to mean that what a director should have known or done is to be judged by reference to a theoretical director who possesses those skills that may 'reasonably be expected' of a director, unless the director is better qualified than this theoretical director, when he is to be judged by reference to his own qualifications. Assuming that John and Kenneth have no special skills, they are to be judged by reference to the theoretical director who possesses those qualifications which can reasonably be expected from a director; the IA 1986 is silent as to what qualifications one can reasonably expect a director to possess and the courts have been reluctant to list what can be expected.

In determining whether John and Kenneth did all that could be expected of them, consider the case of *Re Produce Marketing Consortium Ltd* (1989), hereafter referred to as PMC. In *PMC*, the company had traded successfully for some nine to 10 years and remained profitable until 1980. Thereafter, between 1980 and 1984, the company built up an overdraft, and in 1984 had an excess of liabilities over assets and a trading loss. Between 1984 and 1987, when insolvent liquidation ensued, the trading loss continued, as did the excess of liabilities over assets, but the overdraft approximately halved due to an increase in indebtedness to the company's principal supplier. By February 1987, one of the directors realised that liquidation was inevitable but the company was allowed to trade until October, the decision being justified as allowing disposal of the company's supplies of perishable goods which were held in cold store. Knox J found that the directors should have concluded by July 1986 that liquidation was inevitable because, although accounts were not available until January 1987, their knowledge of the business was such that they must have realised that turnover was down and that the gap between assets and liabilities must have increased. Since the IA 1986 provides that the directors are to be judged by reference to what they know and what they ought to know, Knox J held that they ought to have known the financial results for the year ending 1985 in July 1986 at the latest, so that the fact that these results were not known until 1987 was no excuse. Moreover, the directors had failed to take all steps to minimise loss – the directors had not limited their dealings to running down the company's stocks in cold store, even if this was a justified step. Knox J held that both directors must contribute £75,000 to the assets of the company, this being the loss which could have been averted by speedy liquidation. It could be argued that John and Kenneth were even more reprehensible, since they seemed to be aware that the company was unable to meet its obligations and seem to have done nothing to minimise the company's debts. The loans taken out in 2001 were presumably to prop up the business and there seems to have been no rational business plan operated by the directors to improve the company's position. Assuming that John and Kenneth have funds, an action for wrongful trading seems appropriate.

## PAYING THE CREDITORS
Let us assume that some money has been recovered from the directors. To whom should it, and the other corporate funds, be paid? Consider the four competing claims. Note that if any of them should have been registered as a charge and were not, they become an unsecured debt (s 874 CA 2006), that transactions at undervalue or constituting a preference may not be enforceable (ss 238–241 IA 1986) and that a floating charge created within a specified period of winding up may be void (s 245 IA 1986).

Big Bank plc lent the company £25,000 secured by a fixed charge, duly registered, some 14 or 15 months before liquidation commenced. If this charge is valid, the proceeds of the sale of plant and machinery will be paid to Big Bank, leaving them with a projected shortfall of £3,000 in respect of which they are an unsecured creditor. There seems to be no evidence that this charge was a preference and, even if it was, the **IA 1986** only permits the setting aside of preferential transactions entered into in the six months prior to liquidation (unless the bank was a connected person, which it is not). Big Bank drop out of the liquidator's sums except to the extent of £3,000.

Small Bank Ltd lent the company £15,000 (the overdraft), secured by a floating charge, duly registered, some 9 or 10 months prior to the liquidation. **Section 245 IA 1986** provides that a floating charge created within 12 months of insolvent liquidation (the bank is not a connected person; if it were, the period would be two years) is invalid (the debt remains valid but unsecured) *except* to the extent of any money paid to the company after the creation of the charge and in consideration for the charge. Since Small Bank Ltd lent money to the company, it seems likely that they fall within the exception and that the charge is valid. Thus, the only issue for the liquidator to determine is whether the overdraft arose after the charge and is thus secured or whether all or part of it arose prior to the charge, in which case that part would be unsecured. It seems unlikely that the overdraft arose prior to August 2001. Even if the company had an overdraft at that date of £15,000 or more, the case of *Re Yeovil Glove Co Ltd* (1965) would probably protect the bank. Thus, in this case, if the overdraft existed prior to the charge and the company was allowed to continue using its account after the charge was granted, *Re Yeovil Glove* would apply so that, as money flowed through the account, the old (unsecured) loan would be discharged to be replaced by a new (secured) loan. Thus, Small Bank Ltd have a claim over the assets of the company to the extent of any consideration provided for the charge – probably the full sum.

Small Bank Ltd would, however, be paid after any preferential creditors (**s 175 IA 1986**). The employees of the company are preferential creditors in respect of unpaid wages up to a maximum of £800 per employee (**s 386** and **Sched 6 IA 1986**). Thus, each employee must be paid £800 (£16,000 total) before any other creditors are paid by the liquidator. The balance of their unpaid wages is an unsecured debt, although, on application by the employee, the Secretary of State has the power under the **Employment Rights Act 1996** to pay certain amounts due to the employees.

Thus, the liquidator should pay the costs of the liquidation (£5,000) (the priority of recoverable expenses is contained in the **Insolvency Rules 1986**) and then the employees (£16,000), making a total of £21,000. This leaves assets of £13,000, which must be paid to Small Bank Ltd (owed £15,000), leaving Small Bank Ltd £2,000 out of pocket. If the liquidator obtains any money from John and Kenneth, this is used first to pay Small Bank Ltd its £2,000 and the remainder is divided between Big Bank Ltd (£3,000), the employees (£4,000) and the unsecured creditors, namely, trade creditors. The trade creditors, as unsecured creditors, rank equally and each will receive the same percentage of their debt, according to the funds available. However, under the **Enterprise Act 2002**, amending the **IA 1986**, the liquidator has the power to set aside a portion of the assets that would otherwise be realised to meet the claims of the floating charge holders for distribution to the unsecured creditors (**s 176A IA 1986**). How much can be set aside depends on the value of the company's net property.

# QUESTION 39

You have been appointed liquidator of an insolvent company, Reindeer Ltd, which was founded by Rudolf and which has been engaged in the manufacture of novelties for festivals. The majority of the issued share capital of Reindeer Ltd is owned by Rudolf, who was the sole director of the company, with the remainder being owned by his brother, Gandalf.

What, if anything, should be done about the following, which the liquidation has revealed:

(a)  A year prior to the commencement of liquidation, Reindeer Ltd sold its factory to Elk Ltd for £110,000 (which was its book value) and then leased the premises back from Elk Ltd. Elk Ltd, which is controlled and run by Gandalf, has recently contracted to sell the property for £0.75 million.

(b)  Shortly before your appointment, the company redeemed a floating charge which had been granted to Christmas Bank plc six months earlier as security for the company's overdraft, which was guaranteed by Gandalf.

## Answer Plan

A number of issues for the liquidator to consider, which, as is usual, includes swelling the assets of the company (sale of property, redemption of floating charge) and determining the distribution of the assets (preferential debts).

# ANSWER

As liquidator, you have been asked to consider a number of issues which have emerged in the course of the liquidation of Reindeer Ltd. The substantive issues can be treated separately.

# (A) SALE OF PROPERTY

One duty cast upon a liquidator is to augment the company's assets available for distribution to creditors. In this case, the company has sold an asset at a price which appears to be an undervalue. A number of possibilities arise. Can this transaction be set aside, can the profit on the resale be recovered from Rudolf, Gandalf or Elk Ltd, or can damages be recovered for a foolish commercial decision or for any other reason?

First, it must be seen whether the rise in value of the property sold is attributable to some external factors; if this is the case, the company was unlucky but the transaction is not actionable. If, however, the difference between the sale price and the new price is not so attributable, you may wish to pursue the issue of the sale further. A sale by a company to a third party cannot generally be rescinded merely because the company could have got a better price for the asset, but, if the sale falls within s 238 of the Insolvency Act (IA) 1986, a court can make an order to restore the company to the position it would have been in had it not entered into the transaction. Section 238 IA 1986 covers the situation where the company sells an asset at an undervalue, but the section is applicable only if the transaction falls within the relevant period defined in s 240 IA 1986. The relevant period for a transferee who is a connected person is two years, whereas in other cases it is six months. Thus, the critical issue is whether the purchaser, Elk Ltd, is a connected person. Section 249 IA 1986, which defines 'connected person', treats directors and shadow directors and associates as connected to the company. Elk Ltd is neither a director nor a shadow director of Reindeer Ltd, although Gandalf may well be a shadow director (a person in accordance with whose directions the directors of the company are accustomed to act – s 251 of the Companies Act (CA) 2006), since he seems to play a large role in the affairs of the company. If Gandalf is a shadow director, it might be that the court would lift the veil of incorporation and treat Elk Ltd and Gandalf as one and the same for the purposes of s 238 IA 1986 (a similar approach was manifested in *Aveling Barford v Perion Ltd* (1989)). Alternatively, if Elk Ltd is an associate of Reindeer Ltd, the two year statutory period will also operate. Section 435 IA 1986 defines 'associate' in some detail, but the upshot is that, if Rudolf controls one company and Gandalf another, then Elk Ltd is an associate of Reindeer Ltd either because they are brothers or because Gandalf is a shadow director of Reindeer Ltd. Thus, the sale at the undervalue can be set aside unless Reindeer Ltd could pay its debts at the time of the sale. This seems the simplest way of dealing with the sale of property, but if, for some reason, s 238 IA 1986 is inapplicable, other routes may be open to you.

A liquidator may sue a director if he has broken the duties imposed on him by the CA 2006 (there is no *locus* problem since the power to run the company passes to the liquidator on winding up), although it will not be worth doing so if Rudolf has no money. Is selling an asset at an undervalue a breach of the duty to exercise reasonable care, skill and diligence imposed by s 174 CA 2006)? The conventional formulation of the nature and extent of this duty was that given by Romer J in *Re City Equitable Fire Insurance Co Ltd* (1925), in which he held, *inter alia*, that a director need display only such skill as may reasonably be expected from a person of his knowledge and experience. It is plain that, if Rudolf has made a misguided but foolish decision, he will not be negligent. Arguably, trying to raise funds by selling an asset is perfectly sensible, although failure to have the property revalued seems very misguided. Alternatively, directors are supposed to exercise an independent judgment (s 173 CA 2006) and, if it can be shown that Rudolf simply implemented Gandalf's instructions without paying proper regard to the interests of the company, that might be a breach of duty.

Whether Gandalf can incur liability if s 238 IA 1986 does not apply is uncertain. He may well be a shadow director and the general duties of the CA 2006, as they apply to directors, also apply to shadow directors to the extent provided for by the common law or equitable rules (s 170(5) CA 2006). There are no cases discussing whether the common law or equitable rules on company contracts benefiting directors apply to shadow directors, but if they do apply, there can be no question of approving this sale if it is a misappropriation of a corporate asset. If a director does so appropriate, he is liable as a constructive trustee and must return the property; constructive trusteeship could also be imposed on Elk Ltd if it had knowingly received misappropriated property. While the common law position is uncertain, there is no doubt that the statutory provisions on substantial property transactions are applicable to such persons. Thus, if, as seems possible, he is a shadow director, s 190 CA 2006 will apply to any sale of property to Elk Ltd if that company is 'connected' with Gandalf, since the asset is a non-cash asset of requisite value (over £100,000). Section 252 CA 2006 defines a connected person (the definition differs from the provision in the IA 1986); it includes a company with which a shadow director is associated, so there is no doubt that, since he controls Elk Ltd, Gandalf and Elk Ltd are connected for the purposes of s 190 CA 2006. Section 190 CA 2006 does not prevent Gandalf (via Elk Ltd) from buying a corporate asset from Reindeer Ltd but does require the transaction to be approved by the shareholders in general meeting, and the apparent lack of such a resolution in this case *prima facie* renders the sale voidable (s 195 CA 2006).

While all the shareholders in Reindeer Ltd knew about the transaction, this is probably not a case where knowledge would be regarded as approval. While there are bars to the operation of s 195 CA 2006, there is no statutory time limit on the ability of the company to rescind an improper transaction (a possible advantage over s 238 IA 1986). Further, s 182 CA 2006 requires a director or shadow director to make adequate disclosure of his interest in an existing contract between himself and his company. Failure to disclose his interest in Elk Ltd, even though known to Rudolf, appears to be a breach of s 182 CA 2006, which gives rise to a criminal penalty (s 183 CA 2006).

It should also be noted that, in the case of *Aveling Barford v Perion Ltd* (1989), the facts of which resemble this case, the sale of an asset by the claimant company to the defendant company, which was controlled by the majority shareholder of the claimant company, at a gross undervalue, was held to be an unauthorised return of capital which was incapable of ratification. The defendant company was held liable to account as a constructive trustee.

## (B) REDEMPTION OF THE FLOATING CHARGE

A floating charge granted within 12 months of the commencement of a winding up is invalid, unless the company was solvent at the time, except to the extent of any consideration provided for the charge (s 245 IA 1986). Consequently, the floating charge in favour of the bank was potentially invalid. However, by the time of winding up, the debt which the charge was designed to secure had been repaid. While the charge would have been invalid, the underlying debt would not have been affected by s 245 IA 1986, so that where, as here, the debt has been repaid, the potential invalidity of the charge is irrelevant (*Mace Builders Ltd v Lunn* (1987)). However, a debt paid within six months of winding up may be challenged as being a preference contrary to s 239 IA 1986. This section provides that, where a company has, within the relevant time, given a preference to a person, the liquidator can apply to the court, which can make such order as it sees fit for restoring the position which would be operative but for the preference. Thus, if this repayment is a preference, the liquidator could seek to have the security set aside.

Is this a preference? There is scant case law on this provision, but it seems that the liquidator must establish that the company desired to prefer a creditor *or* a guarantor of one of the company's debts, that is, intended that person to be treated more favourably than other creditors. It seems not improbable that Gandalf would be regarded as having been preferred and the court could make such order as it saw fit, for example, recover the money paid to the bank and leave it to pursue Gandalf if Reindeer Ltd does not pay.

## QUESTION 40

The business of Unfairpack Ltd is the supply of Christmas food and drink hampers to consumers who deposit money with the company in advance of receipt of the hampers. To finance the business, the company obtained a loan from Business Bank plc in 2003 which was secured against the company's entire undertaking, with the title deeds of various properties being left in the company's possession. The instrument creating the charge expressly stated that Unfairpack Ltd was not to create any mortgages or charges upon its properties in priority thereto. In 2004, as security for a loan from Commerce Bank plc, Unfairpack Ltd deposited the title deeds of its distribution depot with Commerce Bank plc. Nine months prior to liquidation, Unfairpack Ltd received further finance from Trade Bank plc, the loan being secured against the company's book debts.

In September 2008, Unfairpack Ltd was the subject of a winding up petition and the company went into liquidation. The liquidator seeks your advice as to the nature of the claims of the creditors of the company and the priority of each creditor. In addition to monies owing to Business Bank plc, Commerce Bank plc and Trade Bank, claims are being made by other creditors, including employees of the company for arrears of wages and salary, Revenue and Customs for unpaid tax and VAT and customers for the failure of the company to deliver hampers.

▶ Advise the liquidator accordingly. Assume that any charge was registered duly at Companies House.

## Answer Plan

It will be necessary for the question to consider the nature of each creditor's claim and to provide an order of ranking in terms of the priority of each creditor. A consideration of the changes made by the **Enterprise Act (EA) 2002** is likely to be required as the date of the company's liquidation is after 15 September 2003, the date amendments to the **Insolvency Act 1986** by the **EA 2002** were brought into force.

# ANSWER

Where a company decides to borrow to expand its business, any creditor is likely to require security. Companies have two forms of security they can deploy – fixed charges, that is, a charge over a specified asset or property, or floating charges, that is, a charge over a class of asset, and current shareholders are largely unaffected by the type preferred. Both types of charge are subject to registration and, if not registered, are void (**s 874(1)** of the **Companies Act (CA) 2006**), although the underlying debt remains valid and becomes immediately repayable (**s 874(3) CA 2006**).

## FIXED CHARGES
A fixed charge may be legal or equitable. For example, if the company charges its real property to its bank by means of a mortgage, the bank has a fixed legal charge over that property. The bank will obtain the title deeds to the property, which effectively precludes the company from dealing with the property without the knowledge and consent of the bank. A fixed equitable charge is less formal and can be achieved by the deposit of title deeds, as in the case with Commerce Bank plc. A fixed charge holder does not claim against the general assets of the company on winding up, he simply

claims against the asset that is the subject matter of his charge, provided that he has ensured that it is of adequate value and he is not in competition with other creditors for the same assets of the company. If the same asset has been used as security for a further loan, then a question of priority will arise. A fixed charge, generally, prevents the company from dealing with the charged asset without the consent of the charge holder and is, thus, an inappropriate form of security for assets which are constantly changing such as stock in trade.

## FLOATING CHARGES

There is no statutory definition of a 'floating charge' and what the parties call 'the charge' is not conclusive evidence of its status (see *Re New Bullas Ltd* (1993); *Agnew v Commissioner of Inland Revenue* (2001); *Re Spectrum Plus Ltd* (2005)), but judicial pronouncements have identified certain factors which are likely to be present if a charge is to be classified as a floating charge. These factors identified in *Government Stock Investment Co v Manila Rly Co Ltd* (1897) and *Illingworth v Houldsworth* (1904) are (a) that the charge is over a class of assets both present and future; (b) that the class is one which, in the ordinary course of business, changes periodically; and (c) that the charge leaves the company free to deal with the charged asset in the ordinary course of conducting the company's business (this freedom need not be absolute). The type of asset frequently subject to a floating charge is goods in the course of production, but it is possible, as here in the case of Business Bank plc, for a floating charge to embrace the whole corporate enterprise (*Re Panama, New Zealand and Australian Royal Mail Co* (1870)).

## NEGATIVE PLEDGE CLAUSES

Since a floating charge leaves a company free to deal with its assets, and dealing may include the creation of further charges, a company may grant a second fixed or floating charge over charged assets. This raises a question of priorities between such charges. As we have seen, a fixed charge will generally obtain priority even if there is notice (which registration provides) of the existence of the prior floating charge, since one of the features of a floating charge is that the company is free to deal with its charged asset. Logically, the same must be true where the second charge is also a floating charge. It could be argued that, where there is no restriction on the creation of later charges, the company's general freedom to deal with a charged asset allows the creation of a later floating charge with priority. Since there is the risk of a later charge obtaining priority, prudent charge holders (for example, Business Bank plc) commonly insert negative pledge clauses in their agreements with companies, a negative pledge clause being a clause specifically precluding the creation of a second charge with priority. Assuming that such clauses are deemed valid, the question that would need to be addressed is whether such clauses are effective. The first charge will retain priority only if the second charge holder has notice of the first charge (which is provided by registration) and of the restriction on the freedom to deal. There is no constructive notice, it seems, of a restriction (a restriction need not, at present, be registered) and, even if a charge holder has actual knowledge of a floating charge, this seems not to be notice of a restriction or to require the potential charge holder to make inquiries (*English and Scottish Mercantile Investment Co Ltd v Brunton* (1892)). Where, however, a potential (fixed) chargeholder (in this case, Commerce Bank plc) searches the Register of charges and obtains actual knowledge of the charge and of any restriction registered with the charge, then Business Bank plc's claim will take priority over Commerce Bank plc's claim. Here, the effectiveness of the negative pledge clause would prove to be as between Business Bank plc and Commerce Bank plc. The negative pledge clause would not be relevant to consider in respect of the relationship between Business Bank plc and Trade Bank plc, as Trade Bank plc has a floating charge (see book debts, below) and, as floating charges rank on creation, Business Bank plc would rank ahead of Trade Bank plc, irrespective of the negative pledge clause.

## BOOK DEBTS

Book debts may be the subject matter of either a fixed charge or a floating charge. Whether a book debt is the subject matter of a fixed or floating charge depends on whether there are any restrictions contained in the instrument creating the charge on how the company can deal with the debts as they become extinguished. If, for example, the company must place the money in a separate bank account and is prevented from using it in the ordinary course of business, the charge created over the book debts would be described as a fixed charge (*Tailby v Official Receiver* (1888)). However, in the absence of such restrictions, charges over book debts are regarded as floating charges (*Re Brightlife* (1987); *Agnew v Commissioner of Inland Revenue* (2001); *Re Spectrum Plus Ltd* (2005)). Given that the question indicates that there are no restrictions present, the preferable view is that Business Bank plc's charge is a floating charge. In *Re Spectrum Plus Ltd*, the House of Lords restated the general position that, in the absence of any restrictions, charges on book debts are regarded as floating charges. With reference to the question, assuming the instrument creating the charge over book debts contains no restrictions on their use, Trade Bank plc's charge is a floating charge.

## VOID CHARGES

Section 245 IA 1986 provides that a floating charge created within 12 months of the onset of insolvency is invalid, except to the extent of any money paid to the company after the creation of the charge and in consideration for the charge. (Where the creditor is a connected person, the relevant period is two years.) As Trade Bank plc provided 'further finance' to Unfairpack Ltd, it seems that the exception applies and that the floating charge over the book debts is a valid floating charge.

## PRIORITY OF CLAIMS

Where a company goes into liquidation, the liquidator will need to rank the creditors in accordance with the priority of their claims and, where a company's liabilities are greater than its assets, it becomes important to ascertain which of the creditors will be satisfied and which will remain unsatisfied, in full or in part. The priority of creditors depends on a number of rules, including new or amended rules introduced by the **EA 2002**, with effect from 15 September 2003.

A fixed charge ranks over any floating charge including any earlier floating charge. This is because it is the nature of a floating charge that a company retains the freedom to grant further security over its assets in the ordinary course of business and this includes the company having the right to grant fixed charges (*Wheatley v Silkstone and Haigh Moor Coal Co* (1885)). As such, fixed charge holders, whether the fixed charge is created before or after a floating charge, take priority over the holder of the floating charge. Where there is more than one floating charge, such holders rank in accordance with creation, and it is immaterial if the second floating charge holder is given priority by the instrument creating the charge (*Re Benjamin Cope and Sons Ltd* (1914); cf *Re Auto Bottle Makers Ltd* (1926)). Where there is a competing claim, fixed charges also rank on creation. Where the earlier charge prohibits the company from granting priority to any later charges, a subsequent fixed charge holder will take priority over the earlier floating charge, unless, as was discussed earlier, the subsequent fixed charge holder has notice of the prohibition (*Re Castell and Brown Ltd* (1898); *English and Scottish Mercantile Investment Co v Brunton* (1892)).

Assuming that Business Bank plc's negative pledge clause is ineffective, Commerce Bank plc's claim would rank first (the fixed charge over the warehouse). If, on realisation, the value of the warehouse is less than the amount owed, Commerce Bank plc would rank as an unsecured creditor for the balance. After the payment of the costs of liquidation, next in line, ranking equally, would be the creditors having a preferential debt in accordance with **s 175 IA 1986**. (The decision of the House of Lords in *Buchler v Talbot* (2004), which allowed a floating charge holder to rank ahead of the costs of liquidation, is reversed by **s 1282 CA 2006** which inserts a new **s 176ZA** in the **IA 1986** to this effect.) The preferential creditors would be the company's employees for unpaid wages and salaries up to a maximum per employee of £800. For any amount in excess of £800, the employee would rank as an unsecured creditor, although, on application by an employee, the Secretary of State has the power under the **Employment Rights Act 1996** to pay certain amounts due to employees. The Crown, however, loses its status as a preferential creditor in respect of any insolvency after 15 September 2003. Revenue and Customs, therefore, will rank as an unsecured creditor. After payment of the preferential creditors, the next in line would be the floating charge holders, namely, Business Bank plc and Trade Bank plc. As there is a competing claim (Unfairpack's entire undertaking includes the company's book debts), there is an issue of priority between Business Bank plc and Trade Bank plc. In this case, as Business Bank plc's floating charge was created before that of Trade Bank plc, Business Bank plc would take priority. Any unsecured creditor, including creditors possessing an unsecured debt, such as Unfairpack Ltd's customers, would rank after the payment of floating charge holders. However, as Unfairpack Ltd has gone into liquidation after 15 September 2003, the liquidator has the power to set aside a portion of the assets that would otherwise be realised to meet the claims of the floating charge holders for distribution to the unsecured creditors (**s 176A IA 1986**). How much can be set aside depends on the value of the company's net property, after the payment of the costs of liquidation and the preferential creditors.

## Common Pitfalls

You need to be precise with this type of question. Make sure you accurately understand the nature of creditors' claims and their ranking. This is particularly the case when discussing fixed and floating charges and whether any charges or transactions are void under the **Insolvency Act 1986**.

## Aim Higher ★

Clearly demonstrate to the examiner that you understand *both* the type of claim each creditor has and the priority of each creditor. There needs to be a balance in your answer between knowledge of the relevant legal rules and the application of those rules.

# Administering the Company

## 8

## INTRODUCTION

The administration of companies is a wide ranging topic, covering such issues as the conduct of meetings, voting rights and resolutions, the maintenance of statutory registers and the role of the company secretary. Indeed, the law relating to the administration of companies, particularly private companies, has been revised significantly by the **Companies Act 2006**. Administration is 'everyday' company law, going on all the time in the background. It is not one of the most spectacular company law areas, concerning dispute and dissension, and questions on it tend to crop up less frequently. Some aspects of administration have arisen in previous chapters – the qualifications and powers of a company secretary, for example, and some are inherent in most questions – the passing of resolutions nearly always arises. This chapter seeks to consider some basic areas of the administration of companies, ending with a brief outline of administration of a failing company.

It should be noted that you either know the material relating to administration or you do not; waffle is impossible. Even if you do know your stuff, it is impossible to display anything better than competence when answering questions on this area. However, some aspects of administration may also be seen as aspects of corporate governance, ensuring that the company operates properly.

## QUESTION 41

Arts and Crafts Ltd is a small company which runs a pottery painting studio. Until incorporation, the business was run as a partnership. The directors are Fiona and Natasha who own, between them, 51% of the shares. Given that their plan is to keep the company small and to concentrate on commercial activities, they seek your advice on whether it is necessary for the company to comply with the annual provision of an audit, accounts and reports and whether it is necessary to hold company meetings.

**Answer Plan**

In the light of Fiona's and Natasha's concerns, the question requires a discussion of the need for an auditor, the content and presentation of reports and accounts and the ability, if any, to conduct shareholder business on an informal basis.

# ANSWER

Fiona and Natasha are concerned about the accounting, reporting and decision making processes applicable to a company as opposed to the unincorporated business they operated in the past. They may think that the running of a small private company imposes too much of an administrative burden upon them as entrepreneurs. Has the **Companies Act (CA) 2006** lessened the burden?

## (A) REPORTS AND ACCOUNTS

**Section 386** of the **CA 2006** requires all companies to keep accounting records, and failure to comply is a criminal offence (**s 387 CA 2006**). The original basis underlying the requirements relating to reports and accounts was that those who have invested in the company should be kept informed of the state of the company and, thus, their investment. These rules on disclosure are immensely detailed but assume that, if the directors have to tell the shareholders certain things, this will, even if shareholder approval is not required, constrain the behaviour of the directors to avoid shareholder disapproval. As explained below, a small company may be able to avoid some of the more onerous reporting requirements. However, the reports and accounts which are required are also designed to provide information for interested third parties, for example employees and creditors, so that their provision can be justified even for a company where there are few shareholders and the directors control the company. Reports and accounts are presented not just to the shareholders but must also be available, via submission to the Registrar of Companies, to the wider public (**s 441 CA 2006** – duty to file accounts; **s 451 CA 2006** – criminal offence for failing to comply with **s 441 CA 2006**; **s 453 CA 2006** – civil penalties for failing to comply with **s 441 CA 2006**). Listed companies also have to disclose information in accordance with the Listing Rules, which also includes the provisions of the Combined Code, while quoted companies are required to comply with the provisions of the **CA 2006** relating to the directors' remuneration report (**ss 420–422 CA 2006**). Quoted companies must also produce additional information in the directors' report relating to 'the development, performance or position' of the company's business (**s 417(5)(6) CA 2006**).

There are strict time limits for the preparation of accounts and their delivery to the registrar. A private company has nine months after the end of the company's accounting reference period to file the accounts, a public company has six months after the end of that period. Small and medium sized companies, however, can deliver abbreviated accounts to the registrar (ss 444–445 CA 2006). Since the purpose of these accounts is to inform the shareholders of the state of financial health of the company and provide an account of the directors' stewardship in the previous year, these accounts must present a true and fair view of the company's financial position (s 393 CA 2006). It is a criminal offence for directors to approve annual accounts which they know do not comply with the Act or to be reckless as to whether they comply or not (s 414 CA 2006). Section 437 CA 2006 requires the directors of a public company to lay the accounts before a general meeting of the company. However, as a private company is not obliged under the CA 2006 to hold an annual general meeting (Arts and Crafts Ltd is a private company), there is no general obligation on the laying of accounts before a general meeting of a private company. Whether or not a meeting is held, all reports, etc, must, within a specified time, be sent to all members and debenture holders (ss 423–425 CA 2006). The CA 2006 requires four documents to be presented to the shareholders and the registrar annually. These are the balance sheet, the profit and loss account, the directors' report (and directors' remuneration report where appropriate) and the auditor's report, unless the company opts to supply a summary financial statement in accordance with ss 426–429 CA 2006. Quoted companies are additionally required to ensure the accounts and reports are available on a website (s 430 CA 2006). Generally, the accounts presented to shareholders will need to comply with the CA 2006 and any applicable accounting standards (s 395 CA 2006), such as the 'CA individual accounts' or the 'international accounting standards' ('IAS individual accounts') (s 396 CA 2006). Directors may also choose to issue other reports, for example a chairman's report, but are not required to do so. Arts and Crafts Ltd must prepare a profit and loss account for each financial year and a balance sheet as at the last day of the year (s 394 CA 2006 – the company's 'individual accounts'). The profit and loss account, which shows such things as the company's trading record and other income and expenditure, is a temperature chart of the company's financial health throughout the year. The balance sheet is a snapshot of the company's financial position on a particular date. Both documents must give a 'true and fair view' of the company's profit and loss for the year and the position at the end of the year (s 393 CA 2006). The Act specifies the content, format and valuation rules to apply to the balance sheet and profit and loss account. Arts and Crafts Ltd is probably a 'small' company, as defined by s 382 CA 2006, i.e. a company with turnover of not more than £5.8m, a balance sheet total of not more than £2.8m and a number of employees of not more than 50. Small companies can avoid the filing requirements relating to the accounts and reports if they are exempt from audit and deliver abbreviated accounts (s 444 CA 2006 – small companies regime). The filing of abbreviated accounts extends to medium-sized companies under s 445 CA 2006. This will probably seem attractive to Fiona and Natasha.

The minimum content of the directors' report is set out in the **CA 2006 (ss 415–419 CA 2006)**. It must include such items as information about the directors, for example the size of their shareholding, and information about the company's business (a business review using key performance indicators), for example the principal activities of the company, any significant changes from the previous year and any likely future developments. The directors' report must also include information about employment and any charitable or political donations (political donations are generally prohibited, unless approved by the company in general meeting – **ss 362–379 CA 2006**). The directors' report, unlike the accounts, is not audited although relevant parts of the directors' remuneration report produced by quoted companies are required to be audited. The Listing Rules require directors of listed companies to include, in the directors' report, a statement that the company is a going concern. This statement must be reviewed by the auditors.

# (B) AUDIT

All companies are required to appoint auditors unless exempt (**s 475 CA 2006**). Small and dormant companies are exempt where the directors of such companies provide a statement to that effect on the company's balance sheet. However, an exempt company must hold an audit if a member or members holding at least 10% of any class of shares demands one (**s 476 CA 2006**). A small company for this purpose is defined by **s 479 CA 2006** – it must not be part of a group (unless a 'small' group), has a balance sheet total of less than £2.8m and a turnover of not more than £5.8m. Further exclusions from the small companies' regime is contained in **s 478 CA 2006**. Arts and Crafts Ltd appears to be an eligible small company and therefore the directors can exempt the company from the need for an audit, unless 10% of the company's members request an audit. The exemption for small companies is aimed at reducing the administrative burdens for small companies.

If an audit is required (**s 485(1) CA 2006** – private companies; **s 489(1) CA 2006** – public companies) the **CA 2006** provides that auditors are to be appointed (other than in the company's first financial year) at each general meeting at which accounts are laid (public companies) or within a prescribed period before the accounts and reports are sent out (private companies). The auditor must be a member of a recognised supervisory body (**s 25 CA 1989**) and be qualified under that body's rules for appointment as an auditor, be independent of the company (**s 27 CA 1989**) and hold appropriate qualifications (**Sched 11 CA 1989**). To remove an auditor requires an ordinary resolution (**s 510 CA 2006**) but special notice of any such resolution is required (**s 511 CA 2006**).

The function of the auditor is to report to the members on the financial statements made by the directors, particularly as to whether they comply with the **CA 2006**, and give a true and fair view of the state of the company's affairs and results for the period under consideration (s 495 CA 2006). In preparing his report, the auditor must satisfy himself that proper accounting records have been kept and that the annual accounts agree with the underlying accounting record. If the auditor is not satisfied that records, etc, are accurate, he must state this in his report. In order to prepare his report, the auditor has a right of access at all times to the books and accounts of the company and can require the company, its subsidiaries and its directors to provide any information required for the performance of his duties. Any failure to provide information must be reported in the auditor's report and it is a criminal offence for an officer of the company to make, knowingly or recklessly, a false statement to an auditor (s 501 CA 2006). Further offences in connection with the auditors' report are contained in s 507 CA 2006. Where information is not provided, the auditor has a duty to try to remedy the omission. As part of the directors' report, directors are required to state that there is no relevant audit information of which the company's auditors are unaware and that all steps have been taken or ought to have been taken to make themselves aware of any relevant audit information and to establish that the company's auditors are aware of that information (s 418 CA 2006). In addition to the statutory duties, the accountancy bodies have laid down a number of accounting standards relating to the auditor's report which should be complied with unless the company can justify departure from them. Additional auditing requirements have been provided for, in respect of listed companies, by the **Companies (Audit, Investigations and Community Enterprise) Act 2004**.

Fiona and Natasha will seek to avoid the costs of an audit if possible. Arts and Crafts Ltd appears to be an eligible small company and therefore the directors can exempt the company from the need for an audit, unless 10% of the company's members request an audit. The exemption is aimed at reducing the administrative burdens for small companies and may be an attractive option for Fiona and Natasha to pursue.

# (C) MEETINGS AND RESOLUTIONS

As a private company, Arts and Crafts Ltd is exempt by the **CA 2006** from holding general meetings. The previous regime under the **CA 1985** of allowing private companies to elect to dispense with the holding of general meetings has been abolished by the **CA 2006**. As with the small company regime in respect of accounts and audit, the **CA 2006** is aimed at further reducing the administrative burden of running a private company, particularly small, private companies. Fiona and Natasha will therefore be able to concentrate more fully on the commercial activities of the company. However, s 303 CA 2006 enables 10% of the members to requisition a general meeting – 5% where more than 12 months has elapsed since the last general meeting – and, as Natasha and Fiona do not command all the votes, they could find that there may still be a burden imposed on them. However, as they own 51% of the shares, they have sufficient control to pass ordinary resolutions, although they will need support of other members in order to pass any special resolution. To avoid unnecessary meetings, **s 288 CA 2006** allows much shareholder business to be conducted by written resolution, although such resolutions must be circulated and recorded properly (**ss 291–293** and **355 CA 2006**). Written resolutions can be passed as either an ordinary or special resolution; they do not have to be unanimous as required by the **CA 1985**. The only resolution which cannot be passed as a written resolution is one to remove a director or an auditor (**s 288 CA 2006**).

## Common Pitfalls

Make sure you keep your answer relevant and provide an appropriate balance between the issues of running a company on an informal basis and shareholder protection.

# QUESTION 42

In respect to the management of a company to what extent do you consider that the provisions of the **Companies Act 2006** achieve the government aim that company law needs to be 'modern, flexible and accessible'?

## Answer Plan

An answer requires setting out and analysing the major benefits to companies the **Companies Act (CA) 2006** is expected to bring. The question does not demand a wholesale look at the **CA 2006** but to consider those provisions that relate to company management. To that extent, the law relating to company meetings, the interests of shareholders and the position of directors needs to be considered, noting any differences between those provisions of the Act applying to public companies and those provisions applying to private companies. It is important to make the distinction between public and private companies, as a main objective of the Act is to ensure that company law, as it applies to public companies, does not by default apply to private companies, as was largely the case with parts of the **CA 1985** and **Table A**.

# ANSWER

The Government's overall objective was to produce clearer law which responded to modern business needs without unnecessary burdens. To this extent, the White Paper

2005 identified four key objectives: (a) ensuring better regulation and a 'think small first' approach; (b) enhancing shareholder engagement and long term investment; (c) making it easier to form and run a company; and (d) providing flexibility for the future. In the light of these objectives, the **CA 2006** is seen as providing a number of 'key benefits' for all companies, but private companies in particular. Overall, the Act is expected to make it easier for small, private companies to transact their business in respect of the procedure relating to meetings and to reform the law relating to meetings for all companies. This is designed as a means of enhancing shareholder protection, by offering companies and shareholders increased flexibility in respect of decision making. The Act also codifies the duties owed by directors to the companies they serve and places the common law procedure relating to derivative claims on a statutory footing.

## ADMINISTRATION AND DECISION MAKING

The law relating to meetings prior to the passing of the **CA 2006** was seen as complicated and containing statutory provisions that were more applicable to public companies than private companies. For private companies, several key benefits were identified, as a basis of reform, reflecting the way small companies operate. First, a separate and simpler model articles for private companies was set out – as provided for by the **Companies (Model Articles) Regulations 2008**, with separate articles for a private company limited by shares (**Sched 1**), a private company limited by guarantee (**Sched 2**) and a public company (**Sched 3**). Secondly, private companies are not required to appoint a company secretary, unless they choose to do so (**s 270 CA 2006**). Thirdly, private companies do not need to hold an annual general meeting, unless they choose to do so (**ss 302–303 CA 2006**), and it is easier for private companies to take decisions by written resolutions (**ss 282–283 CA 2006**). Private companies no longer have to pass an elective resolution dispensing with the requirement to hold an annual general meeting. Written resolutions of private companies can be passed by a majority of all eligible votes (ordinary resolution or special resolution), rather than the unanimous consent of all shareholders as previously required by the **CA 1985**. Fourthly, private companies are no longer prohibited from providing financial assistance for the purchase of their own shares and there are simpler rules on share capital. This is designed to remove provisions that under the **CA 1985** were largely irrelevant to the vast majority of private companies, but without compromising creditor protection.

Other changes include the removal from the **CA 2006** of extraordinary resolutions and elective resolutions and the reduction of the default majority required to agree a shorter notice period at a private company from 95% to 90%.

For shareholders of all companies, the CA 2006 is designed to enable members to benefit from (a) higher quality narrative reporting by quoted companies, (b) a statutory procedure for bringing a derivative claim on behalf of the company against a director for breach of duty, (c) enhancing the rights of persons who hold shares through nominee shareholders, as well as enhanced proxy rights (ss 324–331 CA 2006), (d) shareholders to receive more timely information through electronic communication (e.g. s 309 CA 2006 – publication of notice of general meetings on a website; s 430 CA 2006 – availability of annual reports and accounts of a quoted company on a website) and (e) the notice period for a general meeting, other than the annual general meeting (which is 21 days) to be 14 days unless the company's articles state otherwise or a shorter period of notice is agreed (s 307 CA 2006). In addition, for shareholders of public companies, the Act is expected to enhance shareholder protection in terms of accountability, by requiring public companies to hold their annual general meeting within six months of the financial year end (s 336 CA 2006) and for members to have a right to have circulated a resolution in advance of the annual general meeting, unless considered 'defamatory' or 'frivolous or vexatious' (s 338 CA 2006). (However, a quoted company is allowed a 15 day holding period after the annual accounts have been published. During this period, members will have the right to requisition a resolution for the meeting at which the accounts are to be laid.) Under the CA 2006, members of a company are entitled to requisition a general meeting at the company's expense (ss 303–305 CA 2006) and to have circulated at the company's expense a statement of no more than 1,000 words in respect of any matter referred to in a proposed resolution or other business at the general meeting (ss 314–316), although the company can decline a member's request for circulation where, on application to the court, the court is satisfied that the rights conferred by s 314 CA 2006 are being abused (s 317 CA 2006).

## DIRECTORS

The statutory statement of directors' general duties is designed to make the law in this area more accessible and to bring the duties in line with modern business practice. Apart from the fair dealing provisions of Part X of the CA 1985 (relating to certain types of transactions between a company and a director, such as loans and 'substantial property transactions'), directors' duties were based on case law and not statute. Law reformers had suggested that better compliance by directors with these duties might be better served if the various case law duties were codified by statute. As part of the Department of Trade and Industry's review of company law, the Law Commissions in their report, *Company Directors: Regulating Conflicts of Interest and Formulating a Statement of Duties* (1999) and the Company Law Review Steering Group in its Final Report (2001) proposed that there should be a statutory statement of directors' duties and that directors should be made aware that, in promoting the company's success for the benefit of its membership as a whole, they must take account of long term as well as short term consequences and that they must recognise the importance of relations with employees, suppliers, customers and the community. These recommendations were adopted by the White Paper (2005) and later formed the basis of the directors' 'general' duties contained in the CA 2006. By codifying the duties, it is expected that directors will become more aware of their responsibilities towards the companies they serve, which, in turn, will aid the interests of the company's shareholders.

The 'general' duties specified in ss 171–177 CA 2006 (ss 170–171) form a code of conduct, which sets out how directors are expected to behave. The codification is hoped to provide greater clarity on what is expected of directors and in whose interests companies should be run, as reflecting modern business needs.

The statutory duties are based on, and have effect in place of, certain common law rules and equitable principles but it is expected that the general duties will be interpreted and applied in the same way as the common law rules and equitable principles (s 170(4) CA 2006). As with the existing law, the general duties are owed by a director to the company (s 170(1) CA 2006) and therefore only the company can enforce them. The Act sets out the mechanism for action to be taken by a member to enforce the duties on behalf of the company, in the form of a derivative claim (ss 260–269 CA 2006). The company, of course, at common law can bring a claim against the directors in accordance with the rule in *Foss v Harbottle* (1843). The general duties also apply to shadow directors to the extent provided for by the common law or equitable principles (s 170(5) CA 2006).

## COMMUNICATION

An important aspect of company administration is communication between a company and its members and the submission of company documentation to Companies House. A significant feature of the CA 2006 is the means by which communication by, or to, a company is enhanced by the use of electronic means, such as the use of email and a website. To this extent, the CA 2006 builds on the provisions allowing for electronic communication of the CA 1985 and Table A. The CA 2006 allows for the registration of a company by delivering all the particulars of registration in electronic form and for the administrative requirements of the CA 2006 relating to the giving of notice of general meetings and the circulation of accounts, reports, etc to be complied with using electronic communication, as well as in hard copy format. Where provided for by the Act, Sched 4 to the CA 2006 relates to the use of electronic communication to a company and Sched 5 CA 2006 relates to the use of electronic communication by a company. Lower fees are paid where a company complies with the administrative requirements of the CA 2006 by electronic communication.

## CONCLUSION

The Government recognised that most registered companies are private companies and that most of these are run informally. The provisions of the **CA 1985** and associated subordinate legislation, however, did not fit particularly well with the informal nature of the running of a private company. **Table A** and its forerunner, **Table A** of **Sched 1 CA 1948**, were created for all companies to adopt (**s 8 CA 1985** – if on incorporation a company either fails to have registered articles or fails to disapply **Table A**, **Table A** becomes the company's articles by default), but were considered more appropriate to a public company. New articles for different types of company have been created by the **Companies (Model Articles) Regulations 2008**.

It is too early to say whether the changes introduced by the **CA 2006** will achieve the desired objectives of the government but certainly the language and spirit of the proposed legislation suggests that company law for the future will aid the running of companies within an increasingly competitive environment. In respect of private companies, at least, the Act recognises the informality in which the vast majority of private companies are run. Where changes need to be made to company law in the future, the Secretary of State has the power to make regulations or orders subject to a 'negative resolution' procedure (**s 1289 CA 2006**) or an 'affirmative resolution' procedure (**s 1290 CA 2006**), which will largely prevent the need for primary legislation.

### Aim Higher ★

Extra credit can be expected for discussing other aspects of the changes introduced by the **CA 2006** in respect of company management, for instance, the nature and scope of the office of director (including eligibility), the 'fair dealing' provisions and rules on auditing, accounting and reporting.

## QUESTION 43

Reading plc is a small unlisted public company with an issued share capital of £60,000, divided between Whiteknights and Bulmershe, who each hold 40% of the shares, and Earley, who holds the balance. Whiteknights and Bulmershe, who are also the directors of the company, would like to dispense with the holding of meetings but are uncertain how to achieve this aim and how, if achieved, resolutions could be passed. Earley rarely attends meetings or replies to letters and the directors would like to acquire his shares.

▶ Advise them.

### Answer Plan

This is a question in which a specific administrative problem is addressed – once the right route is identified, re-registration as a private company. It is simply a straightforward question on how to re-register, dispensing with meetings and non-meeting resolutions. A broader question, acquisition of Earley's shares, also arises.

# ANSWER

## (A) MEETINGS

The management of companies is in the hands of the directors, particularly the executive directors, in this case Whiteknights (W) and Bulmershe (B), who conduct the day to day running of the company. However, certain matters, predominantly constitutional issues such as amendments to the articles, can be implemented only with the agreement of the shareholders. The agreement of shareholders can be obtained by obtaining individual assents from *each* of them (*Re Duomatic Ltd* (1969)) but is more usually procured by passing a resolution at a company meeting. A resolution passed at a general meeting binds all shareholders, whether they attended or not and whether they voted for or against the resolution, and the company. A resolution, unlike a decision reached informally by all shareholders, will, subject to registration, bind third parties. A meeting of shareholders, a general meeting, also has a residual power to run the company when the directors are incapable of doing so (*Barron v Potter* (1914)) and it can sack the directors (under s 168 of the **Companies Act (CA) 2006**). Decisions taken at meetings, that is, resolutions, may require a simple majority of those present and voting, or a simple majority of those voting in person or by proxy (an ordinary resolution), but a three quarters' majority of those voting (in person or in person and by proxy) is required to pass a special resolution. The underlying reason for requiring companies to hold meetings is that members can attend to debate, and perhaps be influenced by others, and vote.

Companies have two types of general meetings – annual general meetings (AGMs) and general meetings. For both types, the **CA 2006** requires adequate notice to be given, which can be given in hard copy form, or in electronic form by means of a website (**ss 308–309 CA 2006**). As a public company, Reading plc must hold an AGM within six months of its financial year end. The AGM provides a means for members to receive reports and assessments on the company's performance. However, where a company has only three shareholders, it might be thought, as W and B do, that the holding of an AGM so that the directors (W and B) can report to themselves (and perhaps Earley (E)) is not very sensible and, in practice, many smaller companies fail to comply with the rules on meetings.

Section 303 CA 2006 permits the shareholders to require the directors to convene a meeting, provided that the requisitionists hold at least one-tenth of the paid up share capital carrying voting rights. Any request (in hard copy or electronic form) must state the general nature of the business to be dealt with at the meeting and include any resolution intended to be proposed. However, a resolution may not be properly moved, where it would, if passed, be ineffective by reason of inconsistency, for example, with the company's constitution, or it is defamatory of any person, or it is frivolous or vexatious. The directors of a public company must call a general meeting if the company's net assets fall to below half of the amount of its called up share capital (s 656 CA 2006) to report that fact to the shareholders. The majority of matters which might be the subject of a resolution at a general meeting could be dealt with by a written resolution if Reading plc was a private company. Consequently, it seems that the procedures within Reading plc would be somewhat simplified if the company re-registered as a private company, becoming Reading Ltd.

## (B) RE-REGISTRATION

A public company may re-register as a private company under the procedure laid down in ss 97–101 CA 2006. Reading plc must pass a special resolution (three-quarters majority of those present and voting), alter its name by deleting 'plc' and substituting 'Ltd' and amend its articles accordingly. W and B can achieve this change without the support of E. The company must then apply to the registrar for re-registration and, subject to any application by E, the registrar issues a certificate of re-registration. E, if he did not vote in favour of the change, has the right to petition the court to cancel the re-registration, since he holds in excess of 5% of a class of share capital, provided that he applies within 28 days of the passing of the special resolution. Minority shareholders are given this right because the conversion of a company from public to private may result in diminished marketability of the shares, although this is unlikely in this case given the size of Reading and the fact that it is unlisted. Instead of striking down the re-registration, a court can postpone a hearing to allow the other shareholders in the company, or the company itself, to buy out the dissentient shareholder or holders.

# (C)  WRITTEN AND INFORMAL RESOLUTIONS

If Reading plc re-registered as Reading Ltd, how would the shareholders in a private company reach binding decisions? There are two possibilities. First, the company could call a general meeting for the passing of resolutions by its members. Secondly, the company could pass written resolutions. A written resolution can be passed as an ordinary resolution or as a special resolution (**s 296 CA 2006**) – the requirement for unanimity has been abolished by the **CA 2006**. However, a written resolution is not permitted to dismiss a director or auditor of the company (**s 288(2) CA 2006**). Thus, W and B could conduct the business of the company, insofar as shareholder approval was needed. The written resolution procedure does not validate a decision agreed by all the members informally, that is, one which is not in compliance with written resolution requirements (**s 281(4) CA 2006**) so, if the common law permits unanimous non-written decisions to bind the company, there are two parallel procedures for passing resolutions without formal meetings. The common law is not limited to private companies.

In a series of cases, the courts have accepted that decisions unanimously approved by the shareholders who are entitled to attend or vote at a meeting, whether they all agreed at the same time or consecutively, bind the shareholders and the company (from *Re George Newman Ltd* (1895) to *Re Halt Garage Ltd* (1982)), even if made informally. Difficulties arise when the shareholders purport to give unanimous informal consent to a matter which the **Companies Act** provides must be agreed by a special resolution, particularly when the Act says that such a resolution is the only way to achieve a particular end. The general view is that, where the Act provides that a special resolution is required to do X, such a resolution may be regarded as *a* means of achieving a decision and that a unanimous informal agreement is an equally valid means – although an unregistered informal decision will probably not bind third parties. However, where the Act says that X may be done by special resolution, some writers argue that it can *only* be done by a proper resolution and not informally. Additionally, it is obvious that an informal agreement cannot overcome absolute prohibitions imposed on a company – the shareholders cannot, even unanimously, alter unalterable provisions of the memorandum. In *Re Bailey Hay and Co Ltd* (1971), the judge even held that informal consent could be assumed from acquiescence, and in this case he treated the company as bound by an informal decision which had been positively approved by only two out of five shareholders (the majority had abstained), although it must be said that the three were happy to go along with the consequences of the decision for five years.

Thus, even if E remains a shareholder, there is scope for W and B to dispense with many company meetings and solicit shareholder approval in writing or informally.

# (D) ACQUIRING E'S SHARES

If W and B feel that E is likely to be too obstructive or absent, even if the company goes private, they may seek to acquire his shares either for themselves or with a view to selling them to some third party. They can approach E and offer to buy him out or, if the appropriate procedures are followed, propose that the company buy his shares. However, while W and B can propose the purchase, the decision whether to sell is for E – though, if the price is right, it would seem foolish to refuse. What W and B cannot do is confiscate or cancel E's shares, even if the articles permit such behaviour, unless it is *bona fide* for the benefit of the company and they are exercising the power for the benefit of the company. Nor could a confiscation clause be inserted, unless W and B, as shareholders, voted to insert the provision in the articles *bona fide* for the benefit of the company, which seems improbable. An attempt to expel E might trigger a petition by E under s 994 CA 2006, which might suit W and B very well (apart from the cost), since the normal remedy for disgruntled shareholders is an order for their shares to be bought by the majority or the company, thereby achieving W and B's aims.

# QUESTION 44

In examining the procedures for insolvent companies, discuss the changes introduced by the **Enterprise Act 2002** as a means of facilitating a 'rescue culture' for ailing companies.

## Answer Plan

You will need to explain how the main forms of corporate insolvency and the changes made to the **Insolvency Act (IA) 1986** by the **Enterprise Act (EA) 2002** have met the objectives of the Government in reforming the law on corporate insolvency. A consideration of the law relating to 'old' insolvencies and 'new' insolvencies will need to be made, as the regime relating to old insolvencies is likely to continue to have effect in respect of corporate insolvency for a number of years to come.

# ANSWER

A stated objective of the Government was for the **EA 2002** to bring about changes that would promote a rescue culture for failing or failed businesses. In a spirit of enterprise, the **EA 2002** was designed to promote a reform of personal bankruptcy law and corporate insolvency law so as to enable a swift return to business of failed companies or business people where business failure was caused by commercial factors and not by irresponsible or reckless trading. The amendments to the **IA 1986** by the **EA 2002** on corporate insolvency took effect from 15 September 2003. With the exception of a company voluntary arrangement, the principal procedures dealing with insolvent companies are receivership, administration and liquidation.

## RECEIVERSHIP

Where a company is in financial difficulty, it is the right of a secured creditor to appoint a receiver or administrative receiver to manage the company's assets that are the subject matter of the creditor's security. Receivership involves appointing a person to either sell or collect any income arising from the assets subject to the charge in order to satisfy the outstanding debt owed to the creditor. A receiver is a person appointed to manage the assets that are subject to a fixed charge while an administrative receiver acts as a manager of all or substantially all the assets that are subject to a floating charge.

Receivership is a procedure which is not implemented by the company but by a secured lender (or the courts) in accordance with the terms of the loan. While the procedure cannot be implemented by the company (despite reports in the press which often speak of a company 'calling in the receiver'), it may be initiated by the company in conjunction with a creditor when the company recognises that it cannot continue to trade in its current format. This is not to say that the company can veto the appointment of a receiver, merely that a more orderly and timely process from the viewpoint of the troubled company may be achieved. Receivers may be appointed by a fixed charge holder or by a floating charge holder and in the latter case the receiver is called an administrative receiver and must be a licensed insolvency practitioner. The function of a receiver is to receive income or realise property to which the charge attaches to pay off the charge holder. Receivership does not preclude a creditors' or members' petition to wind up the company being presented. Where a liquidator is appointed, the receiver remains in office and continues to manage and realise the assets to which the charge attaches but is monitored by the liquidator on behalf of the company's creditors. After the receiver has satisfied the client charge holder, the liquidator disposes of any surplus assets, in compliance with the order of priority for the payment of creditors. If the charged asset is insufficient to meet the claims of the charge holder, the balance of the debt is unsecured. A receiver appointed by a fixed charge holder is concerned only with the asset to which the client's charge attaches and he has no general power to run the company. However, a receiver appointed by a floating charge holder has the enhanced powers of an administrative receiver. An administrative receiver has considerable powers designed to enable them to keep potentially successful companies afloat, perhaps by selling the enterprise to another company or by restructuring the company and jettisoning loss-making portions of the business. The enhanced powers of administrative receivers include some of the powers given to liquidators and administrators, but not the powers to re-open or set aside preferences and certain floating charges or to initiate proceedings for fraudulent or wrongful trading. An administrative receiver becomes the agent of the company unless and until the company goes into liquidation. It must be stressed that a receiver's principal duty is to his client and he is not obliged to consider, other than as a secondary matter, the interests of other creditors.

Receivership does not inevitably lead to liquidation but it is obviously not a very promising sign and the EA 2002, by amending the IA 1986, provides several changes to administrative receivership in order to lessen the likelihood of companies going into receivership. With effect from 15 September 2003, the changes introduced by the EA 2002 diminish the right of floating charge holders, typically banks and other lending institutions, to appoint an administrative receiver. This is designed to 'encourage' administration, in order to give the company a better chance of recovery than receivership, which often led to the company proceeding into liquidation. Further, it is possible for an administrator to be appointed out of court, by either the company's floating charge holders, who will no longer be able to appoint a 'qualifying' receiver, the company itself or the directors of the company, subject to certain conditions being met. There are some exceptions to these provisions and the provisions do not apply to a floating charge holder whose charge was created before 15 September 2003.

## ADMINISTRATION

Prior to the IA 1985, a company becoming insolvent was likely to be wound up. There was no formal system in the UK for rescuing a company in financial difficulty and little protection afforded to unsecured creditors. Administration, as a type of insolvency procedure, was introduced. Administration is a relatively recent innovation, designed to permit restructuring of a debt-ridden business – it is comparable with Chapter XI of the American Federal Bankruptcy Code. Administration was introduced to provide a company with 'breathing space' to enable it to continue as a going concern or at least to result in a better realisation of the company's assets than a forced sale on liquidation. Administration may be preferable for the company and creditors to liquidation – it is likely to be cheaper, it may allow the sale of a going concern better than a 'fire-sale' on liquidation, it allows a company currently trading profitably but burdened by debt from past enterprises to trade on with some form of debt moratorium or restructuring operating, and directors, etc, owed money by the company may have better prospects of payment than in a liquidation. An administration order, which can be sought by the company, a company's directors or a creditor, is a court order that, for the duration of the order, the company's affairs are to be managed by an administrator who must be a licensed insolvency practitioner. An administrator becomes, in effect, the board and runs the company on behalf of everyone (unlike the administrative receiver, who acts for the charge holder who appoints him).

Administration, however, was not necessarily a cheap or simple alternative to receivership or liquidation and, as part of the Government's stated intention of rescuing ailing businesses, the EA 2002, by amending the IA 1986, simplified the process of administration. The EA 2002 introduced an out of court mode of appointment of administrator by either the holder of a qualifying floating charge, the company itself or the directors of that company (Sched B1 IA 1986). Further, with a few limited exceptions, so as to encourage administration as opposed to receivership, after 15 September 2003, a floating charge holder can no longer appoint a receiver in respect of any floating charge created after this date. Administration, therefore, is considered by the Government to be the preferred option for ailing companies.

Under the IA 1986, the administrator must perform his/her functions in the interests of the company's creditors as a whole, in accordance with the following three objectives (as amended by the EA 2002) which are in descending order of importance:

(a) To rescue the company as a going concern (the primary purpose);
(b) To achieve a better result for the company's creditors than would be achieved if the company was wound up; and
(c) To realise property to make a distribution to one or more secured or preferential creditors.

An out of court administrator can be appointed by a qualifying floating charge holder. This is a floating charge holder whose charge or charges relate to the whole or substantially the whole of the company's property. A company or the directors of a company can appoint an administrator, but not in circumstances where an administrative receiver has been appointed, a petition for winding up has been presented or where a qualifying floating charge holder has appointed the administrator.

Where a company is in administration, any petition to wind the company up will either be dismissed or suspended until the period of administration is over. An administrative receiver who has already been appointed is dismissed and no steps can be taken to enforce any security without the consent of the administrator or the permission of the court. An administration order cannot be made and neither can an administrator be appointed if the company is in liquidation or is already in administration, although in respect of a liquidation, the court can discharge a winding up order if an administration order is made on the application of a floating charge holder or the liquidator. In respect of the out of court procedure, an administrator cannot be appointed if an administrative receiver is in office nor, in the case of an appointment by a company or its directors, if there are any outstanding winding up petitions or applications for administration in respect of the company.

The administrator may do anything necessary or expedient for the management of the affairs, business and property of the company, including removing or appointing directors. He takes control of all the property to which he thinks the company is entitled and he may pay creditors. He can sell property which is subject to a floating charge, but the charge holder gets the same priority in respect of any property acquired, and by court order, he can sell property that is subject to a fixed charge.

An important feature of administration is that it applies a moratorium. This means that creditors are prevented from bringing claims against the company during the course of the administration. The moratorium, however, applies only from the date of the administration order coming into effect. In order to provide further protection to a company from creditor claims, **Sched BI 1A 1986** provides for an interim moratorium which comes into force on the date of either the application to the court or the date of the presentation of the notice to appoint an administrator. During the period of the interim moratorium, however, it is possible for a winding up petition to be presented to the court and a floating charge holder with a charge created before 15 September 2003 can appoint an administrative receiver.

Despite these changes, it is likely that receivership will continue to exist as a common form of insolvency, as many floating charges were created before the changes introduced by the **EA 2002** took effect.

## PREFERENTIAL CREDITORS

The **IA 1986** gives preferential status to certain unsecured creditors who rank in priority to all creditors except fixed charge holders and the costs of liquidation. In the past, creditors with preferential debts included HM Revenue and Customs and company employees for unpaid wages up to £800 (including any outstanding and accrued holiday entitlement). In respect of any insolvency after 15 September 2003, the Crown loses its preference. Given that a leading petitioner for a winding up was HM Revenue and Customs, it is considered that this change of status for the debts of HM Revenue and Customs will reduce the number of winding up petitions being sought against insolvent companies.

# CONCLUSION

As the law relating to old insolvencies will continue to exist for some time to come, it is perhaps too early to say how effective the changes introduced by the **EA 2002** will be on enabling failing companies to be rescued from oblivion. However, reducing the costs of administration by reducing court involvement is a conclusion that can be drawn from two early cases on corporate restructuring under the new **Sched B1 IA 1986**. The decisions of the court in *Re Transbus International Ltd* (2004) and *Re Ballast plc* (2004) suggest that administrators are being encouraged by the courts to execute administration in a cost effective and efficient way.

**Aim Higher** ★

A good understanding of the differences in insolvency law between the position before 15 September 2003 and the position on or after 15 September 2003 will be to your credit.

# Index